C000259795

 Celti

AN ESSENTIAL GUIDE TO
Celtic Sites and their Saints

Elizabeth Rees

BURNS & OATES
A Continuum imprint
LONDON • NEW YORK

Burns & Oates

A Continuum imprint

The Tower Building	15 East 26th Street
11 York Road	New York
London SE1 7NX	NY 10010

British Library Cataloguing-in-Publication Data

A catalogue record for this book is available from the British Library.

ISBN: 0–86012–318–9

Typeset by YHT Ltd, London
Printed and bound in Great Britain by
MPG Books Ltd, Bodmin, Cornwall

CONTENTS

PREFACE

This is, as far as I know, the first guidebook to some 250 British sites associated with the Celtic saints. The places range from ruined monasteries to holy wells, from caves to Roman and Celtic forts. They are listed and described alphabetically in sections covering Ireland, Scotland, Wales, Cornwall, and the rest of England, with about fifty sites described in each area. A final section of the book outlines the lives of the saints associated with the various places. This is by no means a comprehensive guidebook. It is estimated that there are some 3,000 holy wells in Ireland alone, so this book is a taster. Having made a start by visiting some of these sites, the reader will then be in a good position to explore further.

I wish to thank my sister, Margaret Rees, for her helpful suggestions, and my father, Henry Rees, for preparing the maps. I am also grateful to Margaret for providing decorative motifs taken from early Christian sources. I have received valuable advice from Dr Jonathan Wooding of the Centre for the Study of Religion in Celtic Societies at the University of Wales, Lampeter. Any errors are my own. My final word of thanks is to the Celtic saints who have enticed me to meet them 'at home' in the beautiful locations where they chose to live around the shores of Britain.

Elizabeth Rees

INTRODUCTION

Place-names and church dedications tell us that, in medieval times, Britain was in many ways a landscape of saints. In Ireland, Scotland, Wales, and Cornwall a considerable number of these dedications date from the time of the early Christian saints. These were holy men and women, monks and nuns, priests and bishops, who ministered among the Celtic peoples from the early fifth century onwards. Many lived and prayed within their own tribal kinship group; others set out as pilgrims for Christ, seeking an empty place where they could be alone with God. Their stories were cherished by medieval Christians, and often we know little about a Celtic saint apart from the legends preserved in their biographies or *vitae* (Lives), written by medieval monks. Unfortunately many of these contain few historical facts: the primary aim of their authors was to edify their readers with accounts of astonishing holiness rather than to convey accurate detail.

The coming of Christianity

Much of Britain was Christianized in Roman times. In the second and third centuries, there were Christians in Britain who had been converted and baptized, often secretly, in other Roman provinces, in Gaul or in places further to the east. Christian soldiers also arrived in Britain with the Roman army. Christianity was a permitted religion from AD 260, but Christians worshipped one God and acknowledged neither the gods of Rome nor the deified emperors. This ran contrary to Roman thought and belief, and led to periodic persecutions.[1] The early fifth-century author Gildas tells us of martyrs: Alban in Verulamium (St Albans), and Aaron and Julius, citizens of *Urbs Legionum,* which was probably Caerleon.[2]

Constantine was proclaimed emperor in 306; a convert himself, he was the first emperor to grant liberty of conscience to Christians. In 313 the Edict of Milan announced the restoration of confiscated churches and freedom of worship. The remains of Christian cemeteries and churches indicate that by the fourth century Christians had spread through many areas of England and Wales, into town and countryside.

Introduction

In the Roman Empire, Christianity was centred on urban life. Pastoral care was organized by bishops who lived in towns. British bishops are first recorded in attendance at the Council of Arles in 314. They headed communities in the capitals of the four Roman provinces of fourth-century Britain: London, York, Lincoln, and Cirencester. Bishops were soon found in some twenty other British towns as far north as Carlisle and probably as far west as Carmarthen in south Wales and Exeter in the south-west.[3]

In 1994-5 one of the ancient world's largest basilicas was excavated on Tower Hill, near the present Tower of London. It was built in about 380 and was decorated with black and white marble; its interior was painted with red and white, grey, pink, and yellow designs. This splendid church was probably commissioned by Magnus Maximus, the ambitious head of the Roman army in Britain.[4] Smaller churches have been excavated, scattered through the provinces of Britain. They range from Vindolanda on Hadrian's Wall in the north to Colchester in the south-east.

A number of villas were owned by Christian families who evidently opened their homes as house churches where local Christians could come to worship. Those at Hinton St Mary and Frampton, both in Dorset, had fine mosaic floors decorated with Christian themes. Lullingstone villa in Kent had Christian owners who rebuilt it in about 360. They decorated an upper room over the cellar as a Christian chapel. Its wall paintings appear to represent members of the family at prayer, and other Christian motifs.[5] Eight miles north of Cirencester, a pool in the grounds of Chedworth villa was probably used to immerse candidates for baptism, since three of the stone slabs that surrounded the pool have the *chi–rho* symbol for Christ carved on them.[6] The slabs were later inverted, perhaps by a subsequent non-Christian owner.

Gildas describes the early Church

When Gildas wrote *The Ruin of Britain* in the sixth century, he hints at a long tradition of established Christianity. He describes a Church that is familiar to us in some ways yet strange in others. It was organized on a territorial basis, although parishes still did not exist. Gildas frequently mentions bishops, presbyters, deacons, and clerics in lesser orders. He describes the bishops as skilfully versed in the complexities of worldly affairs; they are men of social and political standing. The clergy have flocks (*greges*) who gather in churches (*domus ecclesiae*) to celebrate the Eucharist. Celibacy is not required of clerics. Gildas speaks of unbelievers (*increduli*) who require missionaries to preach to them. The Church is oriented towards Rome in faith and worship.

Gildas writes about ambitious clerics who travel to Gaul in order to be consecrated as bishops and then proudly return. He depicts the Church during the last years of the declining Roman Empire. His *Penitential* uses Roman weights and measures, and he uses many other Roman terms in *The Ruin of Britain.* Gildas quotes from Jerome's new Vulgate translation of the Bible, but he prefers the Old Latin version, and draws on an early translation of the Book of Job used in Roman times.[7] Gildas thus describes a Church in south Britain which was built on Roman foundations.

Monasteries were a new development, and were to grow in significance in the following centuries.[8] Gildas tells us that King Maelgwyn spent some time in one, and describes its rules, its emphasis on teaching scripture to the young, and the practice of chanting the psalms. He describes bishops who continue to govern the Church, while perhaps living in the new monastic communities. Gildas is very critical of his contemporaries: he was horrified that King Constantine of Dumnonia committed sacrilege by murdering royal youths at a monastery. He condemned another ruler for abandoning his plan of becoming a monk. Gildas considered that society was full of wicked men, but he describes them as being wicked in a Christian context.[9]

Many early Christian sites have their origin as monasteries. How and why did monasticism take root? Gildas tells us how Christians went into solitude. After he describes the martyrdom of early British Christians, he continues: 'The survivors hid in woods, desert places and secret caves, looking towards God.'[10] In Gaul, Bishop Martin of Tours (*c.*316–97) established a monastery at Marmoutier that became a model for successive generations of monks throughout Europe. His friend and biographer, Sulpicius Severus, described it in language similar to that used by Gildas a century later: 'The place was so secluded and remote that it had all the solitude of the desert. On one side it was walled in by the rock face of a high mountain, and the level ground that remained was enclosed by a gentle bend of the River Loire. There was only one approach to it, and that a very narrow one.'[11]

The eastern deserts

There were, of course, no deserts in Gaul, but the Latin word *desertum* means 'an empty space'. In his account of Martin's monastery, Sulpicius was alluding to the tradition of the desert fathers and mothers of the Near East. These men and women left the cities in search of an 'empty place' in which to pray. The monks and nuns of the eastern deserts often chose locations that were remote but not too far from towns. They could therefore exercise hospitality and help their urban neighbours in practical ways. We read in the *Lives of the Desert Fathers*: 'There is no town or village in Egypt ... which is not surrounded by hermitages as if by walls.'[12]

The monk Copres taught peasants how to make their land more fertile; John of Lycopolis predicted the rise and fall of the Nile and the annual yield of the crops. Serapion sent wheat and clothing down to the poor of Alexandria, since those in his neighbourhood were already taken care of. The *Historia Monachorum* describes the monks' dealings with farmers, Romans, merchants, and civil servants in towns and villages.[13] The Greek name *monachos*, or 'monk', means 'one who is alone', but the earliest surviving reference to a monk is in a fourth-century Greek papyrus found in Egypt recording a village squabble in which one of the two witnesses is a *monachos*.

In Gaul, Martin's monastery was in an isolated spot, yet only two miles from Tours, so the bishop was able to commute between his monastic retreat and his episcopal duties in the town. The location of Marmoutier influenced early British monks in their choice of sites. The monastery of Whithorn in Galloway, near the south-western tip of Scotland, lay two miles south-west of the ancient hill fort of Cruggleton and is situated within the bend of a river, although the River Ket beside Whithorn is rather smaller than the Loire.[14] Rivers were major routes, and many British and Irish monasteries are found beside a river and near a chieftain's settlement.

Sulpicius Severus describes the monks at Martin's monastery

as men of prayer who shared all they had: 'No one possessed anything of his own; everything was put into the common stock. The buying and selling which is customary with most hermits was forbidden to them. No craft was practised there except that of copyist, and that was assigned to younger men. The older ones were left free for prayer.'[15] The *Life of Martin* was widely distributed and became a popular text in the early British Church, providing a model of holy living.

The most popular accounts of the Egyptian monasteries were those of John Cassian, whose books spread through Italy and southern Gaul and also reached Ireland. With a companion, Cassian set out for Egypt in about 385 and spent fifteen years learning from men and women whom he met. After a further twenty years of reflection on his experience, Cassian wrote his *Institutes* and *Conferences* for a monastery in Marseilles in about 425. In these books, Cassian explained the aims and methods of monastic life; he helped western Christians to understand the life of eastern, Greek-speaking monks, and to adapt it to their own very different conditions. Cassian's Latin writings were circulated widely and were eagerly read.[16]

A monk's life

What did it mean to be a monk or a nun in the early Church? There was a wide variety of contrasting lifestyles, each of which was an expression of the monastic ideal. You might be a solitary or live in a community. You might remain in your tribal territory, or perhaps feel called to leave it as a pilgrim for Christ. Your life could be extremely austere, or more balanced and moderate. You might devote much time to study, or spend most of your day in hard agricultural labour. There was an interplay between these various extremes: Bishop Samson left his community in order to find solitude with a few close friends and later set out with them as a pilgrim for the love of God.

A group of early writings that throw light on monastic life in early medieval times are the *Penitentials*. These outline a Christian moral code and prescribe penances for specific offences. They provide insight into daily community life and reveal some of its problems. The Penitential ascribed to Gildas describes how monks who commit minor offences should go without their supper, while those who indulge in the more serious misdemeanours of sexual activity and theft should have their food rationed over a longer period: 'He shall have bread without limit and a titbit fattened slightly with butter on Sunday; on other days a ration of dry bread and a dish enriched with a little fat, garden vegetables, a few eggs, British cheese, and a Roman half-pint of milk, on account of the body's weakness nowadays. Let him also drink a Roman pint of whey or buttermilk to quench his thirst, and some water if he is a workman.' By today's standards, this does not sound particularly austere. The miscreant is also to be made less comfortable at night: 'His bed shall be meagrely supplied with hay.'[17]

Monasteries were generally surrounded by an enclosure wall or *vallum*. A few of the earliest sites, such as Iona and Clonmacnoise, are contained within great rectangular earthworks. This may recall the eastern desert monasteries such as St Catherine's on Mount Sinai, whose rectangular fortifications were a protection against fifth- and sixth-century marauders. Many communities, such as that of Old Melrose in the Scottish Borders, where Cuthbert trained as a monk, were situated within abandoned hill forts.[18] Other sites were protected by oval defensive walls.

The rise of monastic communities who followed a fixed rule took place in the later fifth century. This did not entirely replace the older system of territorial bishops, especially in south Wales, where Roman influence was strong. While Martin of Tours created his own form of monastery in north-west Gaul, other communities developed in southern Gaul with a greater emphasis on learning. These monasteries influenced those of Ireland, whose monks in their turn encouraged the growth of monastic life in south Wales. Throughout this time, Irish and British pilgrims returning from the eastern Mediterranean brought back with them their experience of eastern monastic communities.[19] For several centuries, until the ravages of the Vikings, early British Christians developed new and vibrant forms of life and prayer, of learning, industry and art.

Part One
Ireland

Saints of Ireland

AGHABOE, Laois: St Kenneth's cathedral

The settlement of Aghaboe is ten miles east-south-east of Roscrea. It was founded by Kenneth, a friend of Columba, in the sixth century. One of its later abbots, Virgilius, resigned from his position in 739 in order to become a missionary. He travelled to Austria and was bishop of Salzburg from 749 to 784. In 913 the abbey at Aghaboe was plundered by Norsemen. In 1052 a great church was built, and Kenneth's relics were enshrined in it. In 1116 the monastic city was severely damaged by fire; a new church was built in 1189.

From 1111 to 1200, Aghaboe abbey was the cathedral church of Ossory diocese, but the building continued to have a chequered history: in 1346, St Kenneth's church and shrine were destroyed by fire during a Norman attack. The present large-scale building was constructed in 1132 and given to the Dominican order. It was suppressed in 1540, but Dominican friars continued to serve here secretly until the eighteenth century. The building is now a ruin: a few interesting features adorn the otherwise plain walls; there is a delicately carved alcove in the south chapel, with a fourteenth-century ogee arch.

AHENNY, Tipperary: high crosses

Ahenny is six miles north of Carrick-on-Suir. The site is signed from the R697. A minor road leads across the river and up the hillside: follow it until the monastic site is visible in a field to the left. Nothing remains of the monastery that was here except two of Ireland's earliest high crosses. They date from the eighth or early ninth century, and appear to be copies in stone of metal-encased wooden crosses. They are covered with abstract ornamentation, and large bosses are placed where functional rivets would have held a wooden cross together. Carved on the base of the north cross are figures of monks carrying crosses, a man on a pony, horsemen and horses, a procession of seven ecclesiastics carrying croziers, and various animals.

ARAN ISLANDS, Galway: St Enda's monastery

The Aran Islands lie in the Atlantic Ocean south-west of Galway, at distances of between 25 and 30 miles from the mainland. There are three principal islands: Inishmore (12 square miles), Inishmaan (3¹/₂ square miles) and Inisheer (2¹/₄ square miles). They can be reached by sea or air. Aer Arann flies daily to each island from Carnmore, four miles north-east of Galway. There are ferries to the islands from Galway, Rossaveal, Doolin, and, in the summer, from Spiddal.

On the south-west coast of Inishmore is the great stone fort of Dún Aenghus, one of the largest prehistoric fortifications in Europe. There are two other stone forts on the island. North of Dún Aenghus, in the hamlet of Kilmurvey, are the ninth-century church of St Brecan, and *Teampall MacDuagh*, an early church with a nave, dedicated to Colmán of Kilmacduagh. Around Killeany, two miles south of Kilronan, are numerous ruined churches. One is *Tighlagh Eany*, an early church with later features. This is all that remains of Enda's famous monastery, established in the early sixth century. Many of the great Irish monks studied here. The church contains a fine cross shaft decorated with the figure of a horseman and interlaced patterns. Nearby is St Benan's church (*Teampall Bheanáin*). This is one of Ireland's smallest churches, measuring 3 by 2 metres; it may date from as early as the sixth century.

Inishmaan means 'middle island'. It contains an oratory named *Teampall Ceannamnach*. It is 5 by 4 metres, and is built with massive blocks of stone. One boulder spans the entire width of the church.

Inisheer means 'island to the east'. Here, a small chapel is dedicated to a nun named Gobnait; there are remains of a cell and two 'bullaun stones' at the early oratory. Bullaun stones are boulders with a hollow carved in them; their function is unknown, but they are often found at Irish monastic sites. Gobnait was born in County Clare in the fifth century, and was said to have fled to the Aran Islands to escape a family feud. She eventually settled in southern Ireland, at Ballyvourney. Also on Inisheer, the little church of St Cavan, or Kevin, is usually covered by drifting sand, but it is cleared each year in order to hold a service at his tomb, to the north-east of the church. The commemoration takes place on Cavan's feast day, 14 June.

ARDFERT, Kerry: Ardfert cathedral

Dedicated to the sixth-century monk Brendan, the monastery at Ardfert is in his own tribal territory, three miles from the Kerry coast. It is five miles north-north-west of Tralee. Ardfert means 'height of the grave', and much of north Kerry is visible from the low ridge on which the monastery was built. An ogham-inscribed stone and some early graves were discovered in the vicinity of the eleventh-century cathedral.

Ogham is an alphabet using incised lines grouped along two adjacent edges of a monument; its straight strokes were easier for masons to carve than the curved letters of the Roman alphabet. The greatest number of ogham-inscribed stones is found in southern Ireland, where it is likely that a number of Irish people were competent Latin speakers. The concept of incised commemorative slabs came from the pagan Roman Empire, and ogham possibly pre-dates the arrival of Christianity in Ireland. The inventors of this cipher were familiar with the sound-values of spoken Latin, and the alphabet may have been devised by Latin-speaking Irish intellectuals, perhaps as early as AD 300.[1]

A stone church at Ardfert was destroyed by lightning in 1046; some of its masonry survives in the cathedral's north wall. A round tower was built at this time; it collapsed in 1776, and only its base remains. In the twelfth century, Ardfert was declared a diocese. Some time after 1130 a fine Romanesque cathedral was designed, with an imposing west doorway modelled on Cormac's chapel at Cashel. The rest of the cathedral was later rebuilt. There are two smaller churches within the monastic enclosure; the earliest, named *Teampall na Hoe* (or 'church of the Virgin') was constructed in the twelfth century. It has a steeply pitched roof and, unusually, columns with carved capitals decorate its outer corners. A second church, *Teampall na Griffin*, was added beside it in the fifteenth century.

ARDMORE, Waterford: St Déclán's monastery

The village of Ardmore is on the south coast of Ireland, halfway between Cork and Waterford. Déclán established a community here in the early fifth century. *Ard mór* means 'great height', and Déclán chose a site on fertile high ground overlooking a sandy bay. The headland may then have been an island in the mouth of the River Blackwater, before it burst its banks in 803 and made a new channel through Youghal Bay.

The ruined cathedral at Ardmore dates from the ninth century. In the chancel, two ogham-inscribed grave markers date from near to Déclán's lifetime. By the twelfth century, when Déclán's Life came to be written, little was known about his work, and the adventures recounted in his biography may have little basis in fact. However, there were traditions about Déclán's love of solitude and his choice of a 'desert' or place of retreat on the headland 800 metres beyond the monastery. His hermitage was here, in a sheltered spot beside a spring. In old age, he was said to have moved out of the monastic 'city' in order to come and live here. Déclán's desert is still a peaceful place surrounded by trees. In the early morning one can look out across the sparkling sea and watch fishermen in the bay, far below. There are remains of a large ruined church; its east end dates from the fourteenth century, but its west end is earlier.

West of the ruined church is Déclán's holy well. Two small doorways lead down to the spring, where it is possible to bathe. The well house is capped with two late medieval crosses, each bearing a figure of Christ. The well was restored in 1798 and again in 1951. It is visited by countless people, particularly during the week nearest to Déclán's feast day, 24 July. Up to the late 1940s, pilgrims came to spend all night in a prayer vigil at the well.

An account from around 1840 describes the scene on Déclán's feast day: 'The crowd then formed a long line winding up the narrow path that leads along the mountain's brow to St Déclán's chapel ... The scenery was beautiful as we looked over the precipitous cliffs across the bay of Ardmore. On the brink stands the remnant of a chapel, said to be the first built in Ireland. On entering the gate, on your right is the well St Déclán blessed. Then they knelt down and said their prayers ... At twenty different periods, I counted people as they passed. They averaged fifty-five a minute, which gives a total of fifteen thousand persons.'[2] Between the desert and the monastic city, Déclán's Stone is also visited by pilgrims. This is a large erratic boulder which balances on two smaller rocks, and is held to cure rheumatism if one crawls beneath it. In any case, the act of doing so loosens stiff joints!

The twelfth-century *Life of Déclán* relates that when he sensed death approaching he returned from his hermitage to the community, to die among his brother monks: 'When Déclán realised that his last days were at hand, he called for Mac Liag from the eastern Déisi, in order to receive the last sacraments from him. He foreknew the day of his death, and asked to be brought back to his own (monastic) city ... Mac

Liag gave him the last sacraments. He blessed all his people, and when he died, he was buried with honour in the tomb which he had already chosen.'[3]

The chapel of Déclán's Grave is the oldest building of the monastery, although it was restored in the eighteenth century. It is a small rectangular oratory on what may be eighth-century foundations, on the hillside at the edge of the site, where the land slopes down to the sea. Large stone blocks form the lower courses of its walls; its projecting pillars, or antae, would have supported the roof timbers. Generations of Christians have scooped out earth from Déclán's grave inside the chapel, as it is believed to protect from disease.

The round tower and the ruined west end of the cathedral at Ardmore date from the twelfth century. A number of fine but badly weathered Romanesque reliefs have been reassembled and set into the cathedral's west wall; they depict Adam and Eve, the adoration of the infant Christ by the three wise men, and other scenes. The round tower was one of the latest to be built in Ireland. Beautifully proportioned, it rises to a height of 29 metres. Its four tapering storeys are separated by projecting string courses, each resembling a rope. The round-arched doorway is 4 metres above ground level, so that defenders could enter by ladder and pull it in after them, to prevent its use by attackers. An unusual feature of the tower is that inside are projecting stones carved with grotesque heads.

Towers may have served as lookout posts, landmarks, and guides for sailors and travellers on land. Books, chalices, and shrines could safely be stored here, and monks could take refuge in the tower. This one was so strong that it withstood an attack with cannon fire when it was held by the Confederates in 1642, at a time when the native Catholic population struggled against their English Protestant overlords and Oliver Cromwell ruthlessly suppressed the Irish Rebellion. The elegant tower now dominates a peaceful landscape once more.

BALLISADARE, Sligo: St Féchín's church, Kilboglashy

St Féchín's church is four miles south-west of Sligo at the head of Ballisadare Bay, where the river enters the sea. The site is 750 metres north-north-west of Ballisadare, on the west bank of the river. To find it, take the N59 westward from

Ballisadare, signed Ballina. After crossing the river, pass the first shops, continue for 20 metres and turn right. When the surfaced road veers left, continue straight on along an unsurfaced track. Follow this for 50 metres to the church, which is on the right.

The seventh-century church is known as *Teampall Mór Féchín* (or Féchín's great church). It is located on the left bank of the river, overlooking a waterfall, and is now partly covered with ivy. The oldest feature of the building is the western gable and a section of the adjoining north wall. The church is 10 by 20 metres, and has been rebuilt a number of times. The present structure dates from the thirteenth century, and incorporates twelfth-century stonework. A Romanesque doorway has been inserted into the south wall; it is decorated with carved heads. A tympanum, or decorated space above the entrance arch, may have adorned what is now a plain surface. To the west, at a distance of 250 metres, is a fifteenth-century Augustinian church, now almost buried beneath the debris from a quarry.

BRANDON CREEK, Kerry: St Brendan's harbour

Brandon Creek is a tiny harbour at a gap in the cliffs to the west of Brandon Mountain on the Dingle peninsula. Its Gaelic name is *Cuas an Bhodaigh* ('Creek of the Churl'). In *The Voyage of St Brendan*, one of the most popular tales from medieval times,[4] this is where the saint is said to have set sail in search of the Promised Land. According to the story, which was written around 800, when Brendan was abbot of Clonfert, he was visited by a monk named Barrind. This traveller had sailed through thick fog and reached the heavenly Jerusalem, full of precious stones, with all its plants in flower and a river flowing across it from east to west. Barrind describes his experience using words from chapters 21-22 of the Book of Revelation, the last book of the New Testament. Barrind added that he had returned home after a year.

In chapter 2 of the *Navigatio*, (or 'Voyage'), after hearing Barrind's story, Brendan chooses fourteen monks from his own community of Clonfert and tells them that he too wishes to sail to this Promised Land. They eagerly volunteer to accompany him, and Brendan returns to his native Kerry to set out. As a good monk, he avoids visiting his parents, in obedience to Christ's challenge to turn one's back on father and mother for the sake of the gospel.[5] Instead, Brendan and his monks pitch their tent above a narrow creek at a place named Brandon's Seat. At Brandon Creek, Brendan builds a curragh, or wooden-framed boat covered with oxhides. In the boat he and his fellow-monks put a mast and a sail, with supplies of food and water for forty days.

They set sail towards the Promised Land and wander the ocean for seven years. The story is an allegory of monastic life with its annual cycle of labour and worship: they follow a circular route, and celebrate the great festivals at the same places each year.[6] A monastic steward appears at intervals with provisions for Brendan's monks. Each day is punctuated by the monastic liturgy; in an island paradise, the birds sing hymns and chant vespers and the other liturgical offices.[7] The unknown author of the *Navigatio* describes an island of sheep and a paradise of birds which may be echoes of the Faeroe Islands.

BRANDON MOUNTAIN, Kerry: St Brendan's shrine

This mountain, 953 metres high, is named after Brendan; it became a centre for pilgrimage, perhaps as early as the eighth century. At the mountain peak are the remains of cells, a chapel and a holy well. On Crom Dubh Sunday each July, reviving an earlier tradition, pilgrims climb the mountain to visit the shrine at its summit. A 'Saints' Road' led from Ventry Harbour on the south side of the peninsula to the summit of Brandon Mountain. Pilgrims evidently arrived by sea before walking the twelve-mile route that led up the mountain. There are clearly marked paths to the summit starting from Cloghane to the south-east, from Faha, and also from the west.

CARROWNTEMPLE, Sligo: early monastery

This site is five miles south-west of Gorteen and 20 miles south of Sligo. It can be found by driving south from Gorteen on R293. A mile after Kilfree Post Office, turn right, following the sign 'Carrentemple Burial Grounds'. After two miles, the graveyard can be seen to the right. The site contains an enclosure, underground chambers or *souterrains*, the ruins of a medieval church of uncertain date, an old and a new graveyard, and a collection of inscribed stones.

Early maps show that the enclosure was roughly 90 metres in diameter. It is best preserved on its northern side, where it merges with a modern field wall. Inside the enclosure, to the west of the old graveyard, are souterrain chambers with drystone walls, close together and parallel to each other; they are poorly preserved. Souterrains are a feature of a number of ecclesiastical sites. The fine inscribed slabs may represent the work of several artists. There are carved figures, and interlacing typical of Irish art between the eighth and tenth centuries. The Moylough belt-shrine, found nearby, displays a similar style. The stones at the site are replicas of the originals which can now be seen in Sligo Museum and in the National Museum, Dublin.[8]

CASHEL, Tipperary: Rock of Cashel

Cashel lies inland in southern Ireland on the N8, fifteen miles north-north-west of Clonmel. It was the chief stronghold of the kings of Munster for 900 years. Cashel's name comes from *caisel*, an Irish word derived from the Latin *castellum*, meaning a circular stone fort. It is built on a rocky outcrop that dominates the surrounding land. Since pottery dating from the sixth century has been found here, Cashel is an early site. Its first king was said to be Conall Corc, the son of a British mother who had returned from long exile in the land of the Picts. This may imply that Conall came from a group of Irish who had colonized parts of south Wales in around 400 and who were subsequently expelled. At Cashel, Patrick is said to have baptized either Conall or his brother and predecessor.

It is not known how soon there was an ecclesiastical presence at Cashel, but a large church bell survives, dating from the ninth century. It is 30 cm high and 20 cm across and is preserved in Limerick University. A replica of the bell can be seen in the museum at Cashel. In 1101 the ruler of the fortress handed over the Rock to the Church, as the seat of the new Diocese of Cashel. New buildings were constructed, including a round tower, a cathedral, and a magnificent chapel built between 1127 and 1134 by Cormac, King of Cork and Bishop of Cashel. This is the best-preserved Romanesque church in Ireland.

Cormac's chapel has a distinctive Irish character with its small scale and its simple ground plan, without aisles. The barrel-vaulted ceiling of the nave is surmounted by a steeply pitched roof, which serves the dual purpose of anchoring the nave vault firmly by its vertical thrust and of providing space for apartments, perhaps *scriptoria*, over the church. This two-level design seems to be found only in Ireland; there are simpler examples at Kells and Glendalough.

Cormac's chapel also shows the influence of German and English models. Irish monks from the German monastery of Regensburg had returned to Ireland to collect alms for building their church a few years before Cormac's chapel was begun. Dirmicus, abbot of Regensburg from 1121 to 1233, sent four of his monks to help build Cormac's chapel. They included Conrad the carpenter and William: their names sound German rather than Irish. The chapel's twin towers at the junction of the nave and chancel are unique in Ireland; they recall churches in Bavaria and the Rhineland.[9]

There is also evidence of English Norman influence on Cormac's chapel. The groined and ribbed vaulting of the chancel resembles that of Durham cathedral. The *tympana* over the north and south doors, rare in Ireland, also suggest Norman models. The north doorway is richly decorated; its fine *tympanum* depicts a centaur hunting a lion with a bow and arrow. Features of Cormac's chapel were borrowed by architects of other churches in southern Ireland, such as Ardfert and Kilmalkedar, both of which have arcaded wall surfaces like those of Cormac's chapel.[10]

St Patrick's cross formerly stood in front of the cathedral. It has been replaced by a replica; the original is now in the museum. It stands 2.3 metres high and dates from the early twelfth century. The cross is unique in having upright supports to its arms, one of which remains; it is also unusual because it has no ring around the intersection of the shaft and transom. On its west face is a representation of Christ crucified, wearing an ankle-length belted garment. There may have been stones on each side of Christ's head, perhaps with a small angel carved on them. The upright supports might have represented the crosses of the two thieves crucified on either side of Christ. On the east face is a carving of a robed bishop, perhaps Patrick, with his feet resting on an ox head. The cross is tenoned into and supported by a massive base, said to have been the coronation stone of the kings of Munster.[11]

CLONARD, Meath: site of St Finnian's monastery

In the sixth century a monk named Finnian founded a large and famous monastery at Clonard, 34 miles west of Dublin. Finnian chose a central location, only 30 miles from the east coast, so that monks could easily reach Clonard from mainland Britain and Europe. The settlement was in fertile farmland beside the River Boyne; cows grazing the site today are a reminder that the rich pasture could support a large community. There have been sample excavations at the extensive monastic site, but few remains have been uncovered. Down a signed grassy track, a modern church stands within an ancient graveyard. Set in the ground near the church porch is a large rectangular stone basin, which originally contained water for the monastery. Its brackish water was said to cause death to animals but to cure warts.

Another artefact that has survived is an elaborate bucket, only 2.5 cm tall. It is bound with a bronze hoop, and its handle clasps are decorated with fine carving and precious stones. It may have been used to contain holy water. Finnian's relics were enshrined at Clonard until the monastery was destroyed in 887. It was rebuilt in the twelfth century, and its monks adopted the Augustinian rule. A magnificent fifteenth-century font of grey marble limestone survives from the abbey. It can be seen in the apse behind the high altar in the modern Catholic church beside the busy N6 in Clonard village. Lively scenes are carved on its panels: Joseph leads a donkey by its halter as the Holy Family flees to Egypt, and a smiling Bishop Finnian raises his hand in blessing, while an angel beside him holds a Gospel book.

CLONFERT, Galway: St Brendan's cathedral

This tiny settlement is thirteen miles south-east of Ballinasloe, two miles west of the River Shannon. The name Clonfert means 'water meadow of the grave', and well describes the fertile low-lying site where people brought their dead for burial alongside the monks. Brendan is believed to have founded Clonfert in around 558, about twenty years before his death. He is thought to have been buried here. Clonfert was pillaged by the Danes, who sailed up the Shannon from Limerick and burned the monastery in 1016, 1164, and 1179. The earliest surviving feature of the monastery is a cruciform walk of yew trees perhaps planted in the tenth century.

The present cathedral dates from the end of the twelfth century. It is a simple single-chambered building, with *antae*, or pillars, projecting beyond the walls, at each gable. These are a feature of early Irish churches, and were designed to support the roof timbers. The chancel was added in the early thirteenth century, and a beautiful, simple east window was added at this time. A door in the north wall of the chancel leads to a sacristy, in which marks of the wattle roof can be seen in the low plastered ceiling.

Clonfert's magnificent west doorway is perhaps the finest example of twelfth-century Irish Romanesque carving. It was constructed under Bishop Peter O'Moore (1161–71). The door is surmounted by a pediment decorated with carved men's heads set within a geometric design. Some heads are old and bearded, while others are young and clean-shaven. It recalls the ancient Celtic head-cult, in which the entrance to a chieftain's stronghold might be adorned with the potent heads of ancestors or foes. Carved around the doorway are a variety of animals' heads, suggesting Scandinavian influence.

The first stage of *The Voyage of St Brendan* is set in Clonfert (see *Brandon Creek*). As if to illustrate the story, a fifteenth-century mermaid is carved on the chancel arch of the cathedral. She lures unwary monks to destruction as she combs her long, sensuous hair, resting a mirror on her naked body. There was a large monastery at Clonfert throughout medieval times until the Reformation. A State Paper from the reign of Elizabeth I records that before Trinity College, Dublin, was founded, it was proposed to establish the university at Clonfert, since at that time it was known as a seat of learning, and it was in a central location for Irish students. However, the monastery and church were destroyed in 1541, and the monastery was never rebuilt. The church was restored in 1641, but once more fell into ruin. It was eventually repaired in 1900.

CLONMACNOISE, Offaly: St Ciarán's monastery

Five miles south-west of Athlone, in a bend of the River Shannon, Clonmacnoise was founded in about 540 by a young monk named Ciarán. Its name means 'water meadows of the sons of Nós'. Ciarán selected a key point on the broad river, near the Athlone ford and on the esker (or gravel and sand ridge) that forms the great east–west road across central Ireland. Today, passing boats are a reminder that the Shannon, Ireland's longest river, was a major route north and south, so Clonmacnoise was situated at the main crossroads of Ireland.

The water meadows flood annually and provide rich pasture that could support a large community.

Little survives from Ciarán's monastery. Pieces of sixth-century pottery have been found, and in 1990 an ogham-inscribed gravestone was discovered, perhaps dating from the fifth or sixth century. It is the first to have been found in this region of Ireland; the slab lay beneath the new graveyard, at the eastern end of the monastic site. Further excavation of this area revealed a road, traces of houses, corn-drying kilns, and a slipway for boats. At the opposite end of the site, beyond the round tower, underwater excavation carried out in 1994-8 uncovered the remains of a wooden bridge across the Shannon. Tree-ring dating of its oak timbers suggests that it was built in about 804.[12] The construction of a wooden bridge across such a broad river was a remarkable achievement.

Despite Ciarán's early death, Clonmacnoise grew rapidly in importance. Adomnán wrote in his *Life of Columba* (*c.*690) that when Alither was abbot of Clonmacnoise, Columba paid him a visit. He relates: 'When they heard of his approach, everyone in the fields near the monastery came from all directions. Together with those inside the monastery, they most eagerly accompanied their abbot, Alither. They passed beyond the enclosure wall of the property, and with one accord they went to meet St Columba, as if he were an angel of the Lord.'[13] Adomnán hints here that Iona was rather more important than Clonmacnoise!

By the seventh century, Clonmacnoise had a large non-monastic population and had acquired many dependent churches. This led to disputes over property. In about 700 Tiréchán, the biographer of Patrick, complained that the community at Clonmacnoise forcibly held many churches that had been founded by Patrick. In spite of their rapturous welcome of Columba, a further dispute arose between the monks of Clonmacnoise and those of Columba's foundation at Durrow, 35 miles south-east. Monks from the two communities fought each other in 764, and 200 men from Durrow were killed.

There was intensive settlement around the monastery, with circular houses where artisans lived with their families: metalworkers in iron and bronze, gold and silver, and craftsmen skilled in antler-working or comb-making. There were also stone masons who, besides carving crosses, produced some 700 grave markers over a period of 400 years. A piece of scratched bone that was used by an apprentice to practise plaitwork patterns still survives. His attempts were rather unskilled!

Since Ciarán was not of noble birth and his family was not native to the area, he left no dynasty from which abbots might be chosen. His family was not represented among later abbots, and the monastery remained independent of other clans. Chroniclers in the community kept records of significant events from at least the eighth century, and it is possible to compile an almost complete list of abbots from Ciarán's time to the twelfth century. The settlement's churches were burnt down more than thirty times during this period, by accident, by Irish kings, and by Viking raiders.

There are the remains of seven churches and a large cathedral in the enclosure, with three fine crosses and a round tower. Near the centre of the compound is the smallest of the churches, *Teampall Ciaráin*. According to tradition, Ciarán was buried here, and pilgrims used to take home soil from the grave to heal their sick. A relic known as St Ciarán's Hand was kept here until 1684, when the chapel was still roofed. The early tenth-century building has putlog holes in its walls: these held timbers to which scaffolding was tied during the chapel's construction. Its walls are no longer vertical, since so many burials around the founder's tomb have caused the earth to shift.

The round tower stands near the river bank at the west end of the enclosure. Annalists recorded its completion in 1124. However, storms caused damage in the following decades, and in 1135 the top of the tower was struck off by lightning. Close to the round tower is a replica of one of Ireland's most magnificent crosses, the 'Cross of the Scriptures'. The original can be seen in the museum at the site. Its shaft and head were carved from a single piece of sandstone, and an inscription round its base asks prayers for King Flann and for Abbot Colmán who made it. Colmán was abbot from about 904 to 926 and erected the largest of the churches on the site.

Toward the southern end of the enclosure stands the south cross, carved in the ninth century. A damaged inscription on its base suggests that it was commissioned by the father of King Flann, who is mentioned on the Cross of the Scriptures.

Both are made from sandstone, and they were probably quarried in County Clare, transported up the Shannon, and carved here in the monastic workshops. Much of the south cross is covered with abstract ornament, in the form of interlacing and fretwork, spirals and bosses. This style of decoration appears to derive from earlier metal-encased examples. The elaborate bosses echo the shapes and patterns found on metalwork and jewellery of the period.[14]

Built into the enclosure wall to the north is *Teampall Finghin* (or Finnian's church), dating from 1160–70. The ruined stone church has a unique round tower that also served as a belfry. With frequent raids and a very large community, the monks may have felt the need for this second tower, into which they could hurry for protection. The belfry is set at the junction of the chancel and the nave; its conical cap is well preserved. The cathedral incorporates work dating from the tenth to the fifteenth century, and has a sixteenth-century sacristy. Medieval figures of Patrick and two other saints are carved above the cathedral's great north door.

One of the main approach roads to the monastery from the east leads past the Nuns' Church. It is 500 metres east of the main site, and stands within a separate enclosure, surrounded by its cemetery. According to the chronicles, there was a stone church here, which was burnt down in 1082. Its remains are incorporated into an adjoining field wall. The annals relate that the present church was completed in 1127 by Dearbhforgaill, wife of the king of Breifne (now Meath). Its ornate west door was restored in the nineteenth century.

CROAGH PATRICK, Mayo: St Patrick's Mountain

It is unlikely that Patrick visited this mountain, but it has been climbed by pilgrims since the twelfth century. Croagh Patrick is 763 metres high; it is now the site of an annual pilgrimage held in Patrick's honour on the last Sunday in July. The mountain lies six miles west of Westport and rises abruptly from the plain. It can be climbed from Murrisk on the R335, where there is a car park. A small road leads first to a white statue of Patrick, from where a stony track continues. The final climb is up a steep slope covered with quartzite scree. The ascent is strenuous and takes two or three hours. As one climbs, there are magnificent views over Clew Bay to the north and Connemara to the south. There is a chapel on the flat top of the hill; many pilgrims shed their footwear before completing the final stage of their journey.

DEVENISH ISLAND, Fermanagh: St Molaise's monastery

This island is at the southern end of Lower Lough Erne, three miles north of Enniskillen. It has been uninhabited since 1922 and consists of about 123 acres of grazing land. On the island are the remains of a monastery founded in the sixth century by Molaise. There is a small twelfth-century oratory named after him, which may have been built over the first church on the island. It was roofed until the eighteenth century. The stone coffin of Molaise used to be in this chapel; it has now been moved to the Great Church. An impressive round tower, dating from perhaps the twelfth century, is perfectly preserved. It stands over 25 metres high and tapers towards its conical cap. There is a doorway 2.7 metres from the ground, and inside there are five storeys. Visitors can still climb the tower. To the north-west of the round tower is a holy well; an ancient thorn tree formerly grew beside it.

Some 40 metres west of the tower are the remains of the Great Church, dating from the thirteenth century; it served both the Celtic monks and the people of the parish of Devenish. Higher up the hill are the ruins of St Mary's abbey. This was begun by the Augustinians in the twelfth century and reconstructed in the fifteenth and sixteenth centuries. There are remains of a guesthouse, refectory, chapter house, and cloister to the north of the abbey. There is a fine cross, 2 metres high, with an elaborately carved shaft and a crucifixion carved on its east face. It dates from the fifteenth or sixteenth century. The difference in stone and finish between the cross head and its pillar suggests that they were not originally intended to form a single unit.

A small hand bell from Devenish is now in the National Museum, Dublin, and the shrine of Molaise can also be seen there. It was made to contain a copy of the Gospels, but the manuscript has disappeared. The shrine is in the form of a small box made of bronze, covered with ornamental silver plates. On the front is a cross, with symbols of the four evangelists between its arms. An inscription at its base requests 'a prayer for Cennfailad, for the successor of Molaise, and for Gilla Baithin, the craftsman who carried out the embossment'. Cennfailad was abbot of Devenish from 1001 to 1025. The craftsman had restored an earlier house-shaped shrine.

From May to September there is a regular ferry service to the island from Trory, two miles north of Enniskillen. The boat departs from Trory Point, down a short lane at the junction of the B52 to Kesh and the A32 to Ballinamallard. It runs daily; on Sundays it sails only in the afternoon.

DONAGHMORE, Meath: St Cassán's church

A mile north-east of Navan on the N51, Donaghmore is the site of an early monastery, with a well-preserved round tower and a ruined church. Its name means *Domnach Mór*, or 'great church'. *Domnach* is an early Irish word derived from the Latin *dominica*, meaning 'that pertaining to the Lord'. The term pre-dates monastic life, and probably indicates a non-monastic church, of the kind established by Patrick. Scattered across northern Ireland are thirty churches with this name-element; they may indicate where Patrick and his first companions worked.[15]

Patrick was said to have founded a community at Donaghmore and placed it in the care of a monk named Cassán, whose relics were venerated here. The tower has a round-headed doorway 3.6 metres above the ground, with a relief of the crucifixion carved on its keystone. Christ's legs are twisted; a human head has been carved on either side of the architrave or moulded door frame. There are the remains of a small church beside the tower, dating from the fifteenth or sixteenth century, and some early gravestones in the churchyard. The round tower was restored in 1841.

DROMISKIN, Louth: St Lughaidh's monastery

The village of Dromiskin is not far from the N1, near the Irish Sea coast, five miles south of Dundalk. A monastery is said to have been founded here by a disciple of Patrick named Lughaidh. Its remains include an early round tower dating from the ninth century. It has an unusually squat shape, and stands only 17 metres high. The second abbot, Ronan, died when the plague swept through Ireland in 664. There are the remains of a large high cross constructed between 844 and 924, during the reign of High King Finneath.

The monastery was plundered by the Irish in 908, by the

Danes in 978, and again by the Irish in 1043. Among Celtic peoples, tribal ties were strong, and even monks were involved in family rivalries, fighting men of other communities. However, since Dromiskin is near the coast, it was also an inviting target for Viking marauders.

Beside the high cross are the remains of the thirteenth-century east end of the parish church; a fifteenth-century window was later added to it. Nearby is a carved spiral pillar, once part of the church doorway; it dates from the ninth or tenth century.

DRUMCLIFFE, Sligo: St Columba's monastery

This is the site of a monastery founded by Columba around 574. It is five miles north of Sligo city on the N15. The community was frequently mentioned in the Irish annals until the thirteenth century, when it began to decline, and its churches were plundered and robbed. Excavation of the early monastic site has uncovered a wide range of animal, fish, and bird remains, together with seeds of cereals and other plants. Hearths and storage pits indicated considerable domestic activity, and there were cultivation ridges where crops were grown. Craftsmen fashioned items of iron and bronze, antler and bone.[16]

The principal visible remains are a ruined round tower and two high crosses. The tower survives to a height of only 8.3 metres; the rest was demolished, and the stone was used to construct a bridge in the eighteenth or nineteenth century. There is a fragment of a plain cross, and also a fine tenth-century high cross, on whose east face are carvings of Adam and Eve, Cain and Abel, Daniel in the lions' den, and Christ in glory. Carved on its west face are the Presentation of Christ in the temple, two figures, and the Crucifixion. The cross is also decorated with fabulous beasts and interlacing patterns.

FERNS, Wexford: St Maedoc's monastery and well

The town of Ferns is nineteen miles north of Wexford, on the N11. Its name may come from the Gaelic for 'a place abounding in alders'. A monastery was founded here in the second half of the sixth century by a prince-monk named Aedh. He studied with Finnian of Clonard and is said to have established a number of churches in the Irish kingdom of Kinsella, which corresponds roughly with the present diocese of Ferns. His pet-name was Maedoc ('my little Aidan') or Mogue.

In 598 Bran Dubh, King of Leinster, gained a victory at the Battle of Dunboyke and, in gratitude for Maedoc's assistance, gave him land for a monastery at the royal seat of Ferns. The extent of the enclosure's rampart may be indicated by the semicircular wall which bounds part of the ancient graveyard beside the cathedral. Maedoc was the principal bishop of Leinster for about forty years. His staff survives in the National Museum, Dublin, and his bell and reliquary are preserved in the library of Armagh cathedral. One of Maedoc's successors was Moling, who is said to have named the well at Ferns in honour of its founder. The Second Irish *Life of Maedoc of Ferns* states that when a king of Breifne was inaugurated, his wand, or sceptre, was to be cut from the hazel tree beside Maedoc's hermitage.[17]

In 787 the cathedral was referred to as 'the stone church of Ferns', at a time when building in stone was still rare. It became the burial place of the kings of Leinster. During the ninth and tenth centuries, the city and its cathedral were ravaged by the Irish and by the Danes, who plundered the church six times. In 1154 Dermot McMurrough, the last king of Leinster, burned the city and monastery but rebuilt the church in 1169 as an abbey for Augustinian canons. He died in 1171 and asked to be buried 'near the shrines of St Mogue and St Moling' at Ferns.

There are the remains of three high crosses in the graveyard. Parts of the present cathedral date from 1223–43, when the first Anglo-Norman bishop rebuilt it; the rest is more recent. Nearby, a ruined thirteenth-century building may have been the parish church. Maedoc's well lies across the road from the cathedral, a little further down the hill. It is very deep and was arched over in 1847. The spring water flows through a conduit into a stone trough beside the path that leads to the well.

FORE, Westmeath: St Féchín's monastery

The first monastery established by the seventh-century monk, Féchín was on a hillside at Fore. The site is two and a half miles east of Castlepollard and twenty miles west of Navan. In the tenth century a simple rectangular church was built on the hillside. Its west doorway is capped with a giant lintel, decorated with a plain carved cross within a circle. A small graveyard surrounds the church; it contains a high cross and a tower house known as the Anchorite's Cell, with a nineteeenth-century mausoleum built on to it. The monastery was a bishopric until the twelfth century, when the Normans built a large Benedictine abbey in the valley below, and life at Féchín's foundation probably came to an end. The fortress-like ruins of the abbey include a church, two tower houses, part of a cloister, domestic buildings, and a circular dovecote. Further off in the fields are two gates, remains of the old town walls.

Between the Celtic monastery and the Benedictine abbey, a ruined mill is said to stand on the site of one built by Féchín. It is fed by underground streams from Lough Lene, a mile away, on the far side of the mountain. The rivulets emerge from the hillside and flow into a triangular millpond before continuing through the mill. Between the mill and the Benedictine abbey, beneath an ancient ash tree, is Féchín's holy well. It is a triangular structure, its walls formed by three great stone slabs. The well is named *Doaghféighín*, or Féchín's Vat. It is now dry but formerly contained water in which Féchín was said to have knelt in prayer. Delicate children were immersed in the water to be cured through Féchín's intercession. Gnarled roots of the ash tree are now entwined with the stones of Féchín's Vat. Clouties are tied to the tree, as mute prayers for healing.

GALLARUS ORATORY, Kerry: early chapel

Gallarus Oratory overlooks Smerwick Harbour, near the western end of the Dingle Peninsula. It is the only complete early medieval chapel on the mainland; its shape has been compared with that of an upturned boat. A banked wall demarcates the monastery in which it stood, and an inner wall separates the remains of the monks' huts from the chapel. The building dates from around the eighth century and is made from local gritstone. The little church is constructed with unmortared stones, each layer set further inwards, to form a curved roof. Its nine ridge stones are still intact. Often a corbelled roof of this design collapses in the middle, its weakest point, unless its masons are exceptionally skilled. Such chapels are almost all found in Kerry.

The oratory has a low doorway at its western end, with two large lintel stones. A wooden or leather door hung from a pair of projecting stones inside the chapel. At its eastern end, a small circular window splays inwards, to shed morning light on the missal, for the priest to celebrate the Eucharist. We can imagine eager, if weary, pilgrims gathered outside to receive the sacrament, before starting their climb up Brandon Mountain, where they would visit Brendan's shrine at its summit.

GLENDALOUGH, Wicklow: St Kevin's monastery

Glendalough is twelve miles inland, and 25 miles south of Dublin. It can be crowded with day-trippers on summer weekends; it is generally quieter during the week. To find it, take the R755, which runs south from Bray through the hills to Arklow. At Laragh, turn off into a wooded valley, opening out to the west. After about a mile, Glendalough comes into view: it is famous for its scenic beauty as well as its monastic remains, which are built beside a pass through the Wicklow Mountains, and border two lakes. The name *Gleann-dá-loch* means 'glen of the two lakes'.

According to his Latin Life, Kevin founded a great monastery in the lower part of the valley where two rivers meet. Once it was established, he entrusted it to the care of responsible monks and returned to the upper valley, a mile to the west, to live once more as a hermit. Here he built a small dwelling in a narrow place between the mountain and the lake, where there were dense woods and clear streams. This area is known as Kevin's Desert. He was said to have fed on sorrel and nettles. Beside the shore, sorrel of unusually fine quality still grows; nettle broth was considered a valuable food at this time, and sorrel soup is still much prized.

On a promontory overlooking the Upper Lake, the remains of a circular hut known as Kevin's Cell have been excavated, and there are possible sites of other huts further up the hillside. There is an early church, *Teampall na Skellig*, on a shelf above the Upper Lake, close to 'St Kevin's Bed', a cave in the rock face which may have been a Bronze Age mineshaft.[18] According to tradition, Kevin used this as a shelter. The Poulanass River cascades down the hillside into the Upper Lake on its southern shore, and nearby is the Reefert church, in a grove of hazel trees. This appears to have been a church used by the solitary monks who chose to live in Kevin's Desert.

The Reefert church is a fine eleventh-century building with an early example of a chancel arch. A large stone with four interlinked crosses may have been an altar front; it is now in

St Kevin's church in the monastic city. Reefert cemetery is one of the few in which Celtic grave markers are still in their original position, lying flat on the graves, with other slabs and small crosses serving as upright headstones.[19] The name Reefert appears to derive from *Ríg Fearta*, or 'burial place of kings'. The title may date from the late twelfth century when the royal family of the O'Tooles was driven from Kildare into the Wicklow Mountains by the Normans.

After some years as a hermit beside the Upper Lake, Kevin apparently returned to the monastic city to die. His Life relates that he sent a party of monks to the hermitage to pray for him. It describes his burial place, 'to the east of the Lower Lake'. This appears to indicate St Mary's church, at the western end of the monastic city. St Mary's is one of the earliest churches on the site; in the eighteenth century it was still venerated as the place of Kevin's burial. Its chancel was probably built in the tenth century, but its nave is considerably earlier.

It is a common opinion that the monks moved to the lower site only after Kevin's death, but it is equally possible that Kevin himself selected this location. The remains of the monastic city here are extensive, with five churches and a round tower. Another two churches were later built farther down the valley. The main entrance to the monastery is close to the road where it crosses the Glendasan River. The present bridge may stand on the site of an earlier one, which the annals describe as being swept away in the great flood of 1177.

The enclosure is approached by a gateway, the only surviving monastic entrance in Ireland. The impressive building dates from some time after 900. Two fine granite arches survive; its *antae*, or projecting walls at each end suggest that there was a timber roof. The outline of a large, simple cross is carved on a giant slab beyond the inner arch. This marked out the monastery as a place of sanctuary, where criminals could take refuge from the law. Beyond the arches are preserved the large paving slabs of the original causeway into the monastic city.

St Kevin's church is the best-preserved building within the enclosure. Its steeply pitched stone roof is built on the corbel principle, like the beehive huts of Kerry; each stone slopes slightly outwards to throw off the rain. It is similar in construction to Columba's House in Kells. In each, there is a first floor with a loft above, in which monks may have slept. In St Kevin's church there are holes for beams that supported the first floor, 3.8 metres above ground level. A small round tower is built into the west gable; a similar belfry was constructed at Trinity church, farther down the valley, but it collapsed during a storm in 1818.

North of St Kevin's church is a building known as the Priests' House, since priests were buried here in the eighteenth and nineteenth centuries. Set over its doorway is an early carved stone depicting a robed, seated abbot. To his left, an attendant holds a crozier; to his right, a stooping monk rings a hand bell. At the centre of the monastic city is the cathedral, a large building constructed over several hundred years from the ninth century onward. It is referred to in the annals as 'the abbey' and was an imposing building: its nave is wider than that of any other early Irish church. Outside it stands a tall ringed cross of granite.

The round tower dominates the monastic city. Although it is built at the bottom of the valley, it can be seen by travellers approaching from every direction. It is about 30 metres high, and a watchman at the top could spot attackers advancing from either end of the valley, or over the mountains. At the top, four windows face the compass points; below were six floors, four of them each lit by a tiny window. Since a monastery served as a sanctuary not only for people but also for goods and cattle, looting was frequent. Glendalough is first recorded as being burned in 770. Over the next 400 years, annals note its destruction on nineteen occasions. Danes attacked nine times, Irish plunderers once, and three times there were accidental fires.

During the twelfth-century reforms of the Irish Church, Glendalough was handed over to a group of Augustinian canons, but it was destroyed several times and finally suppressed in the sixteenth century. Pilgrims continued to visit the site, especially on Kevin's feast day (3 June). Stone crosses at various points in the valley may mark the route they followed. Their procession ended beside the Upper Lake, in Kevin's Desert. There is now a small retreat centre beside the road above the monastic city, and there are plans to construct hermitages where, once again, people can come to experience the solitude and beauty of the valley.

GOUGANE BARRA, Cork: St Finbarr's monastery

Six miles east-north-east of Glengariff, the R584 passes
through the dramatic Pass of Keimaneigh. For almost a mile
there are sheer rock faces on either side of the road; ferns and
flowering plants cling to crevices in the cliffs. Close to the
head of the pass, a narrow road branches north to Gougane
Barra Forest Park and Lough. This is a dark lough surrounded
on three sides by high hills. It is the source of the River Lee,
which falls in cascades down the rocky hillside and, in times of
heavy rain, fills the whole valley with the sound of rushing
water.

Gougane Barra means 'Finbarr's rocky cave'; it is the site of
a monastery founded by Finbarr in the seventh century, on a
little island in the lough. The island is connected to the shore
by a causeway and contains a cluster of buildings: a tiny chapel
and the ruins of monastic buildings. Eight small circular cells
surround the complex. A modern church has been erected on
the island. An ancient cemetery and Finbar's well can be seen
beside the entrance to the causeway leading to the island.
There is an annual pilgrimage here on the Sunday nearest to 25
September, Finbarr's feast day.

HOLY ISLAND: see INISHCEALTRA

INISHCEALTRA, Clare: Monastery of Sts Colum and Caimin

Inishcealtra, or Holy Island, is twenty miles north-east of
Limerick, in Lough Derg, the largest lake on the River
Shannon. The tiny island is situated in Scarriff Bay, the most
picturesque arm of Lough Derg. In the summer, boats sail here
from the landing stage at Mountshannon Angler Centre, a
mile to the north-east (tel. 016 921615; 086 8749710). Boat
trips can also be arranged from the East Clare Heritage Centre
at Tuamgraney, three miles west of the island.

In the sixth century, a monk named Colum of Terryglass
founded a monastery on Inishcealtra. According to his Life, he
found a lime tree on the island, 'whose distilled juice filled a
vessel, and that liquor had the flavour of honey and the
headiness of wine'. Tea made from lime flowers does taste of
honey; the lime tree is not indigenous to Ireland, however, and
so it is relatively rare. Colum eventually died of the plague. In
the seventh century, Caimin became abbot of the monastery,

which became known as a centre of learning. From 836 onward the community suffered from Viking attacks. The *Annals of Innisfallen* record that in 922 the foreigners 'have thrown into the water its relics and shrines'. At the beginning of the eleventh century, the High King Brian Boru rebuilt some of the monastery, and his brother Marcan became its abbot. Inishcealtra was a centre of pilgrimage from medieval times until the nineteenth century.

It is a peaceful island, with six churches, a hermit's cell, and a round tower. Starting from the landing-place on the north side, one first sees a small building with a simple cell at its west end. South of this is a cemetery, with a small ruined oratory. To the west of this is a larger church with a chancel, called St Caimin's church. Brian Boru added the chancel on to an earlier nave. The windows of St Caimin's church are constructed in various styles: semicircular, square-headed and also triangular – a unique instance in early Irish architecture. To the south of Caimin's church is St Brigit's church. It stands within an enclosure entered from the west through an elaborate doorway. East of St Brigit's church is the larger church of St Mary, and nearby, on the eastern shore of the island, is St Mary's well, set within a stone wall.

The incomplete round tower is 24 metres high, and has a doorway 3.5 metres from the ground. A paved way leads from it to a small enclosure, containing a tiny cell associated with a hermit named Cosgraich. There are fine tombstones inscribed with crosses, dating from the eighth to the eleventh century, and remains of four high crosses. An inscription in Irish on the base of one of them reads: 'the grave of the ten men'. It probably refers to warriors who died while defending the monastery. At various places on the island are five bullaun stones, each with a hollow carved into it; these are often associated with monastic sites, but their purpose is unknown.

INISHMURRAY, Sligo: St Molaise's monastery

The small island of Inishmurray is twelve miles north-west of Sligo, and six miles from the shore. It was abandoned by its inhabitants in 1948, and has a remarkable group of early Christian remains. The monastery was founded by Molaise, probably in the sixth century, and was one of the first to be plundered by the Vikings in the eighth century. Its massive cashel wall, rebuilt in 1880, has led to speculation that the monastery was founded within a pre-existing stone fort. The oval enclosure is divided into three unequal sections. The largest contains the Men's Church (*Teampall na bhFear*) and the tiny early church of Molaise (*Teach Molaise*). A wooden statue of the monk was formerly inside this chapel; it is now in the National Museum, Dublin. Nearby are three examples of a monument known as a leacht. This is a small square stone platform or altar, which often has a pillar erected on it, inscribed with a cross.[20]

In the next section of the enclosure is a large oval building whose roof beams are supported by stones projecting from the wall face. It is known as the Schoolhouse, since the islanders used it for this purpose. Nearby is the Fire House (*Teach na Teine*), a medieval building that contained the community's hearth and is believed to have been the monastic kitchen. There are fifty engraved slabs and pillars in the enclosure and on altars around the island, which were visited by pilgrims as they moved around the island to venerate its holy sites. North-west of the enclosure is the Women's Church (*Teampall na mBan*), and the women's graveyard. North of the enclosure is a small Sweathouse (*Teach an Allais*), which functioned like a sauna.[21]

There is no harbour on the island, but it can be reached by boat in suitable weather conditions. Trips can be arranged privately through Rodney Lomax at Mullaghmore village (tel. 071 66124) or Tommy McCallion at Rosses Point (tel. 071 42391).

KELLS, Meath: St Columba's monastery; St Columba's House

This town is in the valley of the Blackwater, twenty miles west of Drogheda, at the intersection of the N3 and N52. In 807, Columba's monks abandoned their home on Iona in the face of Viking attacks. The abbot of Iona transferred the headquarters of the Columban monastic family network to Kells, 25 miles inland, and better protected from Norse raids. The name Kells derives from the monks' cells at the centre of the early settlement.

Outside the cathedral, four high crosses survive from the Celtic monastery. The south cross was probably erected soon after the monks arrived from Iona. It is inscribed 'the Cross of Patrick and Columba', and stands beside a tenth-century round tower, into which the monks could climb for safety, drawing their ladder up after them. The tower, 28 metres high, must have been used frequently, for the monastery at Kells was plundered at least seven times before 1006. Most round towers have four windows at the top, so that the monks could keep watch in all directions. Unusually, this example contains five windows, each facing one of the five ancient roads that lead to Kells. The unfinished east cross dates from the twelfth century; it shows how plain panels were prepared first and carvings executed later.

To the north-west of the cathedral is Columba's House, which may have been built by monks from Iona in the ninth century. It is a small church with a basement, through which one enters the building, and walls over 1.2 metres thick. The church has a steeply pitched roof, and between the barrel vault and the roof is an attic or croft divided into three rooms, where monks could work and sleep. One can climb up a steep ladder into the croft: it is not difficult to imagine the monks sleeping comfortably above their little church. This may be one of the few buildings to have survived intact from early times. It is kept locked, but the key is held at no. 27, down the road.

When the monks fled from Iona, they brought their treasures with them including, perhaps, the *Book of Kells*, a magnificently decorated Gospel book, which was created on Iona around 800. Its text is a poor version of the Latin Gospels; it is interesting that its scholarship does not match the skill lavished on its illustrations. These were executed in the latest Northumbrian style by monks trained at Lindisfarne. When Kells was plundered in 1006, the Gospel book was stolen and buried for three months. It was retrieved, but had lost its jewel-encrusted cover. It is now in the library of Trinity College, Dublin.

KILDARE, County Kildare: St Brigit's cathedral and well

Situated some thirty miles west of Dublin, Kildare means 'place of the oak'. In the late fifth or early sixth century, Brigit established a community beside this holy tree. The monastery soon grew in importance, and Brigit's early Lives were written to enhance its fame. Around 650, a monk named Cogitosus wrote a biography of Brigit that provides us with a valuable description of Kildare a hundred years after her death. He speaks of a double community of monks and nuns presided over by an abbess. He tells us of an elaborately decorated wooden church, which contained the shrines of Brigit and Conleth, a hermit and metalworker whom Brigit invited to make church vessels for the monastery and to be the pastor for the surrounding people. The two shrines, one on either side of the altar, were adorned with precious metals and gems. There were crowns of gold and silver hanging above them, and the church also contained images, paintings, and partition walls made of boards.[22]

Brigit's relics were venerated at Kildare until it was raided by the Danes in 836. Little survives of the Celtic monastery except the remains of a high cross and a round tower. Just south of the thirteenth-century cathedral, the foundations of a rectangular building were uncovered in 1966. Now named the Fire Temple, this may have contained the convent's communal hearth. A street beside the cathedral is still called Fire Temple Lane. When Gerald of Wales visited Brigit's convent in the twelfth century, he saw a fire, which the nuns carefully tended.

Kildare cathedral is set on a low ridge where three roads cross, and Brigit's monastic 'city' became a large one. In the seventh century Cogitosus described it as 'the chief of almost all the Irish churches'. He added that the king's treasury was in Kildare, and the cathedral must have been worth plundering, as it was raided by the Vikings sixteen times. Kildare seems to have been singled out for its wealth, since it was pillaged more frequently than other Irish monasteries. This suggests a steady flow of pilgrims, who donated generous gifts to Brigit's shrine. Gerald of Wales gives a glowing description of a fine illuminated manuscript, which he called the *Book of Kildare*; it no longer survives but was in the tradition of the *Book of Kells*.

One of the ancient roads leading to Kildare passes through Tully, a mile south of the city. Here is Brigit's well; its water flows into a stream, the site of the convent's water mill. There is no stream in Kildare, and running water was necessary to turn a mill wheel, in order to grind the community's flour. The well is still a place of pilgrimage; it can be found by following a signed road opposite the Irish National Stud. Brigit's well is at the far end of a small meadow; its water flows through a pool, where a stone trough and seats on either side allow pilgrims to bathe. Beside the well, a larch tree is hung with 'clouties' – symbolic prayers for healing. A closer look at the cloutie tree indicates the kinds of cures for which Brigit is invoked: bandages and handkerchiefs, socks and stockings, and children's toys form silent prayers for healing broken limbs, crippled feet, and sick children. Brigit became a patroness of healers, midwives, and newborn babies.

KILKIERAN, Kilkenny: site of Ciarán's monastery; high crosses

At this village five miles north of Carrick-on-Suir there was a monastery dedicated to an early bishop in southern Ireland, Ciarán of Saighir. Its church was on the site where a large later tomb now stands; it was probably surrounded by monks' wooden huts. There are three high crosses at the site: one is unique in design, with its tall thin shaft and stumpy arms; these may have had wooden extensions. The other two crosses are highly elaborate. The ninth-century west cross is particularly fine. On the east side of its base are eight horsemen; the other three sides are decorated with interlacing and geometric patterns.

Further down the hill are the remains of what may have been a second early church, close to a pre-Christian standing stone. Nearby is Ciarán's holy well. A boulder with a cavity containing water is known as St Ciarán's Font; its water is believed to cure headaches.

KILLALOE, Clare: St Molua's monastery

The village of Killaloe is situated twelve miles north-east of Limerick, at the point where the River Shannon emerges from Lough Derg. Killaloe means 'cell of Molua', a monk who died in the seventh century. An early chapel dedicated to him on Friars' Island, a few hundred metres from the cathedral, survived until the area was submerged by the Shannon hydro-electric works in 1929. Molua was succeeded as abbot of Killaloe by a disciple named Flannan.

The cathedral named after Flannan was built in 1185 on the site of an earlier church. It incorporates a Romanesque doorway from the previous building. Beside it is a stone shaft with parallel inscriptions in Irish ogham and Viking runes, translated as 'a blessing on Thorgrim, who made this stone'. This is one of the few examples of Viking runes in Ireland. A chapel dating from the twelfth century, known as St Flannan's Oratory, stands in the cathedral precinct. This is a small

Romanesque church with a finely carved doorway and a well-preserved stone roof. The cathedral formerly housed Flannan's relics.

KILMACDUAGH, Galway: St Colmán's monastery

This extensive monastic complex lies seventeen miles south-south-east of Galway and three miles west-south-west of Gort, on the R460. Kilmacduagh is one of the finest Irish monastic sites, set in green meadows near the shore of a lough, with the Burren Hills on the horizon. In the seventh century Colmán founded a monastery here on land given to him by his kinsman, Guaire the Generous, King of Connacht. Guaire lived in the nearby town of Gort and provided the workmen and materials to build the monastery.

The cathedral is the largest building within the enclosure: it occupies the site of a rectangular seventh-century church. The cathedral's west end, with its lintelled doorway, roof corbels, and steeply pitched gable, was probably built before the eleventh century.[23] Large blocks of stone from the early church can be seen alongside dressed stones of later times. The cathedral's side chapels date from the fourteenth and fifteenth centuries. Colmán was supposedly buried in a shrine outside the cathedral. Nearby, the ruined church of John the Baptist dates from the tenth century. The remains of Our Lady's church stand beside the road that was driven through the site in the eighteenth century. Next to St John's church, the Glebe House was the later bishops' residence. It is strongly fortified, with slit windows for defence. Signs of a crenellated guard tower suggest that a small garrison of soldiers was based here. From an upstairs oriel window, the bishop used to bless pilgrims who gathered here on Colmán's feast day, 29 October.[24]

The most striking feature of the site is a tenth-century round tower, 30 metres high. It is one of the tallest in Ireland, and leans 0.6 metres out of perpendicular. This is probably because it lacks deep foundations: it was built on soft earth, over the site of an early Christian burial ground. When the tower was restored in the late nineteenth century, skeletons were found lying oriented east to west beneath the centre of the tower and below its walls. The tower had seven timber floors, where many people could take refuge. The lower portion of the tower was found to be filled with large and small stones; above this, human bones found in a deposit of ash provided evidence of a disastrous fire. Copper fragments suggested that the monks had taken refuge in the tower, taking their precious church vessels with them.[25]

Viking raiders plundered the site in the tenth century, and the monastery was destroyed by the Normans in the thirteenth century. It was restored by the local chieftain and by Augustinian canons; its cemetery continues to be used for burial by families from the surrounding area. The key of the cathedral and a guidebook to the ruins can be obtained from the caretaker's house across the road.

KILMALKEDAR, Kerry: St Maolcethair's church

A mile north of Gallarus Oratory near the western end of the Dingle Peninsula, Kilmalkedar is one of the few sites in the area that was not taken over by the cult of Brendan; it is dedicated to a local saint of the Corra Dhuibhne named Maolcethair (d. *c.*636). The present church is twelfth-century Romanesque, with arcading modelled on Cormac's chapel at Cashel, but there are considerable earlier remains. At the churchyard entrance is a sundial, important for monks with an organized day of work and prayer. An early eighth-century pillar-stone inside the church has the Latin alphabet carved on it and was probably used to teach literacy to students. To the west of the church, along its ancient causeway, is the graveyard with a simple high cross and an ogham-inscribed stone.

KILREE, Kilkenny: St Rhuidche's monastery

Kilree is ten miles south of Kilkenny and two miles south of the village of Kells. It is probably named after a monk named Rhuidche (pronounced 'Ree'), about whom little is known. The church stands within its ancient oval enclosure bank, which is unusually well preserved. Early grave markers are dotted around the site. Parts of the ruined church may date from the eighth century; the nave and chancel were considerably enlarged in post-Norman times. A round tower, of uncertain date, stands 20 metres high; it has lost its conical top. The tower is built mainly of long, flat limestone slabs, and has a doorway framed with larger granite boulders.

In a field 60 metres west of the church is a high cross carved from granite. It stands over 2 metres high, and dates from the eighth or ninth century. It was once highly ornate, but is badly weathered. In 1259 the church was handed over by the dean and chapter of the diocese to the large Augustinian priory of nearby Kells, which was a daughter church of Bodmin in Cornwall. The parish was later dedicated to Brigit. A holy well named after her can be seen near to Kilree, on the left roadside verge as one drives north from Kilree to Kells.

KILTURA, Sligo: St Attracta's well

Kiltura is five miles south of Bunnanaddan, and fourteen miles south-south-west of Sligo. To find it, take the R294 west from Gorteen. After passing Sligo Agri Supplies, turn left at the crossroads, as for Charlestown. Turn left, left, and left again into a lane. After 60 metres, park at the cottage on your left. The site is across the road, over a fence, beside the stream. It consists of a holy well, a cross-inscribed stone, a memorial slab and a holed stone. These are all within a ring barrow, situated above the west bank of the stream. The eastern side of the barrow falls away into the water. The holy well and stones are on the south-east side of the barrow. The barrow has a raised central platform, and an earthen bank is visible in places.

Attracta's holy well is a tiny artificial inlet leading from the stream. Attracta was a local saint whose feast was celebrated here until recently, with pilgrims visiting her well and the hawthorn trees that encircled the barrow. Above the well is a sandstone pillar 55 cm high, decorated with a plain ringed cross. Nearby is a slab of purple sandstone with a hole through it. This may have acted as an agreement stone where contracts or pledges of loyalty were made by joining hands through the hole and swearing on it. Such stones are also known as Marriage Stones, where couples would promise fidelity while clasping hands through the stone. There is also a nineteenth-century memorial slab to the Cooke family.[26]

LEMANAGHAN, Offaly: St Manchán's hermitage and shrine

Named after a monk named Manchán, Lemanaghan is on the R436 between Clonmacnoise and Tullamore. At Lemanaghan, a former island in the bog is now a low mound, on which are remains of two Romanesque churches and six early grave slabs. Manchán is said to have settled here with his mother, Mella; a small stone oratory is known as her cell. At the lower end of the site a short track leads to Manchán's well, which is approached down a flight of stone steps. Near the well is an ancient ash tree with knotted roots and branches, to which local people tie clouties. Beside the well is a bullaun stone, a feature of many early monastic sites: a large stone with a cavity containing water. It may have been used for washing, or perhaps its water was blessed and used in worship.

Manchán's magnificent shrine was recovered from the bog; it is now displayed in the nearby Catholic church at Boher. The shrine was made around 1130 and contains a number of bones, believed to be Manchán's. It is constructed of yew wood in the shape of a gabled box 48 cm high. It represents a house for the dead and is lavishly decorated with cast gilt bronze and red and yellow fittings. The shrine is ornamented on either side with elaborate metal crosses, each having five prominent bosses. Around the crosses stood fifty elongated human figures, eleven of which have survived. There are intertwined beasts and serpents at the corners and at each end of the shrine, carved in an Irish version of a late Scandinavian style. During processions, the shrine was carried on a pair of wooden poles, threaded through rings mounted at each corner. This is the largest and most magnificent shrine to have been found in Ireland. If the church is locked, the key can be obtained from the presbytery to the right of the church.

LOUGH DERG, Donegal: St Patrick's Purgatory

Three miles south of Donegal, the R232 branches left off the N15 to Pettigo, from where the R233 leads north through desolate countryside to Lough Derg. In the lough lies Station Island, known in medieval times as St Patrick's Purgatory. Although there is no evidence that Patrick came here, every year large numbers of pilgrims visit the site; during the pilgrimage season, from June to August, no other visitors are allowed on the island. A monk named Mobeoc or Dabeoc settled on one of the other islands in Lough Derg, *Oilean na Naomh* ('Saints' Island'), but nothing is known about him.

Lough Derg attracted pilgrims from across Europe from the late twelfth century onward. The Augustinians established a community on Saints' Island and became responsible for the 'Purgatory' on nearby Station Island. The pilgrimage now lasts three days: each person must walk barefoot and eat only one daily meal, consisting of bread and black tea. Participants keep an all-night vigil in the modern basilica and say special prayers at the penitential 'beds', which are the footings of early monks' cells. There are modern hospices providing accommodation. St Patrick's Purgatory is known as 'the hardest pilgrimage in Christendom'.

LOUTH, County Louth: St Mochta's House

The name of this village derives from Lugh, the Celtic sun god. Situated seven miles west of the Irish Sea coast and seven miles north of Ardee, Louth was formerly so important that it gave its name to the county. St Mochta's House (*Teach Naomh Mochta*) is named after a disciple of Patrick who settled with some followers in Meath. It was said that after several years, because of local opposition, Mochta moved north to Louth, where he founded a large monastery and became its first bishop. He died in the sixth century. St Mochta's House is a small church built probably in the twelfth century. It is a fine example of a style unique to Ireland: a vaulted two-storeyed oratory with a roof croft over a barrel vault. The stone roof is supported by the arched vault beneath it, which prevents the building from falling inwards. A stairway leads to the upper floor, where a monk could sleep or study in the croft above the church.

Next to Mochta's House is the ruined abbey of St Mary, thought to have been founded in 1148. Its fine west end dates from 1312, when it was rebuilt after a fire. Across the road, a wall indicates the site of the former twelfth-century abbey of Sts Peter and Paul, established in 1146. A section of the wall was known locally as 'the pinnacle', but the pinnacle collapsed within living memory. On the south side of the village is a mound on which stood a Norman motte, or castle mound, known as the Fairy Mount.

MONASTERBOICE, Louth: St Buite's monastery

This ruined monastery is near the Irish Sea coast on R168, six miles north-west of Drogheda; it may have been a pre-Christian site. It is known in Gaelic as *Mainistir Bhuithe*; this is the only Irish place-name containing the term 'monaster', meaning a monastery. Little is known about Buite, its founder. After his death in about 521, the monastery became a centre of learning. One of its most renowned scholars, Flann, died in 1056. The Irish annals list the deaths of twenty-two of its abbots between 759 and 1122, and mention a probable occupation by Vikings in about 968. They were expelled by Donal, High King of Tara, who, it is recorded, killed at least three hundred Vikings in the process. The monastery remained in existence until 1122.

Monasterboice boasts two of the finest high crosses in Ireland, both dating from the ninth century, and a ruined round tower over 30 metres high without its cap, one of the tallest in the country. Round towers were built in the ninth, tenth, and eleventh centuries by monks as defences against Viking attacks. They had no key-stone for enemies to pull out, so they could not be demolished as speedily as conventional buildings. Because of their height, they were excellent look-outs. Their doorways were several metres from the ground, reached by a ladder, which could be pulled in when the monks were under attack. The only drawback was that if a burning arrow pierced the floorboards inside, the whole column acted as a chimney and became a blazing inferno. When the round tower at Monasterboice was gutted by fire in 1097, much of the monastery's library and its church treasures were burned.

Close to the round tower is the west cross; it is unusually tall, with a height of 6.4 metres. It is richly decorated with 22 panels depicting scenes from the Old and New Testaments. Near the entrance to the graveyard is the south cross, probably commissioned by Abbot Muiredach, who died at the monastery in 844; an inscription reads 'A prayer for Muiredach, by whom this cross was made'. Punctuating the inscription are carvings of two cats: that on the left fondly licks her kitten, while that on the right clutches a bird which it has just killed. The principal theme of the cross is Christ, Lord of heaven and earth. Unusually, the crucified Christ is depicted naked. Two angels support his head, so that it does not hang in symbolic defeat. The four sides of the cross are richly decorated with scriptural themes and abstract patterns.

There is a third ruined cross in the north-east corner of the compound, believed to have been smashed by Cromwell's forces. Beside it is a granite sundial of uncertain date; it enabled the monks to determine times of worship. Within the enclosure there are also two ruined thirteenth-century churches. They probably had no connection with the monastery, which had by then ceased to function.

RAHAN, Offaly: St Mochta's church

This ruin lies in a field in the village of Rahan. It is situated five miles west of Tullamore, beside the River Brosna. A monastery was said to have been founded here by Mochta in the late sixth century; a new community was established on the site in about 760. There are the remains of the transept of a twelfth-century church; it was cruciform, and had a fine round window. The church was altered in the fifteenth century and rebuilt in 1732. A second church was built in the twelfth century; its wall curves inward to support a barrel-vaulted roof. A third ruined church stands in the graveyard at the other end of the field.

ROSCREA, Tipperary: St Cronan's monastery

This town lies in southern central Ireland at the junction of the N7 and the N62. Roscrea grew around a monastery founded by Cronan in the seventh century. Its early buildings were plundered and burnt many times. The present ruins date from the twelfth century. They consist of a round tower, thought originally to have been 24 metres high and, across the road, the Romanesque west front of the cathedral of St Cronan. Above its round-headed doorway is the figure of a bishop, probably Cronan. The rest of the cathedral was destroyed in 1812, to make way for the new parish church. A twelfth-century high cross stood nearby. The monastic site has been bisected by the modern road through the town.

ST MULLINS, Carlow: St Moling's monastery

At St Mullins, six miles north of New Ross, the River Barrow flows between high wooded banks as it runs south to Waterford Harbour. A monastery was founded here by Moling, who was buried here in about 697. The base of a round tower can still be seen, and the remains of a small early church, 2.5 metres long. The upper portion of a high cross also survives, carved in granite in the ninth or tenth century, with a crucifixion scene. On the opposite bank of the river is Moling's holy well. The water passes through a large pool into a well chapel before flowing down to the river. In about 1160 Moling's monastery was annexed to the abbey of Augustinian canons at Ferns. The canons were responsible for building the six medieval churches, now in ruins, that dominate St Mullins; they may also have built St Moling's Mill.

SCATTERY ISLAND, Clare: St Senan's monastery

This island, only half a square mile in area, lies in the mouth of the River Shannon. It can be visited on foot via a ferry which sails from the market town of Kilrush. Information about sailings can be obtained from the Scattery Island Centre, Merchants Quay, Kilrush. The centre is open from mid-June to mid-September. On the island are the ruins of a monastery founded by a monk named Senan in the sixth century. There were formerly seven churches here, but one has been eroded by the sea.

St Senan's oratory is a small, simple building. It has an east window splayed outwards, a unique architectural feature. To the west is Senan's House, where he is said to be buried. *Teampall Mór* (the great church) has a doorway with a massive lintel, and a later east window. On the north side of the island is a small chapel, with two other simple buildings beside it. There is a round tower, one of the oldest and tallest in Ireland, standing 35 metres high. Unusually, its entrance is at ground level, and its doorway has inclined sides. Many pilgrims still visit the holy well, close to the round tower. The island suffered frequent Viking attacks in the ninth and tenth centuries. The monastery was important in the fourteenth and fifteenth centuries; it was destroyed in the reign of Elizabeth I.

SEIRKIERAN, Offaly: St Ciarán's monastery and well

Ciarán was an early Irish bishop who settled at Saighir (now Seirkieran), first as a hermit and later as abbot of a large monastery. This small settlement is seven miles north of Roscrea and 40 miles north-east of Limerick. Ciarán's monastery is set in rolling hills, with panoramic views in several directions. His Life relates how Ciarán tamed a fierce but frightened wild boar that helped him to collect materials with which to build a church. The author adds: 'This boar was the first disciple, as it were a monk of St Ciarán, in that place.' A wild boar often features in the story of a Celtic monk's chief foundation.

Ciarán's Life also relates how he decreed that the fire in his monastery must not go out. When it was allowed to do so, and the monks could no longer cook or warm themselves, Ciarán prayed and the fire lit itself again.[27] The communal hearth was a central feature of ancient rural communities, and was held to be holy. In monasteries, the fire lit on Easter night might be kept alive throughout the following year. In a number of saints' Lives, fire is rekindled at their prayers, to demonstrate God's power. Christian readers would recall that the great prophet Elijah kindled fire through his prayer, after the prophets of Baal failed to do so.[28]

Ciarán's monastery was plundered many times; it later became an Augustinian priory. The walled monastic compound covers ten acres. There are a few remains of the Celtic monastery: the stump of a round tower, an early grave slab, and the base of a high cross. The water which collects in its socket is believed to cure warts. South of the monastery, beside the R421, a signed track leads to Ciarán's well pool. Nearby is Ciarán's Bush: a hawthorn tree to which clouties are tied, as prayers for healing. The aged bush looks strangely out of place with cars driving past on either side.

SKELLIG MICHAEL, Kerry: monastery

The Skelligs are two rocky islets, nine miles west of the Inveragh peninsula. Boats sail to and around the Skelligs from Valencia Island, where the Skellig Experience Visitor Centre at the landing place conveys information about life on Skellig Michael. Phone 066 9476 327 for details of sailings.

Perched on a rocky peak some 200 metres above the ocean, Skellig Michael is one of the most complete Irish monasteries dating from Celtic times. There are the remains of at least six beehive huts, two square stone chapels, and a ruined church, built on terraces on the sloping rock. The windowless huts have walls two metres thick; most of their roofs are still intact. They have survived because of the mild climate here, with its lack of frost. A second hermitage has been discovered on the higher south peak.

There are carved crosses, grave markers, and two wells. The early monastery is reached by a flight of 1,670 stone steps leading up from the sea. It is thought that the monks brought topsoil from the mainland to create small gardens in which they could grow vegetables. The community was raided by the Vikings in the ninth century, and life on the rock was so harsh that eventually in the twelfth century the monks moved to Ballinskelligs on the mainland. In his novel *Sun Dancing: A Medieval Vision* (1997), Geoffrey Moorhouse has reconstructed life in this remote monastery.

SKREEN, Meath: site of Columba's shrine

Skreen, twelve miles south-west of Drogheda and two miles east-north-east of Tara, was originally known as Achall. In 875 the shrine and relics of Columba were brought for safety to the monastery at Achall. The site was renamed *An Scrín* ('the shrine') or *Scrín Choluim Chille* ('Columba's shrine'). The monastery was plundered several times between the late tenth and thirteenth centuries. The shrine itself was stolen in 1027, but was later recovered. The present ruined church may date from the fifteenth century. To the north-east of the church is a late medieval stone cross. Its short arms may have had wooden extensions; a crucifixion is carved in its west face.

SLANE, Meath: St Erc's monastery

The Hill of Slane is eight miles west of Drogheda and twelve miles from the Irish coast. There is no conclusive evidence that Patrick ever visited Slane, but his seventh-century biographer, Muirchú, tells us that he did. Muirchú relates that Slane was the scene of a dramatic confrontation between the saint and the High King who lived at Tara, twelve miles to the south. He describes how Easter that year fell on the same day as the great Celtic fire festival, when every fire had to be extinguished until a new one was lit on Tara at dawn. Patrick gathered his followers on the hill of Slane, to celebrate the resurrection of Christ by lighting the Easter fire. The furious king came to Tara and encountered Patrick, who then emerged victorious from a contest of magic with the king's bards.

Muirchú linked Patrick with Tara at a time when the Church of Armagh was forging an alliance with the rising dynasty of the Uí Néill, who used the ancient capital of Tara as a symbol of their authority. Muirchú wished to place the conversion of Ireland within a theological context: as the Israelites were delivered from their slavery to the Egyptians in a single night, and as Jesus freed the waiting dead through his resurrection on Easter night, so his servant Patrick delivered Ireland from paganism through celebrating the Easter Vigil and lighting the paschal fire.[29]

Soon after Patrick's death, a monastery associated with a bishop named Erc was built on Slane hill. The earliest mention of a round tower in the Irish annals is of one at Slane. The annals state that in 950, Slane's tower was set on fire by the foreigners of Dublin, and the founder's crozier, a bell, and a large number of people, including the lector, or reader, of the monastery, were all burned in it. [30] The 'foreigners of Dublin' were the Vikings who settled there. No trace of Slane's tower survives today. In 1512 Sir Christopher Fleming established a Franciscan friary on the site; its fine bell tower survives. Nearby are the remains of a college founded to serve the church. It housed four priests, four lay-brothers, and four choristers. The college was built round an open quadrangle. Windows, fireplaces, and a double *garderobe*, or toilet, survive.

TISARAN, Offaly: St Saran's church and holy well

The church of Tisaran is six miles south-east of Clonmacnoise. It was founded by Saran, a seventh-century hermit who came from Clonmacnoise. Its original name was *Cill Beg* (or 'small church'). Later it was known as *Tigh Saráin*, meaning 'house, or church, of Saran'. The square medieval building now stands roofless in a field. Saran's holy well, Tobarsaran, is a mile away, on the bank of the River Brosna. It was an important place of pilgrimage in medieval times. The well is signed from the road and lies on the far side of a field.

TULLY: see KILDARE

Part Two

Scotland

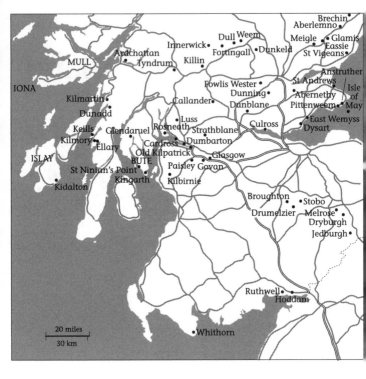

Saints of Central and Southern Scotland

ABERLEMNO, Angus: church and hill fort

Halfway between Forfar and Brechin is Aberlemno, whose name means 'river confluence at the elm tree'. It lies to the south-east of the Pictish stronghold of Finavon. Ninian's followers may have worked here, as nearby Nine Maidens recalls his name, as does Ninewell, a spring below the fort. However, 'nine' at an ancient site may derive from the Gaelic word *nyen*, meaning 'holy'. Three impressive carved Pictish symbol stones stand by the roadside, dating from the late sixth or early seventh century. The largest and finest has Pictish symbols on one side and an interlaced cross with angels on the other. These stones and some early graves indicate that there was a royal burial ground here.[1]

In the churchyard half a mile away, a magnificent early eighth-century royal cross slab depicts a battle between the Picts and the Northumbrians which took place in 685 at Dunnichen, four miles south of Aberlemno. The Picts defeated the Northumbrians, and recovered their territory. Ironically, the other side of the grave-slab is decorated in the latest Northumbrian style with a fine knotwork cross flanked by intertwined beasts and sea-horses, indications that at this time the Pictish Church came under the influence of Northumbria. Nechtán, King of the Picts from 706 to 729, wanted his Christian subjects to abandon their Celtic customs and take on those of Rome, and so in 710 he wrote to Abbot Ceolfrith of Jarrow in Northumbria to seek his help. Bede was a monk in Jarrow at the time and met the Pictish delegation.

Bede records how Nechtán's emissaries asked 'that architects be sent to him in order to build a stone church in the Roman style, promising ... that he and his people would follow the customs of the holy, apostolic, Roman Church as far as they could learn them, in view of their remoteness from the Roman people and language'.[2] Abbot Ceolfrith sent architects to King Nechtán, who built the first stone church in the land of the Picts at Aberlemno. The present church of Aberlemno is modern; however, it has been suggested that a section of the tower at Restenneth Priory, four miles south-west of Aberlemno, may have been constructed by the eighth-century Northumbrian masons whom Bede describes. Its design incorporates a porch with a processional entrance archway through which the monks could walk with dignity down the length of the building. King Nechtán named the stone church at Aberlemno 'Egglespether', or church of St Peter. Those of Meigle and Tealing were also rededicated to Peter, Prince of Rome.[3]

ABERNETHY, Perth and Kinross: St Bride's church

Six miles south-east of Perth, Abernethy is not far from the southern shore of the Firth of Tay. It is an early settlement dedicated to the Irish nun Brigit. A note in the *Pictish Chronicle* claims that it was founded in the mid-fifth century. The note relates that when King Nechtán was driven from his land by his brother Drust he visited Brigit in Ireland and asked her to pray for him. Nechtán was restored to his kingdom, and three years later, Darlugdach, Abbess of Kildare, came to Britain as an exile for Christ. After a further two years, Nechtán offered Abernethy to God and St Brigit. During the Mass of consecration, Darlugdach 'sang Alleluia over the offering'.[4]

Abernethy became the principal seat of the southern Picts, with a Celtic bishop. A stone church was built by King Gartnaith in about 590. Adrian, one of its bishops, was martyred in 875. An imposing round tower was built at the entrance to the churchyard in the eleventh century, one of only two in Scotland. It stands 22 metres high, and indicates the importance of the site as a religious centre. The doorway of the round tower and the window in its belfry are each decorated with a Romanesque arch. There is a Pictish symbol stone near the tower: this symbolic language has not so far been deciphered. Malcolm Canmore and William the Conqueror met at Abernethy, possibly at the church. It remained a Celtic bishopric until about 1273, when government from Rome was introduced.

ANSTRUTHER, Fife: the caves of Caiplie

The small town of Anstruther is on the northern shore of the Firth of Forth, eighteen miles east of Glenrothes. One can reach the caves of Caiplie by turning off the A917 just west of Anstruther, to the tiny settlement of Barnsmuir, beside the shore. Caiplie is half-an-hour's walk along the shore to the south-east, in the direction of Anstruther. The two caves look across the open sea, and were used by monks and hermits from early Christian times until the sixteenth century. The monks enlarged the caves, and on the walls of the larger one, named

'Chapel Cave', they carved small crosses some time between 800 and 1000.

The Christian tradition of living in caves dates back to the time of the desert mothers and fathers of the Near East. They took literally the words of the New Testament Letter to the Hebrews, which describes God's holy ones living in the same manner: 'They were too good for the world and they went out to live in deserts and mountains and in caves and ravines.'⁵ The soft sandstone around the Fife coast created caves in a number of locations, which early Christians used as chapels and as living quarters.

ARDCHATTAN, Argyll and Bute: St Catán's priory

In a beautiful setting on the north shore of Loch Etive, Ardchattan priory is eight miles north-east of Oban. The first church on the site was dedicated to the sixth-century Irish monk Catán. He migrated to the Clyde area, and was said to have been the uncle of Blane. His chief monastery is on the Isle of Bute, beside the Firth of Clyde. The name Ardchattan means 'Catán's hill'. A large Celtic cross slab survives in the priory ruins. The present monastic buildings were constructed in about 1230 by the Vallisculians, who were an offshoot of the semi-eremitical Carthusian order. They also founded Pluscarden and Beauly, farther to the north, in Inverness.

BARRA, Isle of, Western Isles: St Finbarr's church

At the southern tip of the Outer Hebrides, the island of Barra, five miles wide, was a haven for Viking pirates, from where they launched raids in several directions. They also settled there: three place-names end in a Norse suffix meaning a shieling, or summer pastoral settlement. The Norwegians may have lived alongside Celtic Christians, as the island's name, Barra, is a form of Finbarr's name, while an islet to the south is named Pabbay, meaning 'priest's isle' in Norse. Viking sagas describe Norsemen who drove out Barra's Celtic rulers in the mid-ninth century, in order to use the island as a base for plunder, while keeping contact with their relatives in Norway and Iceland.⁶

Cille Bharra, or 'Finbarr's cell', is near the northern tip of the island. A ruined church and two chapels, all dating from an early period, are surrounded by an enclosure wall. Pagan graves of both men and women indicate that the Norwegians brought their wives, but within a hundred years they had accepted Christianity. A grave-slab was discovered at Finbarr's church with an ornamented Celtic cross on one side and an inscription in Norse runes on the other which reads: 'This cross was raised for Thorgerth, daughter of Steinr.' This suggests that the cemetery continued as a Christian burial ground during the Viking period. Cille Bharra remained a popular place of pilgrimage into medieval times.

BIRNIE, Moray: St Brendan's church

Three miles south of Elgin, the old church at Birnie is dedicated to the Irish monk Brendan the Navigator. It is an early foundation. A Celtic monk's hand bell, the Ronnel Bell, is kept at the manse. There are Pictish carvings in the churchyard wall. A number of other settlements are named after Brendan on islands or near the coast, in Scotland, Ireland, and south-western Britain. His cult was popular among sailing peoples, including the Christianized Vikings, and also in medieval times, when sailors rarely learned to swim and so depended on prayer when storms arose.

BRECHIN, Angus: Brechin cathedral

Brechin is 24 miles north-east of Dundee, and eight miles from the North Sea. The eighth-century Pictish King Nechtán sent for Northumbrian stonemasons to build churches in his kingdom, and Brechin cathedral has a fine Northumbrian cross with the Virgin and Child carved at its centre. However, later kings returned to Celtic practices. In the tenth century, under King Kenneth II, the church at Brechin once more followed earlier traditions. A round tower was constructed in the Irish style, and a similar tower was built in Abernethy at this time. That at Brechin is 30 metres high, with a door above ground level for protection; the doorway is flanked by a carvings of two bishops, each carrying a pastoral staff. Brechin became a cathedral only in the mid-twelfth century, under King David I of Scotland. Three magnificent stone fonts at Brechin, Aberlemno, and Restenneth priory are evidence of his royal patronage.

BROUGHTON, Scottish Borders: St Llôlan's chapel

Llôlan is said to have been one of the many Welsh monks who fled from Powys after the Battle of Chester. In the course of the battle, which took place around 613, Ethelfrith, the pagan king of the Angles, massacred many Christians. Llôlan travelled north-eastward, and a tiny chapel at Broughton, eight miles south-west of Peebles, is named after him. It was excavated and roofed in the 1920s. The footings of its walls can be seen, with an arch set low in the present wall; presumably the original floor level was lower. This is one of the few chapels to survive from early times.

Broughton is on the A701 between Biggar and Peebles. To find the chapel, drive north on the A701, enter the village, and pass the B7016 on your left. Stop at the village store on your left and ask for the key to St Llôlan's Cell in the cemetery. Continue to the next exit left. As you turn into it, you will see the old church and cemetery up a lane, through a gate, on the right. The chapel, with its turfed roof, is near the church.

BUTE, Isle of, Argyll and Bute: St Blane's monastery, Kingarth

At the mouth of the Clyde estuary, Bute was attractive to Celtic monks. It was low-lying and fertile, and at the centre of routes from north-east Ireland and south-west Scotland, with Iona to the north-west. The island is sheltered from the ocean and, since it is five miles by fifteen, could support a considerable population. It is so close to the mainland that sheep and cattle could safely swim across. In Celtic times the southern end of Bute was the most populous. There was a fort there and a monastery of some fifty monks, with a surrounding settlement. The community was founded by Catán, who gives his name to Kilchattan Bay, a mile to the north. We know almost nothing of Catán, who apparently arrived from Ireland in the late sixth century. Sources differ as to whether Catán was Blane's uncle or his tutor; as abbot, Catán could well have been both.

Catán's monastery on Bute, now dedicated to Blane, is in a lovely spot in a sheltered valley near the shore. It is surrounded by its original enclosure wall, within which are the remains of a circular fort, a well, and the ruins of monks' huts set against a sheltering cliff. In the cemetery are the footings of a small chapel and a few early crosses. There is a stone bowl, perhaps for washing pilgrims' feet, a traditional ceremony of welcome. Various monk-bishops succeeded Catán and Blane, some of whom met violent deaths at the hands of Norsemen.

The monastery was a centre of culture and craftsmanship: a

tiny ninth-century crucible for casting bronze brooches was found here, and there are designs engraved on slate, which were preparatory sketches made by craftsmen. Norse Christians were buried here: there is a hogback tombstone in the churchyard. A Viking's gold ring and a gold fillet for binding a lady's hair have been found. By medieval times the monks had created an inner cemetery for themselves and an outer one for lay people. There are the remains of the medieval church at the centre of the site. A twelfth-century arch separates the chancel from the nave.

BUTE, Isle of, Argyll and Bute: St Ninian's chapel

St Ninian's Point is on the west coast of the island, four miles south-west of Rothesay. This narrow rocky promontory may be the earliest location on Bute to have been chosen by monks as the location for a chapel. There had been a pagan cemetery on the site; Neolithic flints were found in two hearths below the chapel walls, and, nearby, two small Bronze Age standing stones perhaps mark a chieftain's burial. In late Roman times there was a Christian graveyard here, and in the sixth century a chapel was built of rubble, plaster, and clay. Its inner wall was lined with clay, and its altar had a cavity for relics. The chapel was abandoned after Viking raids but was used again in medieval times.

A mile west of St Ninian's Point is the tiny island of Inchmarnock, which means 'Isle of Mernoc'. For centuries, Christians ferried their dead to Inchmarnock. Scottish people preferred to bury their dead on islands, where their bones would not be disturbed by prowling wolves. Hermits, too, chose to live on islands, where they could be safe from the bears, wildcats, and boar that lived in the northern forests. On Inchmarnock there are the remains of carved crosses from the eighth century onwards, and foundations of a twelfth-century chapel with red sandstone pillars. There were twenty-two St Mernocs, and it is unclear which of these monks gave his name to the island. It is likely to be the Mernoc to whom Kilmarnock, sixteen miles south of Glasgow, is dedicated.

CALLANDER, Stirling: St Kessóg's Mound

Callander is at the foot of the Trossach Hills, fourteen miles north-west of Stirling. The River Teith winds to the south of the Trossachs, and the town of Callander grew beside a shallow crossing-point. A church dedicated to Kessóg once stood here: its walled graveyard can be seen close to the river, beside the road leading into the town. Between the churchyard and a large car park is *Tom na Chessaig*, or Kessóg's Mound: a grassy hillock where the monk is said to have gathered the people and preached to them.[7] The Mound is best approached by entering Callander from the south, on the A81.The ancient cemetery is just over the bridge, and the Mound is beyond it, farther to the left.

CARDROSS, Argyll and Bute: St Mahew's chapel, Kilmahew

Cardross is close to the north bank of the Firth of Clyde, six miles west-north-west of Dumbarton. As one drives north through the town on the A814, Kilmahew is soon reached by following a road to the right. Its chapel is dedicated to Mahew or Mochta, a Briton who was a follower of Patrick. Mochta's charming fifteenth-century chapel at Kilmahew is built on a raised, oval site, beside a swift stream. In the porch is the top of a pre-Christian standing stone on which a plain cross was carved in the sixth century, perhaps to bless what was already a holy site. A piece of a ninth- or tenth-century tomb slab was also found here.

The church still contains its original 'Sacrament house' in a cavity on the inner wall of the sanctuary. The tomb of the benefactor who restored the church in 1467, Duncan Napier, is contained within an alcove, which also doubled as an Easter sepulchre; this was a feature of medieval churches, found on the north side of the chancel. On Good Friday, the Eucharistic wafer was placed here, together with the crucifix from the high altar. They remained in the tomb-like structure until Easter morning. Members of the congregation were often paid to watch and pray continuously at such sepulchres until Easter Day. The tomb was lit by a blaze of tapers and candles, and the watchers sometimes became firemen when church fittings caught fire.

CULROSS, Fife: St Mungo's chapel; Culross abbey

This is a picturesque town with its cobbled streets and sixteenth-century merchants' houses with their gabled roofs. It is six miles west of Dunfermline, on the northern shore of the Firth of Forth. Beside the road leading into Culross are the ruins of a chapel built by Archbishop Blackadder of Glasgow in 1503 in honour of Kentigern's birth. According to legend, his disgraced mother floated ashore here and gave birth to her son. Only the chapel's walls and its altar survive.

The twelfth-century monk Jocelyn of Furness relates that the young Kentigern trained at a monastery in Culross, under its abbot, Serf.[8] The site of Serf's monastery can be found on the hill above the town. Under the ruins of a thirteenth-century Cistercian abbey are traces of an early Christian church, with its altar beneath the present one. A reliquary set inside a niche in the ruined south wall of the nave once contained Serf's bones. A few streets below, a deep well in Erskine Brae was the monastery's source of water; it was covered over in the nineteenth century. Coal is plentiful on both sides of the Firth of Forth, and the monks of Culross became the region's first coal miners. Culross owes its prosperity to this discovery: the coal lay near the surface and was easily transported by sea. Malcolm, Earl of Fife, established the abbey for the Cistercians in 1217.

DEER, Aberdeenshire: St Drostan's church

The settlement of Old Deer is beside the River Ugie, ten miles west of Peterhead in north-eastern Aberdeenshire. The Celtic monastery was probably on the site of the parish church in Deer, not where the later ruins of Deer Abbey now stand, north-west of the village. From Deer, Celtic monks evangelized the region of Buchan. The monastery was established by Drostan, a sixth-century monk who worked in the far north of Scotland: churches dedicated to him are spread over Aberdeenshire, Buchan and across the Moray Firth in Caithness. A fine manuscript survives, named the *Book of Deer*, written in Latin and annotated 200 years later in Scottish Gaelic. It is now in Cambridge University Library.

DRUMELZIER, Scottish Borders: the Altarstone

The hamlet of Drumelzier is eight miles south-west of Peebles, in the upper Tweed Valley. A large boulder at the roadside opposite Altarstone Farm is said to be the place where Kentigern baptized a Celtic bard named Merlin of the Woods, who lived there in exile after the warlord Rhydderch defeated his chieftain in 573. A standing stone in a nearby field is said to mark the bard's grave.[9] There is no authentication for this story, but such incidents could not have been unusual. To find Merlin's Altarstone, take the A72 west from Peebles and turn left on the B712. Pass Stobo and just before crossing the River Tweed, turn right into a minor road, which leads to Broughton. The first farm on the left is Altarstone Farm. The square boulder is in the hedge to the right of the road, opposite the farm entrance.

DULL, Perth and Kinross: Dull monastery

There was a Pictish monastery at Dull, three miles west of Aberfeldy, on the opposite bank of the River Tay. It stood on the site of the present church and was so important that it was considered to be the forerunner of St Andrews University. The valley broadens here; the name Dull means 'meadow' or 'valley'. Three sturdy Celtic crosses survive from the monastery, one beside the road leading to the church, and another two preserved in St Cuthbert's church at Weem, two miles to the east.

DUMBARTON, West Dunbartonshire: Dumbarton Rock

In AD 137 Dumbarton Rock was the site of a Roman military station, perhaps at the end of the Antonine Wall. In 367 the Romans declared the land between Hadrian's Wall and the Antonine Wall to be a province named Valentia, with Dumbarton as its capital. When the Romans withdrew from Scotland in 450, the Britons formed their own kingdom based on Valentia, but excluding eastern Scotland. It came to be known as Strathclyde, and at first Dumbarton remained its capital.

The Britons named their fortress *Alt Clut* or Rock of Clyde: it is a twin-peaked lava plug that towers above the Clyde estuary. The Irish referred to the stronghold as Dumbarton, meaning '*dún*, or fort, of the Britons'. Fragments of sixth-century pottery and seventh-century glass were found during excavations on the Rock. According to tradition, it was the headquarters of a British chieftain named Coroticus. St Patrick wrote two letters to the soldiers of Coroticus.

The two fortified peaks of Dumbarton Rock were separated by a level area with dwellings, halls, a church, and a well. In 731 Bede described it as 'a town of the Britons, strongly defended to the present day'. One of the famous British kings who resided at Dumbarton Rock was Rhydderch Hael, a contemporary of Columba. The Vikings attacked *Alt Clut* in 870, and its inhabitants are said to have surrendered after a four-month siege, when their well ran dry. Carved cross slabs dating from the tenth century found on the Rock indicate that it continued to be used for Christian burial after the Viking conquest. There was a medieval chapel dedicated to Patrick on *Alt Clut*; it was destroyed in the sixteenth century.

DUNADD, Argyll and Bute: Dunadd fort

The rocky fortress of Dunadd is five miles north-north-west of Lochgilphead. It can be reached by driving north from Lochgilphead on the A816. After four miles, turn left along a signed track, and park at the base of the fort.

The Irish Gaels, or Scots, had begun migrating to Argyll in about 300, and at that time they fought alongside the Picts against the Romans in north Britain. They established a hilltop fortress at Dunadd around 500. From this vantage point, their warships commanded the sea route to Ireland, and their army was poised to fight the Picts. Rising from the flat, boggy land beside the River Add, Dunadd made an excellent fortress. A surprise attack was impossible: its main entrance is a natural gully through massive walls of rock, which was closed by great gates with a timber superstructure. Dunadd was at the centre of Dalriada, the kingdom of the Irish Gaels; the king probably stayed here with his retinue on royal progress between his other forts.[10]

A small peak was used as an inner citadel, and carved into the bedrock in front of it are a ceremonial basin and the impression of a foot, dating from the seventh or eighth century. These may have been used for royal inaugurations. Beside the ceremonial footprint are an Irish ogham inscription and a Pictish carving of a boar. Dunadd's chieftains lived in style: a garnet set in red filigree from Anglo-Saxon England was found here, as was pottery from Gaul. Dunadd's craftsmen made jewellery, iron tools, and weapons. A lump of yellow orpiment, a pigment used by monks to illuminate manuscripts such as the *Book of Kells*, was also discovered here. The fort was occupied until AD 1000.

DUNBLANE, Stirling: St Blane's cathedral

Situated five miles north of Stirling, Dunblane means '*dún*, or fort, of Blane'. This hill fort in the land of the southern Picts was built to defend the main route to the north. In the early seventh century, Blane or his followers built a cluster of beehive huts inside the fortress, to the east of the present cathedral, high above the fast-flowing Allan Water. Blane is said to have returned to his island monastery on Bute to die, but his relics were taken to Dunblane, perhaps to preserve them from Viking raids along the west coast in the ninth and tenth centuries. Blane's hand bell is preserved in the cathedral, together with a large tenth-century Pictish cross slab. The twelfth-century belfry was originally separate from the church, and was built for defence as well as for housing bells. It was erected during the reign of King David I, who endowed the bishopric. By the early thirteenth century, the cathedral had become neglected. It was rebuilt by Clement, a Dominican friar who was elected bishop in 1233. The upper storeys of the building were added around 1500.

DUNKELD, Perth and Kinross: Dunkeld cathedral

Dunkeld is fourteen miles north-north-west of Perth. The settlement grew beside the broad River Tay, as a frontier town to the Scottish Highlands, with mountains and wilderness to the north of the town. There was an early monastery here, which became a daughter house of Iona. In 848 King Kenneth MacAlpin rebuilt the church in stone and brought relics of Columba from Iona to Dunkeld. Because Dunkeld was relatively far from the sea, it was safer from Viking attacks than the vulnerable island of Iona. Columba's relics were contained in a small house-shaped shrine known as the Monymusk reliquary. It is fashioned from wood, with gilt and silver ornamentation, and is 105 mm in width. The shrine dates from the seventh or eighth century, and is now in the National Museum, Edinburgh.

The monastery grew in importance as that of Iona dwindled; its abbot was usually a member of the royal family, and the office was hereditary. Abbot Crinan of Dunkeld was a son of the Lord of the Isles, and was the father of King Duncan, portrayed in Shakespeare's *Macbeth*. Dunkeld became the mother church of the region, and Columba's shrine was an important place of pilgrimage until the tenth century, when the Pictish King Constantine II became Abbot of St Andrews, and Columba's relics were removed from Dunkeld to

Constantine's new church. The cathedral at Dunkeld has a fourteenth-century chancel and a fifteenth-century nave. In medieval times, the fast-flowing River Tay was found too difficult to bridge; it had to be forded. A swimming cow was used to entice herds to swim across in order to be sold at the cattle market in Dunkeld.

DUNNING, Perth and Kinross: St Serf's church

According to his medieval Life, Serf's earliest and favourite Christian settlement was at Dunning, on the old road from Perth to Stirling, eight miles south-west of Perth. Serf was a native missionary who was said to have worked among the southern Picts in the district around Stirling. There was an ancient village at Dunning, where six roads meet. Serf is said to have slain a dragon here with his staff; part of the village is named Dray-gon. The story may describe how Serf released the people from the grip of paganism, through the authority of his pastoral staff. Dunning's church has a late Celtic doorway, perhaps dating from the tenth century, and a steeple built in about 1170.

DYSART, Fife: St Serf's church and cave

As the Firth of Forth broadens, east of Edinburgh, Serf is honoured on the northern shore at Dysart, now a north-eastern suburb of Kirkaldy. The name Dysart comes from the Latin word *desertum*, which means an empty place; Serf is said to have lived alone here in a cave beside the shore. It can be found in the grounds of a Carmelite convent; the cave's roof is visible over the convent wall. Across the road is the fortified tower of Serf's medieval church.

EASSIE, Angus: St Fergus's church

Eassie, ten miles north of Dundee, is a village whose church is dedicated to Fergus, a monk who worked at Glamis, three miles to the north-east. Beside the ruined church there is a fine cross slab dating from the eighth or ninth century. The cross is decorated with interlacing. Above its arms stand two angels; below, a huntsman and his hounds chase a red deer stag. On the other side, Adam is depicted, eating the apple of knowledge in the Garden of Eden.

EAST WEMYSS, Fife: hermits' caves

The caves of East Wemyss are on the north shore of the Firth of Forth, five miles north-east of Kirkaldy: *weem* is a transliteration of *uaimh*, the Gaelic word for 'cave'. These red sandstone caves have been inhabited for 6,000 years. There were nine caves here, of which five survive. Three of them contain the largest collection of Bronze Age, Iron Age, and early Christian rock carvings in Britain. Unfortunately, vandalism, coalmining, and erosion of the soft sandstone have blocked access to many of the carvings and destroyed others. On the shore at West Wemyss, a mile to the south-west, is the church of a monk named Adrian; the present building is modern. Adrian was a ninth-century missionary who came to evangelize Fife. He is thought to have been killed by the Danes in about 850.

ELLARY, Argyll and Bute: St Columba's cave and chapel

Ellary is a small settlement on the Knapdale peninsula, near the head of Loch Caolisport. It is eleven miles south-west of Lochgilphead and is reached by driving south on the A83, turning right into the B8024, and turning right again at Achahoish. Large-scale maps indicate that one can reach Ellary from Kilmory to the west, but this is a private road, and the journey from this direction can be made only on foot.

There is a tradition that, after leaving Ireland, Columba sailed up Loch Caolisport in 563 and landed at Ellary. Here he took shelter in a large, airy cave, where there is an altar built of flat stones and a cross carved into the rock wall above, dating from early times. A freshwater pool in the cave is formed by condensation dripping from the roof. There is a stream with a waterfall nearby, and from the cave Columba could have watched seals playing around the islet at the head of the loch. There are the remains of a medieval chapel beside the cave.

By the eighth century there was a monastery a mile away, probably founded from Iona, at a place named *Cladh a Bhile*, or 'burial ground of the holy tree'. We can picture the monks baking bread and conducting funerals, for many early gravestones and querns for grinding corn were found here.

FORTINGALL, Perth and Kinross: St Cedd's church

The ancient settlement of Fortingall lies four miles west of Aberfeldy, in Glen Lyon. Until a hundred years ago, a bonfire was lit here each November on a Bronze Age burial mound, known as *Carn nam Marbh*, to celebrate the pre-Christian Celtic feast of Samhain. This was the forerunner of All Souls' Day, when Christians remember their dead, on 2 November. At Fortingall, the fire was made of furze and sticks; people held hands round the blazing fire, and boys ran into the fields with burning brands. Half a mile from the church, in a field on the opposite side of the road, are three groups of three standing stones.

Beside the churchyard are the remains of Britain's oldest yew tree. It is 17 metres in girth and has grown by producing saplings around its circumference; it has been dated to around 5000 BC[11] and is said to be the oldest piece of vegetation surviving in northern Europe. The church is dedicated to Cedd, a monk from Lindisfarne. Pieces of Celtic crosses have been found here; they are displayed on a window ledge in the church. Protected behind an iron grill is a monk's bell, dating from perhaps the seventh century. It has no tongue but would have been struck. It is one of five such bells to survive in Perthshire. They were used as late as the nineteenth century to bless the sick. Outside the church porch is an early stone font, carved from a massive boulder. It is known as Adomnán's font, after the monk from Iona who is said to have worked in Glen Lyon.

FOWLIS WESTER, Perth and Kinross:
St Bean's church

The hamlet of Fowlis Wester is twelve miles west of Perth. This was an ancient religious site, with a Neolithic burial cairn dating from 3000 BC a mile south of the hamlet, and standing stones nearby. Fowlis Wester lies on the old road to Perth: highlanders drove their cattle through the village to the markets and also sold them here. Beside the road is a replica of a fine Pictish cross carved from red sandstone; the original is inside the church. The unusual protruding arms of the cross indicate Irish influence. It was erected by the followers of Bean, who evangelized this area. Bean was a native monk whose name means 'lively person'. He trained in Ireland, where he is mentioned in a chronicle dating from 800.

GLAMIS, Angus: St Fergus's church and well

In the early eighth century a monk named Fergus is said to have settled at Glamis, ten miles north of Dundee. He was probably a native Pict who studied in Ireland and returned to Angus. His church is close to a pre-Christian standing stone; the cup-marks at its base indicate its ancient origin. The great stone was subsequently christianized: on one side is an interlaced cross, flanked by warriors fighting with hand-axes, and other symbols; on the other side are Pictish carvings of a snake, a salmon, and a mirror. Fergus was said to have lived in a cave, beside a holy well that flows into Glamis Burn. The cave collapsed in the nineteenth century.

There are fragments of three more Pictish cross slabs dating from the eighth to ninth centuries inside the church. A fourth stone from the same period can be seen north of the track leading south from the A94 just east of Glamis. On the front is a cross decorated with interlace and key patterns. An angel and a bird-headed man flank the upper arms of the cross, while two deer and two hunting dogs flank the shaft. Below the dogs is a triple disc or cauldron, with flower symbols. On the back of the slab are a red deer stag and a snake symbol.

GLASGOW: St Kentigern's Cathedral

According to the twelfth-century *Life of Kentigern* by Jocelyn of Furness, Kentigern was bishop of Glasgow, where he had founded a monastery. He spent the last years of his long life among his brothers. Jocelyn records a tradition that Kentigern's death occurred on 13 January, at the end of the octave, or week, of celebration following the feast of the Epiphany. He died comfortably in a warm bath, symbolic for Jocelyn's readers of the bath of baptism. The story demonstrated that Kentigern was reborn into heavenly life. In the Eastern Churches, candidates were immersed for baptism on the feast of the Epiphany. The festival recalled how the wise men followed a star to Bethlehem, and how angels appeared to guide them. Jocelyn weaves these strands into his story: 'While the morning day-star shone forth, an angel of the Lord appeared with unspeakable splendour, and the glory of God shone around him. And for fear of the angel, the guardians of the holy bishop (Kentigern) were astonished and amazed and became as dead men, being unable to bear so great glory.... The gentle bishop had been accustomed each year to baptize a multitude of people on the feast of the Lord's Epiphany. When its octave was dawning, a day very pleasing to St Kentigern and his adopted sons, they carried the holy man to a bath filled with hot water, which he first blessed with the sign of the cross.' Kentigern died peacefully in the bath, was dressed in his bishop's clothes, and was buried in the cathedral, 'on the right side of the altar, beneath a stone'.[12]

Kentigern's tomb is in the crypt of Glasgow cathedral. Arcading from the plinth of his thirteenth-century shrine can still be seen. Built into the wall of the crypt is the well that provided his monks with water for both drinking and washing. The first stone-built cathedral was dedicated in 1136 in the presence of King David I; the present building dates from the thirteenth century.

GLENDARUEL, Argyll and Bute: Kilmodan church

Glendaruel is in Cowal, five miles north of the northern tip of Bute. Kilmodan church is nearby, signed from the A8003, west of the road. Kilmodan means 'cell of my Aidan', and is named after Modan, the monk who is also commemorated at Dryburgh and at Rosneath. Modan's chapel in Cowal was on the hillside to the east of the charming eighteenth-century church that now stands in the valley below. Eleven gravestones in Kilmodan churchyard were carved in the fourteenth and fifteenth centuries by sculptors who had come from Ireland to work on the abbey buildings of Iona. Since they worked from pattern books, their style can easily be recognised. They used traditional motifs for grave slabs: men in armour, priests, mythical creatures, and interlaced designs. On simpler slabs, a sword or a pair of smithing tongs show the occupation of the dead person. The valley beside the church is named Glendaruel or 'glen of the red river'. It received its name after bitter fighting in 1098 between the Scots and the Norse forces of Magnus Barelegs, which caused the river to run red with blood.

GOVAN, Glasgow City: St Constantine's church

Now engulfed by the city of Glasgow, Govan lies on the south bank of the river Clyde, three miles west of Glasgow city centre. Excavations here have revealed an early stone church with a surrounding enclosure wall and ditch. It is dedicated to Constantine, a king turned monk who is said to have founded a monastery here in the late sixth century. He may be the king to whom two Cornish churches are dedicated and the Constantine who was martyred at Kintyre in 576. An impressive ninth-century stone sarcophagus perhaps formed part of his shrine. It portrays a stag hunt and various other decorative animals.

The monastery at Govan had a fine school of sculptors: in the church are a large number of carved crosses and a magnificent collection of tenth-century Viking hogback tombstones, each representing a house with a curved roof, wooden shingles, and mythical beasts clasping the gable ends. Another Viking slab portrays a cross surmounted by a sun in splendour, each ray ending in an animal's head. On the reverse side, a piper on horseback skirls the bagpipes as he perhaps leads troops into battle. There must have been a cemetery at Govan in which Viking chieftains were buried. The church is normally locked, but the key can generally be obtained from the caretaker in the large building to the right of the churchyard, on the main street.

HODDOM, Dumfries and Galloway: site of Kentigern's church

Hoddom, twelve miles east-south-east of Dumfries, was the site of a fort belonging to a chieftain named Rydderch Hael. According to tradition, he invited Kentigern to address his people from Kinmount Hill, above the River Annan. The monks built a church close to the bridge over the river; only its cemetery survives. It is reached by a short footpath from the main road. Excavated in 1991, this was an early ecclesiastical site, contemporary with Whithorn and Ruthwell. It was situated at a bend in the river, like Whithorn and St Martin's monastery of Marmoutier, on a meander of the River Loire. The site at Hoddom was bounded by an outer group of buildings for non-monastic craftsmen, as at Whithorn.[13] Pieces of three elaborate Northumbrian crosses were found here.

INNERWICK, Perth and Kinross: St Adomnán's bell

On the north bank of the River Lyon, Innerwick is seventeen miles west of Aberfeldy. Preserved in the nineteenth-century church is a Celtic hand bell, known as the Benrudh Bell; it is said to have belonged to Adomnán. It was abandoned for 200 years in the churchyard and then recovered. Just over the

Bridge of Balgie, a mile to the west is the site of *Milton Eonan* ('Adomnán's mill'). A mile to the east is Camusvrachan, traditionally the place where, when the plague struck, Adomnán prayed with the people and sent them up to their summer shielings, away from the polluted river. The plague then ceased.

IONA, Isle of, Argyll and Bute: St Columba's monastery

Iona is an island three miles long, a mile off the western tip of the larger island of Mull. It can be reached from the Scottish mainland by taking the ferry from Oban to Mull. A bus crosses the island; its journey ends at Fionnphort, where a small boat takes passengers a mile across the Sound to Iona. If you take the first ferry out from Oban in the morning, and catch the last ferry back in the evening, there is time for a couple of hours on Iona. In order to visit the island at greater length, you must arrange to stay in Mull, or on Iona itself.

One tradition relates that Columba was given the island of Iona by Conall, king of Argyll, as a site for a monastery. We know a considerable amount about life in Columba's community, because in about 690 the ninth abbot of Iona, Adomnán, wrote a *Life of Columba* and preserved for us many details about the activities of the monks. The earliest surviving text of the Life was written on Iona by Dorbbéne, a monk who succeeded Adomnán as abbot and died in 713. We are fortunate to possess such an early copy, written on goatskin parchment in a heavy Irish hand.

Columba lived in a hut built on planks on a small rocky mound in the monastery compound. The mound can still be seen in front of the large Benedictine abbey that was later built on the site. This may also be the 'little hill overlooking the monastery' from which, according to Adomnán, Columba gave his final blessing to the monks before his death.[14]

Adomnán describes the monks walking across the island with their farm implements on their backs, to reach the sandy plain on the west side of the island where they grew their crops, using seaweed as fertiliser. He tells us of the white horse that carried the milk churns from the cow pasture, and he mentions expeditions to larger islands to fetch wood for building, since there were no trees on Iona. Adomnán pictures the monks writing manuscripts, and praying in the small church, where Columba's clear voice could be heard above the others. He could also be recognized by his white cowl, or hooded cloak, for the other monks wore unbleached cowls.

The Life refers to 55 sea voyages back and forth between Iona and Ireland. Monks and pilgrims came to visit or to join the community. Those travelling from Scotland crossed the island of Mull and then shouted across the Sound to Iona for a brother to ferry them over. From his hut on planks, Columba could see them coming. On arrival, guests had their hands and feet washed.

There are few remains of Iona's Celtic monastery. St Odhráin's chapel is the earliest building to survive on the island. It dates from the twelfth century and stands within what was probably the first Christian burial ground on Iona. It is named after an early monk who may have lived here before Columba's arrival. Odhráin's oratory resembles Irish chapels of the period, with a single doorway in the west wall, decorated with chevron and beak-head ornament. It was probably rebuilt as a family burial vault by Somerled, king of the Isles, who died in 1164.[15]

In 1979 excavations were carried out in the early seventh-century boundary ditch between the little hill on which Columba's cell was built and Odhráin's cemetery. Objects were discovered that would have been in use at the end of Columba's lifetime, including heeled shoes and other leather goods, and elegant wooden bowls that had been turned on a lathe in the monastic workshops. The monks also produced fine quality metalwork, and glass ornaments.[16]

The great rectangular ramparts which surrounded the monastery can still be traced: they were constructed around the time of Columba's death; alongside them was a hedge of hawthorn and holly. The tiny chapel in front of the Benedictine abbey is built on Celtic foundations and may mark the site of Columba's shrine. There are three elaborate high crosses and a winding path of large stones, known as the 'Street of the Dead'. Chieftains were brought to Iona from the Scottish mainland for burial, and this was the track along which they were solemnly carried.

Outside the rampart, 300 metres to the north-east, are the remains of another Celtic cemetery, named *Cladh an Disirt* in Gaelic. It was entered through an impressive gateway framed by two large stone pillars. These supported a giant lintel, which has now fallen. The cemetery was enclosed by a wall, and beside it was a hermitage, whose superior is named in a twelfth-century list of monastic officials. There are the remains of a medieval stone chapel beside the entrance to the cemetery.

Columba died on the island in 597. Iona suffered a number of Norse raids; in 806, during their third attack, Vikings killed 68 monks, and the remainder of the community decided to transfer to Ireland. They acquired the monastery of Kells in eastern Ireland and left Iona, taking their belongings with them.

ISLAY, Isle of, Argyll and Bute: Kidalton cross

Kidalton is six miles east-north-east of Port Ellen, near the south-eastern end of Islay, in the Inner Hebrides. The magnificent Kidalton cross is the only Scottish high cross to survive intact at its original site. It is a ring cross with a central boss, decorated with figures and decorative scroll motifs. Below the boss, the Virgin and Child are flanked by angels. The monastery at Kidalton was dedicated to 'the Fosterling', who may have been Columba's foster-son and successor, Baithene. Just before Columba died he was copying out Psalm 34, and he requested that Baithene finish the task; in this way he indicated that Baithene should succeed him as abbot.

JEDBURGH, Scottish Borders: Jedburgh abbey

The abbey of Jedburgh is 42 miles south-east of Edinburgh; it is set on a hilltop above the fast-flowing Jed Water. In 638 the Angles of Northumbria captured Edinburgh, then Galloway and Fife, until the Picts defeated them in 685. During the time that the Northumbrians ruled this area of Scotland, an Anglian monastery was established at Jedburgh by Aidan of Lindisfarne. A group of monastic sculptors worked here from the eighth to the tenth centuries. Some of their carvings survive, including five free-standing crosses and the end panel of a magnificent house-shaped stone shrine. The panel depicts a tree of life, with birds and animals among swirling vine tendrils. The shrine probably enclosed the relics of Boisil (d. c.661), an Irish monk who became the second abbot of Melrose. The ruined Norman abbey dates from the twelfth century. It was established by King David I and given to the Augustinian canons.

KEILLS, Argyll and Bute: St Cormac's chapel

Keeills is twelve miles south-west of Lochgilphead, at the southern end of the B8025. It is an isolated chapel at the end of a narrow ten-mile tongue of land in Knapdale, bordered by the often rough waters of the Sound of Jura to the west and the sheltered waters of a sea loch, Loch Sween, to the east. In summer, Keills can be swathed in mist; in winter, the Atlantic winds howl from the north-west. Only thirteen miles to the north, where the Sound of Jura meets the Atlantic Ocean between Jura and Scarba in the Gulf of Corryvreckan, there is a whirlpool that the Celts believed was the entrance to the underworld. Keills was easily accessible by boat: an old landing stage survives beside the deep water on the north side of the peninsula; the chapel is on the sheltered southern slope.

Keills was originally called *Cill Mo-Charmáig*, or 'my Cormac's cell'. An islet named Eilean Mór, four miles to the south-west, was also dedicated to him.[17] It is uncertain which Cormac this might be; a number of saints bore this name. The present chapel dates from the late twelfth or early thirteenth century. In Celtic times there was a school of sculptors here, for among the carvings preserved in the chapel there is a half-finished cross which was abandoned when the stone fractured, as well as another stone on which masons practised carving letters and patterns.

On the hillside 45 metres north-west of the chapel there was an elaborate eighth-century high cross, resembling those on Iona. Only a large monastery would have commissioned such a fine monument. A replica now stands on the windy hillside; the original has been brought into the chapel. At its centre is a nest-like boss surrounded by four lions, with the archangel Michael above it and a seated saint or evangelist below. The remaining surface is covered with intertwining creatures and abstract designs.

KILBIRNIE, North Ayrshire: St Brendan's church

The name-element *kil* denotes a monk's cell, and such a settlement is often an early one. Kilbirnie Old Kirk with its medieval tower, twelve miles south-west of Paisley, replaces an earlier church dedicated to Brendan. St Brennan's Fair used to be held here on 28 May. There were seventeen St Brendans, but the monk honoured here appears to have been the most famous of them, the Irish monk Brendan the Navigator. There are many churches named after Brendan, particularly around Britain's sea coasts: sailors liked to invoke his protection. Other Scottish examples are Kilbrannan on Islay, Kilbirnie near Beauly (Inverness), Birnie (Moray), Kilbrandon (in Lorn, on Mull, and on Islay), and Boyndie (Banff). He was a patron of the Isle of Bute: Butemen were called 'Brandans', because sea travel was a way of life for them.[18]

KILLIN, Stirling: St Fillan's mill

The town of Killin is at the south-western end of Loch Tay, 28 miles north-north-west of Stirling. The Irish monk Fillan is said to have settled here beside the rushing water of the Dochart Falls. According to his legend, recorded in the *Aberdeen Breviary* (1507), Fillan felt called to 'wander for God', so he resigned from his monastery on the Fife coast and travelled eastwards into the Highlands. He is believed to have built a mill at Killin. Monks who trained in Ireland knew how to construct mills and grind flour; they developed a horizontal mill wheel, which could be used where there was little water, and they brought their technology to the British mainland.

According to tradition, Fillan sat on a stone under an ash tree near the mill at Killin to preach to the local people. The mill became the focal point of the settlement. In a small community, the miller supervised the sowing of seed and the cutting of peat to fuel the mill's oven, which might also be the village bakery. Fillan's feast day, 9 January, is still a holiday for the mill-workers at Killin. The modern parish church houses a seven-sided Celtic font, carved from a huge boulder. In the grounds of the large hotel next door are the ruins of the medieval church and cemetery dedicated to Fillan.

The saint had a reputation for curing the sick. His eight healing stones have always been kept at Fillan's Mill, which now houses the Breadalbane Folklore Centre. These large black and grey stones, smoothed by the river, were considered to heal different parts of the body. A large skull-shaped stone with two 'eye sockets', for example, was invoked for diseases of the head. People still come to hold Fillan's stones and pray for healing.

KILMARTIN, Argyll and Bute: St Martin's church

Near the Scottish west coast, nineteen miles south of Oban, Kilmartin (or 'cell of Martin') may have been a foundation made from Iona by Columba's monks. It was probably dedicated to Martin of Tours. The earliest mention of a church on this site dates from the fourteenth century, but there are four early Christian crosses here: three simple Latin crosses, and a richly carved free-standing cross probably dating from the tenth century.

In a shelter in the churchyard is a fine collection of fourteenth- and fifteenth-century grave slabs carved by a group of sculptors who worked around Loch Awe. These men came from Ireland to Iona in the fourteenth century to construct the abbey buildings; when their task was finished, they moved to the Scottish mainland and continued to carve in the same style. This group of tombstones was brought from nearby Poltalloch. If the church is locked, the key is held at no. 16, Kilmartin.

KILMORY, Argyll and Bute: St Máelrubha's church

The hamlet of Kilmory is on the Knapdale peninsula, two miles north of the Point of Knap, facing the island of Jura. Kilmory is fourteen miles south-west of Lochgilphead, and is reached by a minor road that runs through Knapdale Forest and along the east side of Loch Sween. Kilmory means 'cell of St Mary', but the small church was originally dedicated to Máelrubha, a monk from north-east Ireland who worked on the Scottish west coast.

The church dates from the early thirteenth century. It houses some early Christian decorated crosses and later ones carved, like those at Kilmartin, by Irish sculptors from Iona. Later, they travelled throughout Argyll with their pattern books, and local masons continued designing works in the same style until the mid-sixteenth century. Their work is plentiful in this locality because much of the stone for the west Highland crosses was quarried beside Loch Sween. Kilmory church houses the MacMillan cross: this was created in the fourteenth century, but executed in twelfth-century Romanesque style. It is an elaborate wheel cross with a figure of the crucified Christ at its centre.

LUSS, Argyll and Bute: St Kessóg's church

Luss is a town on the western shore of Loch Lomond, eleven miles north-north-west of Dumbarton. Its church was the site of Kessóg's shrine in medieval times; Kessóg was said to have been an Irish prince-monk from Cashel. He founded a monastery on the 'Isle of the Monks' (*Inchtavannach* in Gaelic) in Loch Lomond, a mile south-east of Luss. Older people still call it 'Isle of the Two Bells', referring to the bells with which the monks summoned one another to prayer in the chapel. The wooded island is a mile long; it was an ideal location for a monastery, being sufficiently isolated to afford an opportunity for prayer but close to the lakeshore, providing easy access to centres of population.

The small town of Luss grew beside the mouth of Luss Water, at the point where it flows into Loch Lomond. In the churchyard, two sixth-century grave markers, each carved with a Latin cross, and a seventh-century four-holed cross indicate the continued presence of Christians at Luss. An impressive Viking hogback tomb can also be seen in the churchyard, embellished with neat rows of imitation roof tiles. It is designed to represent a house of the dead; arcading rises from a row of columns around its sides.

The grave slab dates from the Norse invasion led by King Hakon of Norway and is a reminder of one of his most daring raids. In 1263 Hakon's longships sailed into the Firth of Clyde and continued northward through Loch Long. The boats were then hauled overland to Loch Lomond, across the tarbert, which was the narrow strip of land at the head of an isthmus, a useful short-cut between two stretches of water. The village of Tarbet is still there. Loch Lomond lies only one and a half miles to the east of Loch Long, and from their new vantage point the Norsemen proceeded to ravage Luss and much of the surrounding countryside. King Hakon then travelled twenty miles round the coast to fight the Battle of Largs. The hogback tomb at Luss may commemorate one of his warriors.[19]

Kessóg was said to have been murdered at Bandry, a mile south of Luss. Local Christians built a cairn of stones over the place where he fell. It was destroyed when the shore road was constructed in 1761. A carved stone head, perhaps representing Kessóg, was found beneath it; the small sculpture now rests on a window ledge in the church at Luss, which continued to be the centre of Kessóg's cult. In 1315, King Robert Bruce declared the church and its surrounding area a place of sanctuary, an offering 'to God and the blessed St Kessóg for ever of three miles round the church as by land and water'.[20] Here criminals could take refuge from the law and presumably go into hiding on the islands and in the glens.

Kessóg's shrine was visited well after the Reformation. The remains of a medieval chapel can be seen in Luss churchyard.

MAY, Isle of, Firth of Forth: site of St Ethernan's church

Traces of the earliest church yet to have been found on the Scottish east coast were discovered in the last decade on the Isle of May, six miles east-south-east of Anstruther. The church may date from the ninth century, and is the first in a sequence of buildings on the site of the island's later Benedictine abbey. Excavations in 1996 uncovered an extraordinary mass-burial mound, on which the first church was built. The mound contains Christian graves dating from Celtic times, but the artefacts found suggest that the site may have been in continuous use for 3,000 years, perhaps from the Bronze Age onwards.

The early church was a small square building with drystone foundations similar to those on the west coast of Scotland and to those in Ireland dating from the seventh to the tenth centuries. It may have been built as a chapel to house the remains of Ethernan, an early missionary who is believed to have lived and died on the island. The Benedictine abbey was constructed in the twelfth century, and the saint's relics drew thousands of pilgrims from then onward.

The abbey's cloister was built into the ancient burial mound, bringing numerous bones to the surface. These were left to litter the area; at this time, it seems, little reverence was accorded to the bones of unimportant people. Ethernan's grave has not been found. In the abbey itself, an unusual ten-seater communal lavatory was found at the rear of the monastic dormitory, probably designed for the use of pilgrims.[21]

From Easter to September, a boat sails daily to the Isle of May from Anstruther harbour. The departure time depends on the tide. The journey takes an hour; passengers are able to spend three hours on the island. For further information, contact the Isle of May Sailings Company, tel. 0133 310103.

MEIGLE, Angus: site of Pictish monastery

One of the last Pictish kings was Ferat, who reigned from 839 to 842. He had a royal estate at Meigle, twelve miles north-west of Dundee, and there was a Pictish monastery on the estate. We know the name of one of the monks who worked as a scribe in the royal villa at Meigle: he was called Thana.[22] This was a pre-Christian holy site: cup and ring marks dating from 3000 to 2000 BC decorate two giant boulders here. The two great rocks flanked the north gate of the churchyard, and were in place by the late eighth century. Like the other twenty cross slabs found at Meigle, they are formed of old red sandstone, a soft rock easy to carve. One of the two large stones stands 2.5 metres high. One side is perhaps modelled on a much smaller, jewelled cross: its circular stone 'jewels' are carved in high relief, and its cross-shaft is decorated with lively animals.[23]

The reverse side features the Old Testament story of Daniel in the lions' den. This subject appealed to Celtic Christians: Daniel's struggle to tame ravenous lions reminded them of Christ who conquered the forces of death. Daniel's heroic feat also symbolised the battles in which Celtic warriors were often engaged. Daniel appears, flanked by two lions, on the eighth-century cross of St Martin at Iona. On the stone at Meigle, Daniel wears a long, pleated skirt or kilt. His arms are outstretched as he tames the lions; his gesture also reminds us of Christ on the cross. Two lions paw at his skirt, while another pair lick his face. Above Daniel are an angel and huntsmen with their hounds. Below him, a centaur chops down a tree and a wild beast eats an ox whose undevoured, horned head is still visible. The mighty slab may once have stood inside the church, as it has side tenons, designed to slot into cavities in the wall.[24]

The church was magnificently decorated. Part of a sculptured frieze survives, in which clawed beasts appear on either side of a mermaid with a twisty tail. The panel perhaps adorned the outside wall. On another slab, which was fortunately copied before it was lost, a driver holds the reins of two horses pulling a carriage. Two passengers sit comfortably behind him under an awning, above the twelve-spoked chariot wheels. The stone panel formed part of a low screen that may have separated the chancel, where the priest presided at the Eucharist, from the nave, where the congregation stood. The 27 carved stones, dating from the eighth to the tenth centuries, can be seen in Meigle museum, which occupies the old schoolhouse near the centre of the small town.

MELROSE, Scottish Borders: Melrose abbey

The town of Melrose is 30 miles south-east of Edinburgh. The ruins in modern Melrose are of a Cistercian abbey founded in the twelfth century. The earlier foundation of Mailros (or Old Melrose) was on a bend of the River Tweed, two and a half miles east of the Cistercian abbey. Like many insular monasteries, it was built within an abandoned hill fort. It was probably founded by Aidan of Lindisfarne, with monks from Iona, and its first abbot was Eata, one of Aidan's Anglo-Saxon converts.

Cuthbert trained as a monk here, as Bede relates. An old monk, Sigfrid, from Bede's own monastery of Jarrow, could remember the day in 651 when a youth named Cuthbert rode up to the enclosure gate at Melrose and leapt down from his horse. He handed its bridle to a servant, together with his spear, in order to enter the church and pray. The prior, Boisil, was standing at the monastery door and noted young Cuthbert with approval. He asked why the youth had come, and the eighteen-year-old replied that he would prefer life in the monastery to life in the world. Boisil welcomed Cuthbert kindly, told the abbot, and received permission for Cuthbert to have his head shorn and be enrolled among the brothers.[25] The site of Old Melrose is on private land; the Cistercian abbey is open to the public.

OLD KILPATRICK, West Dunbartonshire: site of St Patrick's church

Old Kilpatrick, three miles east-south-east of Dumbarton, is one of the sites that claims to be the birthplace of Patrick (c.390 – c.461). The line of the Antonine Wall can be seen on the bluff above the town: this marked the northern boundary of Roman Britain, although it had been abandoned as a fortification two hundred years before Patrick's birth. A Roman garrison based at Old Kilpatrick controlled the river Clyde. The fort, at a site now occupied by the bus station, commanded a view of shipping for miles, both upriver and out toward the sea. Christianity may have continued here as the Roman town declined. Down the hill, 300 metres beyond the garrison, a modern church stands on the site of an earlier one, which became a dependency of Paisley abbey in the twelfth century. Beside the church is St Patrick's healing well.

ORKNEY: Birsay monastery

The Brough of Birsay, 20 miles north-west of Kirkwall, was an important Christian centre in Pictish and Viking times. Access is by a tidal causeway. The site includes an early monastery, and the later St Peter's cathedral built by Thorfinn the Mighty, the Norse Earl of Orkney. Magnus, Earl of Orkney, was buried here before his relics were transferred to Kirkwall. Magnus was the grandson of Thorfinn; he was treacherously murdered by his cousin Haakon in 1116, and was venerated as a martyr. St Magnus Cathedral in Kirkwall was built to house his relics.

PAISLEY, Renfrewshire: Paisley abbey

This ancient settlement, close to present-day Glasgow airport, lies 9 miles west of Glasgow city centre, beside the White Cart River. The name Paisley may come from the Latin word *basilica*, meaning a church, so this may have been a Roman Christian settlement. There was a pre-Christian cemetery on the site, overlaid by the graves of Christians buried facing east. In the second half of the sixth century an Irish monk named Mirrin founded a community here. Excavation has provided evidence of a stone chapel and enclosure wall dating from the seventh or eighth century.

Pilgrims continued to visit Mirrin's shrine, and in the twelfth century, Benedictine monks from a daughter house of Cluny were brought to Paisley from Much Wenlock in Shropshire. A fifteenth-century stone frieze in Paisley abbey church illustrates scenes from Mirrin's life: a panel portrays him as prior of the monastery of Bangor in north-east Ireland, and another shows him reviving a monk who had died of heat stroke while working in the fields. A third section depicts Mirrin praying in his cell at night, illumined by a ray of heavenly light.

The abbey was founded in 1163 by the High Steward of Scotland. The fifth High Steward supported Scottish independence, and so the English set fire to the complex in 1307. The seventh High Steward became the first Royal Stewart, from whom Queen Elizabeth II is descended. There are extensive remains of the Cluniac monastery, including a vaulted chamber containing the main drain, constructed in about 1350. The abbey was largely rebuilt in the fifteenth century. A slate survives from its choir school, with the earliest surviving Scottish polyphonic music scratched on it, dating from around 1450.

PITTENWEEM, Fife: St Fillan's cave

The small town of Pittenweem is on the north shore of the Firth of Forth, seventeen miles east of Glenrothes. The town's name means 'place of the cave'. Around the south coast of Fife there are a number of caves where hermits lived: at Dysart, at East Wemyss, and at Caiplie, a mile east of Pittenweem. A cave was warm in winter and cool in summer, and if it looked out to sea, it encouraged prayer. The rock plug containing Fillan's cave stands among fishermen's cottages in Cove Wynd, a steep road leading down to the old harbour. The cave was restored in 1935; it is a large one, with two outer chambers, the second of which branches into two more. An altar has been erected in the cavern to the right, while a freshwater pool in the left-hand one provided Fillan with drinking water. He is said to have left the cave to become abbot of a nearby monastery, where he remained for some years.

The door at the entrance to the cave is kept locked. The key is obtainable from the Gingerbread Horse Coffee Shop, 9 High Street.

PORTMAHOMACK, Highland: St Colmán's church

Ten miles east of Tain, Portmahomack is on a tongue of land on the northern shore of the Moray Firth. Its name means 'my little Colmán's harbour'. There was an important Pictish and Christian centre here. Between the eighteenth century and 1995, gravediggers unearthed thirteen fragments of Christian Pictish carved stones from this area; they are now in the National Museum at Edinburgh. In 1990, aerial photography revealed a D-shaped enclosure ditch encircling the church, like that on Iona. It was radiocarbon-dated to the second to sixth centuries. There appears to have been a Pictish monastery here; its simple carved grave-markers resemble those found on Iona.

Remote mapping in 1994 and 1995 revealed a *souterrain*, or underground chamber, and the foundations of buildings and hearths in the fields around Tarbat Old Church, above the village; there was evidently a Pictish settlement here. The name Tarbat or Tarbert frequently occurs in Scotland (see LUSS, above). Tarbat church is built over an earlier chapel, and among the cross slabs found in the graveyard is one with an inscription to Rethaide, abbot of Fearn. The ruins of Fearn abbey are seven miles south-west of Portmahomack. The site at Portmahomack is currently being excavated, and has provided evidence of occupation from pagan Pictish, Christian Pictish, Norse, and medieval periods, dating from the second century to the fifteenth.

In 1997 the greater part of the nave of Tarbat church and the floor of its crypt were excavated. This revealed a sequence of burials from the sixth century onwards, followed by the construction of a stone church. Incorporated into the foundations of the church were nine decorated carved stones, dating from the ninth century; these had evidently been discarded by the time the church came to be built. Together with fragments collected from the crypt and elsewhere, the current number of carved stones found at the site is 140. In the same year, excavation was begun in the adjacent Glebe Field. A medieval trackway was found; it led from a marshy area up toward the church and was flanked by buildings and iron-working pits. On a large fragment of old red sandstone, a rural scene with a family of cattle had been carved in the ninth century. Other objects suggested that the area had also been in use in the eighth century and earlier.

ROSEMARKIE, Highland: St Moluag's church

Rosemarkie is a mile north-east of Fortrose, and eight miles north-east of Inverness, on the shore of the Moray Firth. The parish church of Rosemarkie stands on the site of a Celtic monastery dedicated to Moluag, a monk from north-east Ireland who sailed to Scotland and founded a community on the island of Lismore in the sixth century. A fine Pictish cross slab was found at Rosemarkie; it is now in the Groam House Museum. There is a tradition that Curitan was buried at Rosemarkie. He was a Celtic monk who followed Roman practices and helped Nechtán, King of the Picts, to reform the Pictish Church in the eighth century. A medieval abbey was founded at Fortrose, around which the town of Fortrose has grown.

ROSNEATH, Argyll and Bute: St Modan's church

Across the Firth of Clyde, four miles north-north-west of Greenock, Rosneath enjoys a beautiful situation next to Gare Loch. The Gaelic for Rosneath means 'headland of the sanctuary' and suggests a pre-Christian holy place. Modan was a sixth-century disciple of Columba, who may have been born in Argyll. He is said to have ended his days as a hermit at

Rosneath. Modan is an affectionate name meaning 'my Aidan'. There is a fine Celtic cross preserved in Rosneath church, which is open on Sundays for services. The remains of the medieval church, with a belfry dating from 1610, can be seen behind the modern one. Here, pilgrims visited Modan's shrine and venerated his relics. Local pastors were named after him: a Michael Gilmodyn ('Michael of Modan's church') was a priest here in 1199, as was Gilmothan, son of the sacristan, in 1294.

RUTHWELL, Dumfries and Galloway: the Ruthwell Cross

There was an early Christian monastery at Ruthwell, which is ten miles south-east of Dumfries. Later, a magnificent cross was erected here. In eighth-century Northumbria, Celtic culture became fused with that of both the ruling Angles and the Viking invaders. The Ruthwell Cross is an outstanding example of this; it was perhaps set up on the seashore in the early eighth century as a boundary-marker between the Anglians of Northumbria to the east and the Britons of Galloway and Strathclyde to the west.

The cross now stands in Ruthwell church. It is 5 metres high; its carvings express the rich faith of its unknown sculptor. Beneath a figure of Christ in glory appears a traditional Celtic theme: St Antony and Paul the hermit, breaking bread in the desert. The loaf they share symbolizes the breaking of bread at meals and in worship that lies at the heart of monastic life. Women are also carved on the cross: the angel Gabriel greets Mary, and Mary Magdalen tenderly washes the feet of her Lord. Along the side-panels, birds and beasts play among vine tendrils.

The central figure on the cross is Christ portrayed as a triumphant warrior, with a moustache in Germanic style, not a beard. He wears a cloak and sash, and clasps his hands, at peace. Inscribed both in Latin and in Anglo-Saxon runes is a poem, *The Dream of the Rood*. Its theme is one dear to warrior peoples: Christ, the young hero, fights a great battle, wounded and bloodstained, yet victorious. The story is told by the rood, or tree of the cross:

> I raised a great king,
> Liege-lord of heaven ...
> I dared not bow down.

Men reviled us both.
I was all moist with blood
Which poured from his side ...

I saw it all,
Overwhelmed with grief,
Wounded with arrow shafts.

They laid him down, limb-weary.
They stood at the corpse's head:
They saw the Lord of heaven.'

ST ANDREWS, Fife: St Andrews cathedral

The Celtic name for St Andrews, on the Fife coast, was
Kilrimont, or 'church of the king's mound'. This suggests the
presence of a royal fort. There are traditions of a monk named
Rule who lived in a cave by the shore, now known as Lady
Buchan's Cave. In the sixth century, an Irish monk named
Kenneth, who was a friend of Columba, used St Andrews as a
base from which to evangelize the southern Picts. The
monastery is first recorded in 747, when Irish annals note the
death of its abbot. Fifteen years earlier, in 732, Bishop Acca of
Hexham was driven from his diocese and came to live at
Kilrimont. He brought with him relics of St Andrew, which
his predecessor, Wilfred, had obtained from Rome. The
precious relics of the apostle enhanced the prestige of
Kilrimont, which was later renamed St Andrews.[26]

Fine Pictish crosses were carved at this time by the monastic
stonemasons, and an elaborate house-shaped shrine was created
in about 800, perhaps to contain the bones of one of the
Scottish kings, since scenes from the life of the Old Testament
King David are carved on its panels: the young David pastures
his father's sheep and breaks a lion's jaw with his bare hands.
In 943 King Constantine II retired from office and became
abbot of Kilrimont's monastic community. The church of St
Rule was built to serve its monks. In the late tenth century,
when Norsemen began to raid Iona and the Scottish west coast,
leadership of the united kingdoms of the Scots and Picts was
transferred to Kilrimont, which was in a safer location on the
east coast.[27]

King Alexander I, who reigned from 1107 to 1124,
attempted to convert the Celtic monks of Kilrimont to Roman

ways. He tried to appoint a bishop who would help him to reform the Church, but the first two bishops he chose were unwilling to do so. The King achieved a measure of success with his third candidate, Robert, prior of the Augustinian abbey of Scone. Bishop Robert determined to establish a community of Augustinian canons at Kilrimont, who would transform it into a model Roman cathedral chapter.

The Celtic monks opposed their new bishop so fiercely, however, that Robert was unable to carry out his plans until 1144, over twenty years later. The Celtic clergy, consisting of about thirteen monks and some priests, all of them married, were invited to join the new community, but they declined. They were given a permanent home in the church of St Mary on the Rock, whose foundations can be seen outside the cathedral walls, close to the shore. The building was on the edge of the promontory, overlooking the harbour. Many of the carved cross slabs now in the visitor centre were found here. In 1248 the community at St Mary of the Rock was recognized as an independent college of diocesan priests.[28]

The very large site contains a number of buildings. At the heart of the medieval city is the cathedral, on a headland to the east of the settlement. It was begun by Bishop Arnold in about 1160 and grew to become the longest and greatest church in Scotland; only its shell remains. Beside it is a thirteenth-century priory built for the Augustinian canons who served the cathedral. Its predecessor, St Rule's church, stands alongside it, dominated by its plain twelfth-century tower. The entire complex is enclosed within a great precinct wall. North-west of the cathedral is the medieval bishops' castle, on an easily defended cliff-top site.

ST BOSWELLS, Scottish Borders: Dryburgh abbey

Just outside St Boswells, four miles south-east of Melrose, Dryburgh abbey is tucked inside a bend in the River Tweed. The medieval abbey is built on the site of a chapel dedicated to Modan, an early missionary whose cult survives in Stirling and Falkirk. He was said to have ended his days as a hermit in the mountains near Dumbarton, where the church at Rosneath is dedicated to him. The vaulted chapel of St Modan at Dryburgh was originally the library and vestry of the medieval monastery. This was founded in 1150 for Premonstratensian canons brought here from Alnwick in Northumberland by the

Constable of Scotland, Hugh de Moreville. A twelfth-century chapter house survives, decorated with patterns painted on the wall plaster between its stone arcading. The ruined refectory contains a fine rose window. Dryburgh abbey lies to the north of the town, and its location is clearly signed.

ST VIGEANS, Angus: St Féchín's church

Vigeanus is the Latin form of Féchín, the name of a seventh-century Irish holy man from Sligo. He did not travel to Scotland, but his followers did, and several churches are dedicated to him. The hamlet of St Vigeans is a mile north of Arbroath, close to the Angus coast, sixteen miles east-north-east of Dundee. The church stands on a hillock, and an important Pictish monastery grew around it, where a school of sculptors carved a large number of grave slabs between the eighth and tenth centuries. Twenty-five stones survive, including one that depicts two monks carrying leather book satchels on straps round their necks; each holds a staff.

Another eighth-century cross slab is one of the few Pictish stones with an inscription. A later ninth-century mason commemorated 'Drostan, in the time of Ferat and Fergus'. King Ferat reigned from 839 to 842, and Drostan may be the monk who founded a monastery at Deer, further north in Aberdeenshire, 10 miles west of Peterhead. Fergus, the third person named in the inscription, was a native Pictish monk who settled at Glamis. The stones are housed in a small museum in the street below the church.

SHETLAND ISLANDS: Papil, West Burra: the Monks' Stone

Papil is six miles south-west of Lerwick; it may have been the principal monastic site on the Shetland Islands. The Monks' Stone was found here; it can be seen at the Shetland Museum in Lerwick. It shows a procession of five monks moving toward a high cross. Four are on foot and one, perhaps the abbot, rides a pony. Each carries a staff and a book satchel to contain a book of the gospels. The stone formed the side panel of a shrine. Another Pictish sculpture, the Papil Stone, depicts monks below a wheel-headed cross, with various Pictish symbols.

Further north in the Shetland Isles, an early monastery has been surveyed at Birrier on the island of Yell; it contained fourteen buildings. At Outer Brough, a rock stack beyond

Fetlar, the foundations of sixteen buildings have been traced, and an enclosing wall. In the far north at the Kame of Isbister on the isle of Unst, remains of a monastery survive, including the foundations of nineteen buildings, but these are accessible only by helicopter.[29]

SKYE, Isle of, Highland

Near the north-western tip of the peninsula of Trotternish on Skye, Kilmuir contains the Skye Museum of Island Life and an old church and graveyard. As you drive south from Kilmuir, you pass the drained *Loch Chaluim Chille*, or Columba's Loch. A stony mound now marks the former island of Columba. The foundations of an enclosing wall, beehive huts and two chapels can be seen on the hillock.

Near the head of Loch Snizort Beag, fourteen miles south of Kilmuir, is the little village of Skeabost. In the mouth of the River Snizort as it enters the loch is St Columba's Island, on which are the ruins of a Celtic and a medieval chapel. This is believed to have been an early foundation made by the monks of Iona. The island was the headquarters of the bishopric of the Isles from 1079 to 1498.

On Skye's second northern peninsula, Vaternish, a mile north of Fairy Bridge, is Annait or 'mother church', which is one of the oldest Christian settlements on the island. A monastery was built on a ridge between two deep gulleys, through which streams cascade. Its cashel wall can be clearly seen, with the foundations of a chapel and several beehive huts. The founding monk's name has been lost, and the site has not been excavated.[30]

At Borline on Loch Eynort, in the south-west of Skye, is the early monastic site of Kilmoruy. Its name means 'cell of Máelrubha', and it was related to this monk's famous monastery at Applecross, on the mainland opposite Skye. The shaft of a high cross stands in Kilmoruy churchyard. It depicts the crucifixion on one side and an abbot on the other; this probably represents Máelrubha, although the cross was carved well after his lifetime. On the mainland, the burial ground of Applecross chapel is all that remains of this important monastery, which was destroyed by the Vikings within a century of Máelrubha's death.

STOBO, Scottish Borders: St Kentigern's church

Stobo is a hamlet in the upper Tweed Valley, five miles south-west of Peebles, just north of the river. Eleven dedications to Kentigern and his followers in the Lothians have given rise to the suggestion that Kentigern may have originated from, or worked in, this area.[31] The church is on a hillside above the village; it dates largely from the twelfth century. Stobo became the mother church of Upper Tweeddale; until the Reformation it was linked with Glasgow cathedral.

STRATHBLANE, Stirling: site of Kessóg's church

Strathblane is ten miles east-north-east of Dumbarton. The name of this settlement means 'strip of land beside the River Blane'. Towering above the church is a rocky outcrop known as 'Earl's Seat'; this was part of the ancient earldom of Lennox, of which Kessóg was said to have been a bishop. The church was erected beside the settlement's ancient holy place: a large stone that marks a Bronze Age burial site. The present church is modern and is open only for services. The standing stone can be seen in the churchyard.

TYNDRUM, Stirling: St Fillan's pool and priory

Sixteen miles east of Oban, Tyndrum is a small Highland settlement beside the River Dochart. This strip of land beside the river is known as Strathfillan, after the Irish monk, Fillan, who is said to have died and been buried here. Two miles south-east of Tyndrum, where the A82 passes Auchtertyre farm, a shallow stretch of the river is named Fillan's Pool. It was believed to cure insanity: deranged people were bathed in the river, wrapped in straw, and then taken to Fillan's priory, half a mile to the south-east. Here they spent the night with their head in the stone font, with Fillan's bell placed above them. Cures were sought as late as the nineteenth century.[32]

Fillan's ruined priory with its walled cemetery can be seen on Kirkton Farm. To find it, take the A82 heading north-west from Crianlarich. Turn right up a signed track to Kirkton Farm, over a slender bridge. Park facing the ancient cemetery, which is on a mound. The remains of the ruined priory can be found beneath trees to the left. Return to the A82 and continue north-westward. Stop where the road crosses the river Dochart, beside a track on the right, which leads to Auchtertyre Farm. Do not drive up the track. Instead, with the track to your left, walk from the A82 towards the river. Fillan's pool is now visible, near the opposite bank.

WEEM, Perth and Kinross: St Cuthbert's church and cave

Weem is a mile north-west of Aberfeldy, on the opposite bank of the River Tay. Cuthbert may have visited this area during missionary journeys from the abbey of Melrose in the Scottish Borders. The name of the settlement means 'cave' (*uaimh* in Gaelic). The cliffs rise steeply above the Tay valley, and Cuthbert's cave is little more than an overhanging rock, where water seeps into a freshwater pool. According to the Irish *Life of Cuthbert*, he built a chapel and a cistern here, as a place to rest and pray while evangelizing the Picts in the surrounding area.

The well is now called St David's well, after a local fifteenth-century laird, Sir David Menzies, who gave up his comfortable life and came to live as a hermit here. The cave is found by taking the steep track that starts near St Cuthbert's church in the valley below, beside the main road. Do not follow the path to the top of the hill but turn left, and the cave will soon be signed. The chapel below contains two sturdy eighth-century crosses from the nearby Pictish monastery at Dull. The key to the church is held at the nearest house, which is set back behind the church, to the right.

WHITHORN, Dumfries and Galloway: St Ninian's shrine

The small town of Whithorn is near the coast, 40 miles south-west of Dumfries. We know little about the pre-Columban bishop, Ninian. Writing much later, Bede tells us how Ninian established a monastery at a place called *candida casa* (Latin for 'white, or shining, house'). In Old English this was translated as *hwit aern*, from which is derived the modern name of Whithorn. Bede writes: 'The southern Picts, who dwell on this side of the [Grampian] mountains, had ... embraced the truth by the preaching of Ninian, a most pious bishop and holy man of the Britons, who had been regularly instructed at Rome in the faith and mysteries of the truth, whose episcopal see is named after St Martin the bishop, and is famous for a stately church (where he and many other saints are laid to rest). It is still in existence. The place belongs to the province of Bernicia, and is generally called the White House, because he there built a church of stone, which was not usual among the Britons.'[33]

A stone church suggests one built in the Roman, or continental, style. Excavation has provided evidence of successive churches on the site dating from the sixth, seventh, and eighth centuries. When Bede mentions St Martin the bishop, he is referring to Martin of Tours, who developed monastic life in Gaul after learning how monks lived in the Near East. Excavations conducted by Peter Hill in the 1990s yielded potsherds indicating contact with Europe over a long period: fragments from the Mediterranean dated around 500, Gaulish pieces from about 550, and Frankish and Gaulish plain ceramic ware from about 600. There were pieces of eight glass bowls from the eastern Mediterranean, or Spain or Rome, dating from the fifth or sixth century. There were also fragments of fine African red slipware imported from Carthage in the mid-sixth century.[34]

A fine collection of inscribed stones can be seen in the small museum at the site. One is an early fifth-century memorial stone carved in a style developed in Gaul. It was erected for a man named Latinus by the descendants of Barrovadus, who may have been the local chieftain. It perhaps marked the gift of this site to the Church. Another monument, the 'Petrus Stone', formerly stood on high ground south-east of the monastery. It reveals traces of three different periods. First, a damaged, dressed face from an earlier inscription or design may have been removed. The violence of its removal suggests that it was no longer welcome. Second is a stemmed cross-of-arcs, designed like a petalled flower, dating from the seventh century. It is symmetrically placed and carefully executed. Finally there is an irregularly placed inscription of three lines reading LOCI PETRI APUSTOLI. It proclaims the *locus*, or place, of Peter the Apostle. This can probably be attributed to the Northumbrians and reflects the popularity of St Peter following the triumph of the Roman party at the Synod of Whitby (663/4). The stone may have stood beside the old road from Whithorn to the Isle of Whithorn, and was perhaps associated with a chapel.[35]

The Anglo-Saxons established a bishopric at Whithorn, constructing a church and a large monastic complex. Today, wooden posts indicate the outline of the church, built in about 750, and two timber halls, which would have had bowed walls and curved, ridged roofs. The first Saxon bishop, Pecthelm, was a correspondent of both Bede and Boniface, the English-born archbishop of Mainz. The Northumbrians popularized Ninian's cult, to legitimize their control of the Britons in Galloway. One monk wrote a poem about Ninian's life and miracles, and sent a copy to the Northumbrian scholar Alcuin at Charlemagne's court. Alcuin thanked him and sent back a silk veil for Ninian's shrine. Below the chancel of the twelfth-century priory at Whithorn, excavations have revealed the stone coffins of Northumbrian clerics. Several fine carved crosses also date from this time, including the Petrus Stone.

In the twelfth century King David I of Scotland brought the Scottish Church more fully under the control of Rome. He encouraged religious orders to take over native foundations, and Whithorn became a priory of Premonstratensian monks. The Cistercian abbot Ailred of Rievaulx, who had been educated at King David's court, wrote a *Life of Ninian*. He had access to a now lost British Life, but he admits that he despised its 'barbarous language'. He describes Ninian carrying out centralizing policies of which King David would approve: 'Then [Ninian] began to ordain priests, consecrate bishops, distribute other clerical honours and divide the whole land into parishes'.[36] However, Ailred also travelled to Whithorn and collected stories about Ninian from the Galloway region, which then belonged to Ailred's own diocese of York.

Ninian is said to have used a cave as a quiet retreat. It is on the seashore 5 miles south-west of Whithorn and is approached by an ancient path. Seven Celtic and Northumbrian crosses are carved on its walls; the earliest of these may pre-date the Northumbrian conquest of Galloway, which took place in about 730. This suggests that the cave soon became a place of pilgrimage. To find it, take the A747 west from Whithorn, following signs to St Ninian's cave, Physgill. Park where the road ends. Follow the path to the right through Physgill Glen for half a mile. Turn right at the beach; the cave is ahead of you.

The Isle of Whithorn, which is now joined to the mainland, lies three miles from the town on the opposite shore. It was probably associated with the monastery throughout its history. There are traces of a Celtic fort on the island, around the ruins of a thirteenth-century chapel in which pilgrims arriving by sea could give thanks for their safe arrival.

Part Three
Wales

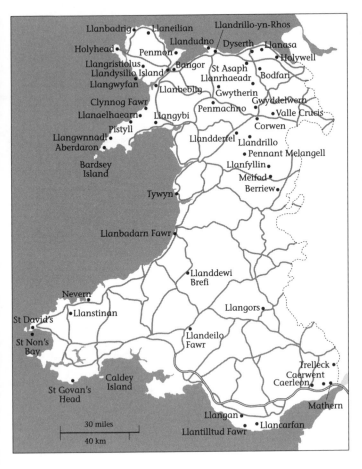

Saints of Wales

ABERDARON, Gwynedd: church of Saints Hywyn and Lleuddad

Close to the tip of the Lleyn peninsula, Aberdaron was traditionally important as the place of departure for pilgrims to Bardsey Island. The church is dedicated to two of Cadfan's followers, Hywyn and Lleuddad. Hywyn was said to have been Cadfan's steward, and chaplain to the monks on Bardsey Island. According to sources of late date, Lleuddad succeeded Cadfan as abbot of Bardsey. A field on the island was known as 'Lleuddad's Garden'; on the mainland, a cave at Aberdaron is named after him, and a well in Bryncroes parish, four miles east of Aberdaron. Its water was renowned for curing sick people and animals.[1]

The lower course of the church at Aberdaron has been buried by drifting sand. It has a Norman porch, and by the twelfth century it had a sanctuary seat: this was a stone chair in which those taking refuge from the law could claim immunity before sailing to safety in another land. This was a *clas* church: a monastery without a rule, whose headship was hereditary. The Normans destroyed the *clas* system since they preferred to control the churches in their territory, but because of its remoteness Aberdaron remained a *clas* church until the Reformation. In the fifteenth century the church was doubled in size to accommodate pilgrims.

Great numbers of people made the difficult crossing to Bardsey Island throughout medieval times. They travelled along the Lleyn peninsula, and spent the final night before their sea-crossing at Aberdaron. The hospice where they slept is known as 'The Great Kitchen' (*Y Gegin Fawr*); the present building dates from about 1300. Here travellers could rest in comfort before their rough journey by sea. There were two embarkation points near Aberdaron: one of these was at Brach-y-Pwyll, where the foundations of a chapel are visible in the turf above the shore. Down among the rocks is Ffynnon Fair ('St Mary's well'), a freshwater spring visible at low tide, but it is difficult to find. Here travellers could fill their water bottles before they embarked.

BANGOR, Gwynedd: St Deiniol's cathedral

Deiniol established Bangor beside the Menai Strait, on land given to him by Maelgwyn, Prince of Gwynedd. Its community was destroyed by the Vikings in 1073. All that now survives are pieces of some ninth- or tenth-century stone crosses carved with geometric designs. They can be seen in the cathedral, which became the centre of one of Britain's earliest dioceses. Deiniol's son gave his name to a small settlement across the Menai Strait in Anglesey, Llanddaniel Fab (or 'church of Daniel the Younger'). Unlike Deiniol's magnificent fourteenth-century cathedral, his son's church is hidden behind a row of houses in the village that bears his name.

BARDSEY ISLAND, Gwynedd: site of Cadfan's monastery

One can visit Bardsey Island in the summer by boat, weather permitting. The island is south-west of the Lleyn peninsula. The Welsh name for Bardsey is *Ynys Enlli* ('Island in the Currents'). It lies only two miles offshore, but because of the strong currents in the Sound the sea journey can be as long as six miles. Cadfan is said to have established a monastery here, although the site may have been used only as a Lenten retreat by monks living on the mainland at Aberdaron or at nearby Capel Anelog, where two gravestones were found dating from the late fifth or early sixth century. The tombstones refer to two priests and 'many brothers'; they can now be seen in Aberdaron church.[2]

On Bardsey, graves that may be those of early monks are clustered around the ruined tower of a thirteenth-century Augustinian monastery. There are also circular foundations of monks' huts; their date is unknown. The earliest contemporary reference to the monastery is a record of the death of a monk in 1011. The steward of the thirteenth-century community was given the title *Oeconomos*, an early Greek word originating with the desert monks of the East. This archaic title may have been used by the Celtic monks on Bardsey.[3] Several types of herb still grow around the houses on the island, perhaps descendants of those grown by the monks.[4]

It is often said that after the Saxon King Ethelfrith massacred twelve hundred monks at Bangor-is-y-Coed on the river Dee, he destroyed their monastery, and the surviving monks fled to Bardsey. However, this statement cannot be traced back beyond the early nineteenth century. Bardsey is a Norse name meaning 'Bardr's Island': in the tenth century it may have become the base of a Viking pirate chief. If so, the monks would have fled or been killed or kidnapped. They appear to have returned, however, as the lower half of a cross dating from the late tenth or early eleventh century depicts a monk wearing a pleated robe that almost reaches his ankles.[5]

In medieval times, Bardsey was called the 'Isle of the Saints' after the monks who were buried there; it became a famous centre for pilgrimage. Today, hermits once more live and pray on the island. In summer, when the sea is calm enough, a boat sails to Bardsey from Pwllheli on Saturdays; it picks up passengers at Aberdaron en route. For information about sailings, phone 01758 730740.

BERRIEW, Powys: St Beuno's church; St Beuno's stone

Beuno's medieval Life relates that, after his father's death, a local prince gave Beuno the small settlement of Berriew, five miles south-west of present-day Welshpool, as a site for his first monastery. Its name (*Aber Rhiw* in Welsh) indicates that Berriew grew beside the river Rhiw where it flows into the Severn, near the Roman road to Wroxeter. Beuno's church is set in a Celtic oval churchyard; it was rebuilt in the nineteenth century. The monolith known as *Maen Beuno* ('Beuno's Stone') is a pointed Bronze Age standing stone in Dyffryn Lane, a mile from Beuno's church. This perhaps marked the settlement's ancient holy place and here, according to tradition, Beuno preached to the people at the beginning of his missionary career. To reach it, drive through Berriew, passing the Red Lion Inn on your right. At the junction with the A483, continue across the main road into Dyffryn Lane (unsigned), past a few houses and a lay-by. Beuno's Stone is on the right, beside the hedge.

BODFARI, Denbighshire: St Deifor's church and well

Bodfari, three miles north-east of Denbigh in north Wales, features in the twelfth-century *Legend of Winifred*. She is said to have left Holywell with a group of nuns, and travelled inland, first to Bodfari, where they stayed with a monk named Deifor, and eventually to Gwytherin. The name Bodfari means 'dwelling (*bod*) of Deifor'. His church is on a hillside above the Roman road from Chester to Caerhun, which was a fort guarding the River Conwy. There was a Roman posting station at Bodfari and a small settlement. The Normans rededicated

Deifor's church to St Stephen. Huge buttresses anchor the medieval church into the hillside. The key of the church can be obtained from the Post Office across the road.

A thirteenth-century manuscript mentions Deifor's well, 100 metres down the road from the church, opposite the site of the Roman station. The well can be seen within a concrete surround, beside the road. Even after the Reformation, villagers went in procession from the church down to the well, where the Litany, the Ten Commandments, and the Epistle and Gospel were read. The poorest people in the parish offered a chicken after walking nine times round the well: a cock for a boy or a pullet for a girl. Children were also 'dipped to the neck at three of its corners, to prevent their crying at night'.

CAERGYBI (Holyhead), Anglesey: St Cybi's church

According to Cybi's thirteenth-century Life, Maelgwyn Gwynedd gave the monk permission to build a church at Caergybi. In the Lives of Patrick and other saints, a chieftain, on conversion to Christianity, often handed over part of his fortified homestead to the Church. Maelgwyn gave Cybi a late third-century Roman coastal fort, and the church sits neatly inside it, well protected by its Roman enclosure wall with towers at each corner. Inside the south corner of the fort is *Eglwys-y-Bedd*, 'the church of the grave'. Cybi was said to have been buried here. The chapel over his tomb dates from the fourteenth century. The large medieval parish church is thirteenth century. It was rebuilt in the late fifteenth and early sixteenth centuries; its elaborate porch contains fine carved stonework and a fan-vaulted roof. The whole complex lies near the centre of old Holyhead.

CAERLEON, Newport: St Cadoc's church

Caerleon is beside the River Usk, two miles north-east of Newport, in south-east Wales. Here, where the tidal river was still navigable, the Romans built the legionary fortress of Isca. Troops could assemble here, their supplies easily transported by land or sea. The name Caerleon means 'Camp of the Legions', and Cadoc's church is near the centre of the ruined fort. Bede tells us that in the third century two Roman soldiers were arrested at Caerleon and executed for their Christian beliefs. They belonged to the Second Augustan Legion and were named Julius and Aaron.[6] They were buried south-east of the town, across the river, in the Christian portion of the Roman cemetery. In medieval times, a chapel dedicated to Julius and Aaron stood on the site; it lies in the present parish of Christchurch.

When the Romans withdrew in the early fifth century, local dynasties of Welsh chieftains ruled. Cadoc sprang from one of these dynasties, and a number of churches named after him are associated with Roman forts and settlements. Cadoc's church in Caerleon is at the centre of the old town. Part of a ninth-century high cross survives, decorated with bird-like angels and interlaced patterns. It stood at the crossroads, outside the churchyard. The Roman ruins in Caerleon provided immense supplies of good building stone, and almost all the town's older buildings utilize recycled Roman material. Incorporated into the fifteenth-century tower of Cadoc's church are red sandstone blocks, orange brick tiles and yellow freestone, all of Roman origin.

Cadoc's church at Caerleon is built over the Roman *principia*, or legionary headquarters, where the imperial standards were kept and statues of the emperor were venerated. On this site the Christian soldiers, Julius and Aaron, would have refused to worship the deified emperor. Beneath the churchyard, the fine mosaic floor of the *principia* was discovered. It depicts a labyrinth; around its border, a stylized tree of life emerges from a vase. The mosaic is now preserved in the museum across the road. We can imagine Julius and Aaron standing within the maze, having to choose between life and death on account of their beliefs.

Not far from the church are the legionary barracks where Julius and Aaron would have slept, and the giant amphitheatre where the soldiers trained. After their arrest, they would have been taken to the civil settlement of Caerwent, 8 miles to the east, to be tried by the judiciary. As Roman citizens, they would not have been subjected to the sadistic indignities of the amphitheatre games at Caerleon. Instead, they were probably beheaded, in about 304. Ironically, within ten years, the converted emperor Constantine gave Christians freedom to worship.

CAERWENT, Monmouthshire: St Tathan's church
Caerwent is ten miles east of Newport in south-east Wales. A monastery was founded here by an Irish monk named Tathan.

Cadoc was said to have studied here as a youth. Caerwent was an ancient tribal capital, and was the largest centre of civilian population in Roman Wales. One can still walk round its impressive walls with their defensive towers. There was a Christian community here in Roman times, and evidence of two house churches has been found. One house was redesigned to include a nave, an eastern apse, a porch, and sacristies. In the second house, a sealed urn contained a pewter bowl with the *chi–rho* symbol for Christ scratched on it, and other vessels that were perhaps used for the meal that followed the Eucharist in the fourth century.

Two hundred years after the Romans withdrew, Tathan built a church near the centre of the ruined Roman town. An ancient yew tree stands in the churchyard. Roman masonry is incorporated into the church walls, and a Saxon font has an inverted Roman column for its base. There is a section of Roman mosaic in the church floor. The present church dates from the thirteenth century; it has a fifteenth-century tower. Tathan probably died in Caerwent. His monastery lies beneath the vicarage orchard, where a housing complex has now been built. Another early monk, Malo, was said to have been a native of Caerwent and abbot of its monastery. He went to Brittany as a missionary and gave his name to St Malo.

CALDEY ISLAND, Pembrokeshire: the monastery

This island is three miles south of Tenby, at the south-western point of Carmarthen Bay. There are frequent daily boat crossings on weekdays throughout the year; the journey takes about 20 minutes. There are Saturday sailings from mid-May to mid-September, but none on Sundays. This enables the Cistercian monks who now live on the island to enjoy its tranquillity once a week. At high tide, boats leave from Tenby harbour; at low water they depart from the landing stage on Castle Beach. Tickets can be obtained from the Caldey Island kiosk at the top of Tenby harbour.

The monastery on Caldey Island was a daughter house of Llanilltud Fawr in the Vale of Glamorgan, 40 miles south-east. At this time, Caldey Island was known as Ynys Pyr after its first abbot. The *Life of Samson* describes Pyr's undignified death: walking back to his cell one night, the drunken abbot fell into the monastery's well and was drowned. Dubricius had authority over the community, and appointed Samson as abbot to replace Pyr. There are many caves around the island's coastline; the monks may have lived in these and in wattle huts clustered around a church, close to the spring which still supplies the island with abundant fresh water.

Near the centre of the island are St Illtud's church and the remains of a Norman priory, with a distinctive stone watchtower. The present church with its floor of cobble stones dates from the thirteenth and fourteenth centuries. Located against the south wall of the nave is a grave slab inscribed in ogham *Magl Dubr* ... '[the stone of] the tonsured servant of Dubricius'. It also bears a Latin inscription. Writing in about 1811, the antiquarian Fenton says that the stone was dug up in the ruins of the priory 'many years ago'.

Ynys Pyr was a foundation of some significance: a fragment of sixth-century pottery from the eastern Mediterranean, and the base of a seventh-century jar from Gaul were found near the tiny parish church of St David, which may be built on foundations dating from Celtic times; its site was then just above the high water mark. Linked with the monastery was a community of nuns on St Margaret's Island, which adjoins Caldey. At that time it was possible to walk across low-lying marsh to St Margaret's from the mainland at Penally.

CLYNNOG FAWR, Gwynedd: St Beuno's church and well

The impressive church at Clynnog Fawr is on the northern coast of the Lleyn peninsula, ten miles south-west of Caernarfon. Beuno is said to have spent the last phase of his life at the monastery that he established here, before his death in 642. The small freestanding chapel is probably built on the site of his church and may have contained his tomb. Until the eighteenth century, pilgrims came here to Beuno's shrine to pray for healing. A late Celtic sundial stands beside the outer wall of the chapel. It is carved on the southern face of a pillar stone, pierced with a hole into which the gnomon was inserted to cast its shadow. This is one of Britain's earliest sundials, and would have been used by the monks in their ordered life of work and prayer.

The settlement became known as Clynnog Fawr, 'Great Clynnog', and a large medieval church was built alongside Beuno's chapel. It was extended just before the Reformation to accommodate the crowds of pilgrims who came here to begin walking the Saints' Way, a route that led along the Lleyn peninsula to Bardsey Island at its tip.

Inside Clynnog church is 'Beuno's chest', hollowed out from a single tree trunk. People put offerings into Beuno's chest to atone for crimes; they also offered money from the sale of animals that they considered to belong to Beuno. At birth, some Welsh calves and lambs have a slit in their ears, known as 'Beuno's mark' (*Nôd Beuno*), as do Jersey cattle today. Until the late eighteenth century, farmers brought these animals to the churchwardens on the Sunday after Whitsun; they were sold, and the money was placed in the chest. Beuno's well is 200 metres south-west of the church, beside the main road. A flight of stone steps leads to a pool of clear water in a square, open-roofed stone well house. It supplied water for the monastery and became a famous healing well.

CORWEN, Denbighshire: church of Saints Mael and Sulien

The town of Corwen is in mid-Wales at the foot of the Berwyn Mountains, beside the fast-flowing river Dee. It grew alongside an important route for travellers through the centuries. This was the Roman road along which Welsh drovers also herded their cattle. It later became the A5, the main road from London to Holyhead. The name Corwen means 'stone church' (or, literally, 'choir-white'). This is a Welsh version of the English name Whitchurch, and denoted an important stone church, at a time when others were more simply constructed of timber. Corwen church is built on an ancient holy site, beside a prehistoric standing stone, named in Welsh 'the pointed stone in the icy corner'. When the building was enlarged in medieval times, the ancient stone was incorporated into the wall of the porch.[7] In the churchyard is a large Bronze Age boulder with seven cup-marks. The boulder was 'christianized' some time between the ninth and the twelfth centuries and used as the base for a tall cross.

DYSERTH, Denbighshire: St Cwyfan's church and well

Dyserth is three miles south-east of Rhyl, near the north Welsh coast. It is one of four settlements with churches dedicated to a disciple of Beuno named Cwyfan. His church at Dyserth is close to a high waterfall. The name Dyserth comes from the Latin word *desertum*, which means 'an empty place'. This is the western equivalent of the Greek *eremos* or 'desert hermitage', an ancient monastic word that was used by the monks and nuns who went into the deserts of Syria, Egypt, and Palestine in search of a solitary place to pray.

European pilgrims were impressed by the wisdom and holiness of these desert mothers and fathers, and wished to follow their example. Since there were no deserts in Britain, monks searched for a similar 'empty place' on a rocky headland or small island, or in a remote valley. Scattered across Ireland, Scotland, and Wales are places named Dyserth, or *Díseart* in Irish.[8] Each indicates an 'empty place' where a person could search for God in solitude. Cwyfan or his unknown follower chose a magnificent location for his 'desert', within sound and sight of the waterfall's spray. The pool at its foot provided water for drinking and washing, and a place in which to immerse candidates for baptism.

Watercress, valued as food by Celtic monks, grows thickly in the cold stream flowing past the church. Inside, the remains of two elaborate Celtic crosses indicate that a community continued on the site. Half a mile north-west of the church is Cwyfan's well, now dry. Until seventy years ago, people still fished for trout in the well. Fish in wells were regarded with awe and respect, and were considered to bring healing.[9] To find the well, with the church on your right, continue along the road. Turn right at the main road. The well is soon visible in a square stone well house, beside the road, on the right.

GWYDDELWERN, Denbighshire: St Beuno's church and well

There is a cluster of dedications to Beuno around the village of Gwyddelwern, which lies on a Roman road, eight miles west-north-west of Llangollen. Beuno is said to have founded a community here. Since *gwyddel* means 'Irishman', the name of the village indicates that it was settled by Irish immigrants. Groups of farming families in search of land for pasture migrated from Ireland to Wales in early times. There is a Celtic yew tree in the churchyard. Beuno's somewhat neglected holy well is just inside a field beside the road, half a mile to the north of the church. Its chute is covered with corrugated sheeting, and the water pours into a trough. People used to bathe in the well, believing in its miraculous powers. Its water was brought to the church for christenings. Older inhabitants remember this being the only water supply for the village.

GWYTHERIN, Conwy: St Winifred's church

According to her medieval Life, after leaving Holywell Winifred travelled inland with a group of nuns, until she reached the remote settlement of Gwytherin. The hamlet is twelve miles south of Colwyn Bay, in the valley of the river Cledwen. As one drives toward it, Snowdon's peak is often visible, across the Vale of Conwy. A monk named Eleri was said to have founded a monastery at Gwytherin. His mother, Theonia, was its first leader. Gwytherin was already a holy place: above a burial mound, two yew trees now over 2,000 years old were planted on an east–west axis, aligned with the rising and setting sun.[10] Between them is a row of four pre-Christian standing stones. In the fifth or sixth century, one of these was reused as a tombstone by a Christian family, for inscribed on it in Latin is '[The stone of] Vinnemaglus, son of Senemaglus'.

Near this spot, Eleri founded his community, and in time Winifred succeeded Theonia as abbess. Winifred died here, and in the eighth century her bones were enshrined in a house-shaped wooden reliquary, decorated with ornamental metalwork. Gwytherin's single-chambered church was rebuilt in the nineteenth century. A late Celtic grave slab inscribed with a cross is set in the chancel step, and nearby is a medieval chest, carved from a single tree trunk, for offerings at Winifred's shrine. There was a flourishing monastery here in medieval times: it was a double community for both monks and nuns. A survey of 1334 mentions abbots at Gwytherin. The churchyard was larger than it is today; it included Winifred's *capel y bedd*, or chapel of her grave. In the seventeenth century, the antiquarian Edward Lhuyd wrote that it was still standing; it was demolished early in the following century.[11]

HOLYHEAD: see CAERGYBI

HOLYWELL, Flintshire: St Winifred's chapel and well; St Beuno's church and well

According to her twelfth-century Legend, Winifred established a convent of nuns at Holywell in north Wales, near the Flintshire coast, fifteen miles north-west of Chester. Here,

Winifred's well was known for its healing properties and has attracted pilgrims throughout the centuries. In the fifteenth century King Henry V walked the 50 miles from Shrewsbury to Holywell. When King Edward IV made a similar pilgrimage in 1480, Tudur Aled wrote: 'Garlands on garlands decked the way; thousands trampled down the greensward.' He noted how the king reverently sprinkled soil from the shrine on his crown. Lady Margaret Beaufort, King Henry VII's mother, built the present chapel with its star-shaped pool in 1483, to replace the earlier Norman chapel. A carving on a corner roof-corbel shows a pilgrim carrying an invalid on his back; the sick are still carried through the bathing pool in this way.

Jesuits and other priests lived at Holywell throughout penal times, when Catholics could be fined or imprisoned for worshipping openly. The well became a centre of resistance to the 'new religion' of Protestantism. Daniel Defoe wrote that priests were 'very numerous' here but had to appear in disguise. In May 1719, hearing that Catholics intended to celebrate St Winifred's day, the authorities sent in dragoons who seized the priest during the Eucharist, together with the church plate and richly decorated statues. In 1722 the church was confiscated and became a day school; 'however, to supply the loss of this chapel, the Roman Catholics have chapels erected in almost every inn, for the devotion of the pilgrims that flock thither from all the popish parts of England'.[12]

In the eighteenth century, Lancashire pilgrims visiting Holywell crossed the Mersey by boat, walked across the Wirral and the often treacherous sands of the Dee estuary at low tide, and climbed the narrow valley to Winifred's well. The ancient landing stage at Holywell can still be seen; here, local fishermen bring in their catch. The pilgrims travelled in groups, and lit beacons on the Wirral to signal for a boat on their way home.[13] In 1795 Thomas Pennard visited the shrine and wrote: 'In the summer, still a few are to be seen in the water in deep devotion up to their chins for hours, sending up their prayers.'

In the following century, opposition to visiting the well waned, and the town council became aware of its possibilities. A hospice for pilgrims was opened in 1870, and at a meeting of the town council in 1896 the chairman stated, 'In the past year, 1,710 pilgrims, many sick and pitifully afflicted, were housed at the hospice.... Of these, upwards of 500 were examined and registered by the medical attendant, and I am assured by him that a great many remarkable cures were obtained.' To this day, many continue to come to the shrine for healing.

Winifred's Legend relates that her uncle, Beuno, came to Holywell where he obtained land from her parents on which to build a church. This may have been on the site of the fifteenth-century parish church, on the hillside above Winifred's well. Across the road, on top of Castle Hill, Beuno's well is almost inaccessible beneath undergrowth. It flows into a stream on the embankment that surrounds the hill fort, where it is possible that Winifred's family may have lived.

LLANAELHAEARN, Gwynedd:
St Aelhaearn's church

This village lies six miles north of Pwllheli and is situated at the foot of Yr Eifl. The mountain, which rises to a height of 564 metres, is famous for its well-preserved Iron Age hilltop village. The settlement below is named after Aelhaearn who, according to Beuno's Life, was one of three brother monks who were followers of Beuno. Inside the church, set into the wall, is a sixth-century memorial stone inscribed in Latin: 'here lies Aliortus, [a man] from Elmet'. The gravestone was found in a field beside the churchyard named 'the Garden of the Saints'. Elmet was a distant Celtic kingdom around present-day Leeds. A family from the Leeds area settling in the Lleyn peninsula must have been even more unusual in Celtic times than it would be today, giving rise to this unique early Christian epitaph. It hints at a group displaced from northern Britain in the face of Saxon conquest. Early written sources preserve a similar tradition.

In the churchyard, another Romano-Celtic grave marker commemorates a Christian named Melitus. It stands to the right of the path as you approach the church. The nave is Norman, with a sixteenth-century north chapel and a seventeenth-century south chapel. The chancel was rebuilt in the nineteenth century. The key to the church can be obtained from no. 4 on the main road, named Bodawel.

LLANASA, Flintshire: church of Saints Asaph and Cyndeyrn

Cyndeyrn is Welsh for Kentigern, so this church is named after the bishop of Glasgow and his Welsh student, Asaph. The name Llanasa means 'church site of Asaph'. The village is in a sheltered valley near the north Welsh coast, six miles east of Rhyl. It is possible that this is an early foundation established by monks from St Asaph. The present double-chambered church was built in the fifteenth century; an asymmetrical bell turret was constructed at this time. In 1540, when the monasteries were dissolved at the Reformation, two fine stained glass windows were brought to Llanasa church from Basingwerk abbey in Holywell. The window over the altar depicts four saints, including Beuno dressed as a bishop. The saint to his right is Beuno's niece, Winifred, with a scar round her throat, although she is named, probably incorrectly, as St Catherine.[14] The church also contains the fourteenth-century tombstone of the father of Owain Glyndwr, the last Welsh fighting prince who rose against the English. He died in 1416.

LLANBADARN FAWR, Ceredigion: St Padarn's church

Llanbadarn is a southern suburb of Aberystwyth, on the Welsh coast. Padarn was an early monk; he may have preceded David, who also has dedications in this area.[15] According to medieval tradition, Padarn persuaded the local chieftain to give him land between the rivers Rheidol and Clarach, where he built Llanbadarn Fawr on a hillside. The site is near Sarn Helen, an ancient route continuing the line of the Roman coastal road. The trackway is named after Helen, the wife of Magnus Maximus. For twenty years, Padarn was bishop and abbot of the monastery at Llanbadarn Fawr. A pre-Christian standing stone carved into a cross can be seen in the church. There is also a narrow granite pillar cross, 3 metres high, carved in about 750, on which a worn figure with a crozier may represent Padarn.

Llanbadarn Fawr had close links with Ireland, and it may have become a reformed Culdee community (see PENMON). Unlike other Welsh monasteries in the south-west, it became a centre of learning. By the eleventh century, under Abbot Sulien the Wise, its library was larger than those of Canterbury Cathedral or York Minster. Sulien was twice bishop of St David's;

his four sons also became monks at Llanbadarn. The eldest, Rhigyfarch, wrote a *Life of David*. Another, Ieuan, later archpriest of Llanbadarn, illustrated Rhigyfarch's Psalter and wrote a poem about his father Sulien, wistfully recalling the former greatness of the monastery, which by then had perhaps been absorbed into the sphere of influence of St David's.

LLANBADRIG, Anglesey: St Patrick's church

Llanbadrig is a church on a clifftop, fifteen miles north-east of Holyhead, on the north coast of Anglesey. Patrick did not become a popular figure in Wales, where only three churches are dedicated to him, including that of Llanbadrig. Half a mile out to sea is a rocky islet named Ynys Badrig ('Patrick's Isle'); on the mainland, a cave with a freshwater well, halfway up the cliff, is also named after him. The medieval church contains a pre-Christian standing stone, which was decorated in the seventh or eighth century with carvings of a palm tree and two crossed fishes. They symbolize Christians, as the Greek letters that spell the word 'fish' also represent a title for Christ: they form the first letters of the title 'Jesus Christ, Son of God, Saviour'. The palm represents a tree of life; these symbols are also found in the Roman catacombs and in churches of the Near East.

To find Llanbadrig, take the A5025 east from Cemais. At Neuadd, take the track left down to the cliffs. You soon reach Llanbadrig. The church is open from May to September, 10 a.m. to 12 noon and 2 p.m. to 4 p.m.

LLANBEBLIG, Gwynedd: St Peblig's church; Segontium Roman fort

Peblig, or Publicus, was a son of Princess Helen and Magnus Maximus. The only church dedicated to Peblig is close to the Roman fort of Segontium, on the eastern edge of Caernarfon. It is likely that Helen and Magnus Maximus were based with the Roman troops at Segontium at some point, and it is possible that Peblig was with them. 'The Dream of Maxen Wledig' in *The Mabinogion* gives an early account of Caernarfon, filtered through medieval eyes.[16] Segontium was built in AD 77 and remained the military and administrative centre of north-west Wales until 394. Up to a thousand soldiers were stationed here. The medieval church of Llanbeblig is usually locked, but a Roman altar can be seen in the churchyard. Llanbeblig is on the A4085 Portmadoc Road, on the same side of the road as the Roman fort, a little lower down the hill.

LLANCARFAN, Vale of Glamorgan: St Cadoc's church

The site of Cadoc's chief monastery can be seen at Llancarfan, four miles north-west of Barry, in the Vale of Glamorgan. There were several great monasteries in the area, including that of Illtud at Llanilltud Fawr, only five miles to the west of Llancarfan, and that of Docco at Llandough, now a northern suburb of Penarth, farther to the east. Llancarfan was beside a stream, not far from the sea, which has now receded. It may have been an ancient port, safely upstream, hidden from pirates. The Celtic monastery probably lies below the field to the south of the medieval church; a well in the next field was also associated with the monastery.

The medieval *Life of Cadoc* by Lifris of Llancarfan describes how, before selecting his site, Cadoc and his monks spent the night in prayer; in the morning a white boar appeared, to indicate where he should begin building. This is a recurring theme in stories of Celtic saints' foundations: the boar was a sacred animal to pre-Christian Celts, and in the Lives of Celtic saints a white boar becomes a messenger from God. The pig foundation tales take place in a timeless world of pseudo-history. In the *Life of Cadoc*, a large white boar leaps out from a thicket, frightened by Cadoc's approach. It shows him where to build a church in honour of the Trinity, with a dormitory and a refectory. However, this is an Anglo-Norman pig, for a dormitory and a refectory, are features of a Norman monastery rather than a Celtic one.

The name Llancarfan means 'church of the stags', from a legend about Cadoc: when he asked two monks to till the ground near the monastery they refused, but a pair of stags appeared from the woods and dug the soil with their antlers. The monastery was ravaged by the Danes in 988. After the Norman conquest of Glamorgan in 1090, the monastery was dissolved, and the church was annexed to Gloucester Abbey. The present church dates from the thirteenth and fifteenth centuries. It contains a fine rood screen of carved oak, dating from the Perpendicular period. In the last few years, medieval wall paintings have been discovered beneath the white wall plaster.

LLANDDERFEL, Gwynedd: St Derfel's church

Llandderfel, four miles east-north-east of Bala in mid-Wales, is set on a valley slope, near the headwaters of the river Dee. Here, Derfel was said to have retired as a hermit. Until the Reformation there was an ancient wooden statue in the church, of Derfel mounted on a horse, or possibly a red deer stag. Thomas Cromwell, whom King Henry VIII made responsible for the confiscation of church property, sent agents throughout Britain to seize goods and 'abolish Popish practices'. There is a record of Cromwell's agent in Wales writing to his master in 1538 for instructions about Derfel's statue, because 'the people have so much trust in him that they come daily on pilgrimage to him with cows or horses or money, to the number of five or six hundred on April 5th' (Derfel's feast day). Cromwell had the statue of Derfel brought to London to be burned at Smithfield, but the rider's wooden mount can still be seen in the church porch. It stood in the chancel beside the communion table until 1730 when the rural dean, who disliked the presence of images in church, removed it and sawed off half the animal's head.

The wooden horse was still brought out each Easter Tuesday around the time of Derfel's feast and carried in procession to the Wake Field, where it was fixed to a pole for children to ride. Despite the damage it has sustained through the centuries, the recumbent beast retains considerable character, with its deep eye sockets and most of a head half-turned over its right shoulder. The small church has a magnificent oak rood screen, carved in about 1500. Llandderfel was sufficiently remote to remain a centre for Catholic worship; the last Mass in north Wales until recent times was celebrated here. The church is on a rise, near the end of the village. The key can be obtained from the former vicarage, now a nursing home, up the road, across from the church.

LLANDDEWI BREFI, Ceredigion: St David's church

This village is seven miles north-east of Lampeter. Its name means 'David's church beside the River Brefi'. David rose to a position of leadership during a synod that took place here in about 545. The Synod of Brefi appears to have been a religious tribal gathering to refute the heretical teachings of Pelagius. This British theologian taught that people could reach heaven by their own efforts, without the help of God's grace. His emphasis on personal responsibility appealed to British chieftains, with their strong sense of self-reliance.

Brefi was a natural place for an assembly: three Roman roads converge nearby, and they continued in use long after the Romans departed, although by the mid-sixth century they were probably becoming overgrown. At the synod, no one could make their voice heard over such a large crowd. David was a clear, convincing speaker, and was brought from nearby to address the gathering. When David's biographer, Rhigyfarch, relates this detail, Welsh readers would recall that a victorious bard could silence his opponents, just as only David could quieten the crowd and convince them of the errors of Pelagius.[18]

Inside Llanddewi Brefi church there is a fine collection of early gravestones dating from the seventh to the tenth centuries. Set into the outer wall of the church are two fragments of an inscription dating from the fifth, sixth, or seventh century: this may be the first surviving reference to David. The antiquarian Edward Lhuyd examined the complete stone, and concluded in 1722 that it read: 'Here lies Idnert, the son of James, who was killed while defending the church of holy David from pillage.'[19] The fragments can be seen in the west wall of the church, on the north side.

LLANDEILO FAWR, Carmarthenshire: St Teilo's church and well

Teilo was a monk who established a community at Llandeilo Fawr, above the river Tywi. The extent of the Celtic monastery is outlined by the very large churchyard of three and a half acres. It is bisected by the town's main street, which may follow the line of a Roman road. A spring rises near the east end of the church, and flows into a large chamber beneath it. This may be the site of a baptistery in which converts were immersed. The spring provided the town with its water until the nineteenth century; today it bubbles into an alcove on the outside of the churchyard wall.

Teilo was buried at Llandeilo Fawr. His cult became popular in south Wales: thirty-three churches are named after him. Remains of two finely carved crosses from the late eighth century show the continuing importance of the community. A magnificent Irish or Mercian Gospel book, illuminated in about 730, was given to the monastery around 820 'for the good of his soul' by a man named Gelhi, who had bought the book from a certain Guyal in exchange for his best horse.[17] The Gospel book contains stylized figures of the four evangelists: Luke holds a pastoral staff modelled on those carried by abbots of the Near East, and there are whole pages of intricate eastern-style 'carpet' decoration in which fish, dogs, and pelicans are intertwined.

The monks wrote entries in Welsh in the margins of the Gospel book, recording gifts to the bishop of St Teilo. These records of land transactions and legal settlements are some of the earliest surviving examples of written Welsh. The Gospel book was perhaps paid as tribute to a Saxon king, for some time after 850 it was in the ownership of St Chad's cathedral, Lichfield, where it still remains.

LLANDRILLO-YN-RHOS, Conwy:
St Trillo's chapel and well

Trillo's chapel is a mile north-west of Colwyn Bay on the north Welsh coast, at Llandrillo-yn-Rhos, whose name means 'church site of Trillo on the promontory'. The chapel is situated improbably below the Victorian promenade, close to the shore. Inside the tiny thirteenth-century building, in front of the altar, is a rectangular pool. This encloses the freshwater spring that Trillo or his unknown follower used for drinking, bathing and baptizing converts. Beside the chapel are the remains of his circular hut. Further up the hill from the beach, the parish church is also dedicated to Trillo.

LLANDUDNO, Conwy: St Tudno's church and well

Little is known about Tudno, to whom a church is dedicated on the headland of the Great Orme (Old Norse for 'great worm', or sea-serpent), above the modern town of Llandudno. A limestone cave containing a freshwater spring on the shore below the church is named after Tudno, and there is another ancient well near his church. The Great Orme was well known in early times: copper was mined here from the Bronze Age to the nineteenth century. Tudno attracted bardic legend: one of the thirteen treasures of Britain was said to be Tudno's whetstone, which sharpened the sword of a hero but blunted that of a coward!

A stone church was built here in the twelfth century; the carved bowl of its font still survives. In medieval times,

Llandudno was still a cluster of farms around Tudno's church, and it remained a small community until a holiday resort grew along the strand below in the nineteenth century. A flock of feral goats has been reintroduced on the Great Orme. They roamed wild in Celtic times and feature in the lives of the monks. However the goats that one sees here today are from Kashmir; they have been on the Orme since the 1890s. The key of the church is held at the farm below the churchyard. To find Tudno's well, walk up the road past the church and take the second footpath on the left toward Pink Farm, signed 'Ski Llandudno'. The well is on the right, 100 metres along the track, just inside a field.

LLANDYSILIO ISLAND, Anglesey: St Tysilio's church

At some point in his life, the prince-monk Tysilio is said to have become a hermit on a tiny island named after him in the Menai Strait. It can be visited by walking down through the woods, a little beyond the Anglesey end of the Menai Bridge. There is a small car park at the approach to the woods. On the island, a single-chambered church dating from the fifteenth century probably stands on the site of a Celtic chapel. Many dead are buried around Tysilio's church. The islet is reached by a causeway, from which one can watch curlews, oystercatchers, and a colony of terns. In spring, the island is golden with primroses.

Behind the church are the Swellies, dangerous tidal currents. An eighteenth-century traveller, Thomas Pennard, described how 'as a very young man, I ventured myself in a small boat into the midst of the boiling waves and mill-race current'. The next settlement along the coast is Llanfairpwllgwyngyll, whose full name describes both the Swellies and Tysilio's tiny church. When translated it reads: 'Church of St Mary by the pool with the white hazels, near the fierce whirlpool by the church of St Tysilio, near the red cave'. In spite of continuous traffic over the Menai Bridge, Llandysilio Island has retained its peaceful atmosphere through the centuries.

LLANEILIAN, Anglesey: St Eilian's church

Llaneilian is a village on the north-east coast of Anglesey, a mile east of Amlwch. In medieval times, the sick came to be cured at Eilian's shrine; it is of plain panelled wood, and still survives. The church dates from the fifteenth century, with a fourteenth-century chancel, from which a stone passage leads to Eilian's chapel. This is a small room, 4.5 by 3.5 metres. Eilian's shrine is here; formerly, pilgrims used to crawl through it as they prayed for healing. There is a fine fifteenth-century oak rood screen in the chancel. A feature of the church is its twelfth-century spired tower; there is a medieval preaching cross in the churchyard. Eilian's holy well near the shore was a place of pilgrimage; it was also a famous cursing well, and was used as such into the eighteenth century. However, it is difficult to find.

LLANELWY: see ST ASAPH

LLANFYLLIN, Powys: St Moling's church and well.

This small town is in mid-Wales, eighteen miles west-north-west of Shrewsbury. It is dedicated to the Irish monk Moling and was possibly founded by one of his followers. The church was rebuilt in red brick in 1710. On the hillside 300 metres above the church is Moling's well. Its large well chamber could be used for baptism by immersion. An account of 1894 describes how people tied rags to branches beside the spring, as prayers for healing. On Trinity Sunday they came to drink sugared water at the well. The water was drawn by the girls, after which the lads paid for cakes and ale at the inn. This was a survival from a medieval pilgrimage to the well, around the time of Moling's feast in June.[20] Sugar-water or liquorice water was often made at wells to improve the flavour of mineral-rich healing waters, and to symbolize life's sweetness. Sweetened water was also considered to be a tonic.

To find the well, with the church on your left, continue along the main street. Soon there is a sign to turn right for the well. Turn up this street, and right again at the top. Continue up the hill, park, and continue on foot for another 100 metres. As the track bends to the left, the well is on the right, beneath a great sycamore tree.

LLANGAN, Vale of Glamorgan: St Canna's church

This is a village twelve miles west of Cardiff. Llangan means 'church site of Canna', who was said to be a Breton princess associated with Cadfan. Aerial photography has revealed a circular churchyard within a larger circular enclosure, just north of the present church. Near the porch is the upper portion of a disc-headed cross slab, 1 metre wide and 1.3 metres high, carved from sandstone. It dates from the late ninth or tenth century, and depicts the crucifixion, in Byzantine style. Christ is alive (until the twelfth century he was portrayed as living, rather than dead), with open eyes and extended arms. He appears to be bearded and wears a loincloth. Christ is flanked by the smaller figures of soldiers with a sponge (left) and a spear (right). The style of carving is reminiscent of similar scenes on Irish metalwork. There is only one other similar cross in Wales.

There are fragments of another Celtic cross in the church porch, and a plain medieval tub font in the church. In the graveyard is a beautiful preaching cross carved in the fourteenth or fifteenth century. The parish of Llangan West in Pembrokeshire is also dedicated to Canna, where a holy well and a boulder named Canna's Chair are named after her. People were cured of the ague and of intestinal complaints by throwing pins into the well, bathing, then sitting in the chair, a process that was sometimes repeated for fourteen days in order to effect a cure.

LLANGORS, Powys: St Paul Aurelian's church; Llangors crannog

Llangors is a small town six miles east of Brecon in south-east Wales, in the foothills of the Black Mountains. The full name of the settlement was Llan yn y Gors, or 'church in the marsh'. It is dedicated to Paulinus, or Paul Aurelian, a sixth-century Welsh monk. Two other chapels in the parish are named after Paul Aurelian: one is Llanbeulin and the other is Llan y Deuddeg Sant (or 'church of the twelve saints'), referring to the twelve monks who accompanied Paul Aurelian.[21] It would have been appropriate for Paul to establish a community at Llangors, which appears to have been the royal burial ground for the kings of Brycheiniog (now Brecon), who may have lived in the crannog in nearby Llangors Lake.

A charter of Llandaff, ostensibly from the eighth century, but probably tenth-century in origin, states that King Awst of Brycheiniog and his sons gave a royal estate corresponding to the present parish of Llangors to Bishop Euddogwy. It records that King Awst requested that he and his sons might be buried at Llangors. Another Llandaff charter tells of a meeting at the monastery in Llangors around 925 between King Tewdwr of Brycheiniog and Bishop Libiau, to settle a dispute over food rent. Inside Llangors church at the west end there is an inscribed gravestone dating from the sixth or seventh century and an early cross slab decorated with pockmark patterns. The font dates from about 1300. The building is fifteenth-century and was restored in the nineteenth. The key to the church can be obtained from the vicarage, which is set back from the road, behind the church.

Llangors Lake is half a mile south-east of the village and is the largest natural lake in south Wales. A crannog is situated 40 metres from the northern shore of the lake. This is an artificial island; today it measures 40 metres across and is covered by trees and reeds. It was formerly occupied by buildings, which may have periodically housed the *llys* (court) of the king of Brycheiniog. Manuscript B of the Anglo-Saxon Chronicle relates that shortly before midsummer in 916, the Saxon King Aethelflaed sent an army to Wales to destroy the palace on the lake; they captured the queen and thirty-three of the king's followers. In the 1190s Gerald of Wales, in his *Journey Through Wales,* recorded a folk memory of the destruction of the island palace of Llangors. Local inhabitants said that there was a town beneath the waters of the lake; sometimes the city could be seen floating in the surface of the lake. They said that the lake sometimes turned bright green and occasionally scarlet.

A sixteenth-century manuscript reports that local people observed 'sometyme, greate peeces of tymber and fframes of houses ffleeting upon the water' (*De Mirabilibus Cambriae*, 'The Wonders of Wales'). This refers to the remains of timber planks forming the crannog's palisade, which was then still prominent. The crannog was observed in the late 1860s by two local antiquarians, Edgar and Henry Dumbleton, after the lake level had been lowered. They described a substantial mound of boulders lying on top of brushwood, reeds and sand. They noted that the south and west sides of the mound were edged by one or two oak palisades.

Prompted by these accounts, a team from the University of Wales College of Cardiff excavated Llangors crannog in 1989-90. They concluded that the island had been periodically extended from an initial platform. Timber from earlier structures was incorporated into later ones. Dating of one sample gave a tree ring sequence of 747–859, indicating construction in the ninth and early tenth centuries, 300 years before the Norman conquest of this part of Wales. In 1925 a log canoe had been found here; dated to about 800, it is now in the museum at Brecon. The crannog at Llangors is the only one to have been identified in England or Wales, although there are many in Scotland and Ireland. Crannogs were principally defensive in purpose. Most show gaps in their palisade, usually facing the shore, where boats could land. Some, like that at Llangors, were reached by a causeway. The occupants usually lived by farming around the lake shore and by fishing.

Crannogs were constructed by driving piles into the mud. The island was built up in layers of various available materials until it rose above the surface of the water. The name crannog is derived from the Irish word *crann*, meaning a tree; this refers to the common use of timber in their construction. During the excavations of the 1880s, bone, charcoal, and a few fragments of leather, pottery, and metal were found. The excavations in 1989–90 recovered evidence of animal husbandry and cereal cultivation. Smelting was suggested by fragments of fired clay from furnace linings or hearths and slag. A bone comb and rare pieces of textile were found. The fine quality of its weave and the carefully planned construction of the entire site indicate that Llangors was the home of one of the leading families of ninth- and tenth-century Wales. The construction of the site required an ability to call upon a high level of specialized knowledge and resources.[22]

LLANGRISTIOLUS, Anglesey: St Cristiolus's church

The church of Llangristiolus, in Angelsey, is visible from the busy main road to Holyhead. It is eight miles west of the Menai Bridge. Cristiolus was said to be a follower of Cadfan who worked among the people of central Anglesey, which was then mainly marshland. The single-chambered church is on a ridge outside the village, with a view over the low-lying fields. It has a tenth-century tub-shaped font, carved with geometric designs by local Celtic craftsmen. These sculptors moved around in the course of their work: there is a similar font at Beuno's church in Trefdraeth, two miles to the south-west, and a more elaborate example in Beuno's church at Pistyll on the Lleyn peninsula. Llangristiolus church was rebuilt in the fifteenth century; its chancel dates from the early sixteenth century. The key to the church can be obtained from the house next door.

LLANGWYFAN, Anglesey: St Cwyfan's chapel

There is another Llangwyfan in Denbighshire named after this monk, who was a follower of Beuno. Llangwyfan on Anglesey is a tidal islet, north of Aberffraw. The island is less than an acre in area, and in summer the grass of the raised churchyard is studded with pink thrift and golden birdsfoot trefoil. The isolated rock is connected to the mainland at low tide by a causeway 200 metres long. The single-chambered church dates from the fourteenth to the sixteenth century, and contains some Norman stonework. The Eucharist was celebrated here until the mid-nineteenth century, when the tide and weather allowed. The priest was entitled to demand from the proprietor of Plas Llangwyfan on the mainland a tithe of two eggs, a penny loaf, half a pint of beer and hay for his horse. The church is usually locked.

To find it, take the A4080 out of Aberffraw, heading north-west for Holyhead. After a mile, turn left along a rough road into a motorbike racing area. Go through its entrance kiosk, where you can check directions. Continue along the road and fork right. Park where the road ends. Cwyfan's islet is ahead of you.

LLANGWYNNADL, Gwynedd:
St Gwynhoedl's church

Gwynhoedl, or Vendesetl may have been a Romano-British monk from south Wales who travelled north as a missionary.[23] Llangwynnadl is ten miles west of Pwllheli, on the north coast of the Lleyn peninsula. It became one of the main stopping places on the Saints' Way to Bardsey, since it was a short walk from there to Aberdaron, the crossing point to Bardsey Island. A medieval monk's hand bell survives from the church: it is of cast bronze and is 17 cm high; its handle has animal-headed terminals. It is now in the National Museum of Wales, Cardiff.

Gwynhoedl's tombstone is at Llanbedrog, four miles south-west of Pwllheli, on the south coast of the Lleyn peninsula. However, the people of Llangwynnadl were keen to claim that their saint was buried among them, and a Latin inscription carved round a pillar in the nave around 1520 reads, *S.Gwyn hoedl iacet hic,* 'St Gwynhoedl lies here.' At the same time, a second and third nave were added to the church, to accommodate the crowds who came. A fine new font was also carved, featuring the heads of King Henry VIII and Bishop Skeffington of Bangor. Across the small river that flows past the church to the sea, a large field was named *Cae Eisteddfa*, or Hospice Field. Here pilgrims could camp before continuing their journey to or from Bardsey Island.

LLANGYBI, Gwynedd: St Cybi's church and well

The village of Llangybi is six miles north-east of Pwllheli on the Lleyn peninsula. The author of Cybi's thirteenth-century Life tells us that Maelgwyn Gwynedd granted him land for a settlement here. At the edge of a wood in a valley 500 metres from the church is the most complete Celtic well house in Wales. A small rectangular room built round the well adjoins a larger room enclosing a pool fed by the spring. The pool is surrounded by a paved walk; its dry stone walls, 6 metres high, and its corbelled vaulting are similar in style to those of early Irish cells. Some of its giant stones are likely to date from Cybi's time; the well house has stood untouched since at least the twelfth century.

To approach the well, pilgrims used two stone causeways across the damp field. A large sacred eel lived in the well, where the patient stood barelegged. If the eel coiled itself round the patient's legs, it was believed that a cure would follow. The spring water possesses mineral properties and cured a wide variety of illnesses. A register of cures made in 1766 describes how a man who had been blind for thirty years bathed his eyes for three consecutive weeks and recovered his sight.

In the eighteenth century, seven people were cured of blindness caused by smallpox. The lame came to Llangybi on crutches or were wheeled to the well in barrows. When they were cured, they gratefully left their crutches and barrows around the well, where they were noted by an observer in the early eighteenth century. Water was carried away in barrels and bottles for use as medicine. A party of smugglers returning from a night's work with casks of spirits explained when challenged by an excise officer that the casks contained water from *Ffynnon Gybi*![24] Until the eighteenth century, the church contained a chest, *Cyff Cybi*, for thank-offerings from pilgrims cured at the well.

LLANILLTUD FAWR (Llantwit Major), Vale of Glamorgan: St Illtud's church

This was the most famous Celtic monastery in Wales. It is situated in the Vale of Glamorgan, 9 miles west of Barry, close to the south coast of Wales. It is hidden in a small river valley, where it would have been out of site of pirates. Nearby St Donats provided a natural harbour. Inside the church there is a fine collection of monuments from the Celtic monastery. One of the earliest of these, the St Illtud (or Samson) Cross, may date from soon after Illtud's death. Its shaft, which was probably once capped by a wheel cross, contains two Latin inscriptions. The east face reads: 'Samson placed this cross for his soul', and the west face reads, '[For the souls of] Illtud, Samson the King, Samuel, Ebisar'.

There is a pillar inscribed to an abbot named Samson, and a cross with a disc head inscribed in Latin half-uncial script: 'In the name of God the Father and the Holy Spirit. Houelt prepared this cross for the soul of Res, his father.' Houelt was probably Hywel ap Rhys, a ninth-century king of Glywysing, the land between the river Tawe and the river Usk. The monastery was so important that kings were brought here for burial. Hywel was a subject of King Alfred of Wessex in 884. The Houelt cross dates from the late ninth century; its shallow triangular key-patterns, arranged in two paved bands, recall motifs found in illuminated manuscripts. Both the inscription and the style of decoration resemble examples of the same date in Ireland. This suggests that the Houelt cross may have been the work of an Irish sculptor, or of one trained in Ireland. It is carved from local gritstone, and is 1.9 metres high.

Today there are two medieval churches at Llanilltud Fawr, built end-to-end. The Celtic church probably stood on the site of the present west church, in which the crosses now stand. This was rebuilt by the Normans in about 1100. The archway over the south door dates from this time. The Norman font also survives; its bowl is decorated with fish-scale patterns. In the thirteenth century the east church was built for the canons of the medieval monastery, while the parishioners probably continued to worship in the west church. Behind the modern rood that decorates the chancel arch of the canons' church are the remains of fourteenth-century wall paintings. There is a fine fifteenth-century reredos of carved stone behind the high altar of the east church.

In the fifteenth century the west church was rebuilt; its arched roof of oak dates from this time. In time, however, the west church fell into ruin. John Wesley preached here in 1777 and recorded in his diary: 'About eleven, I read prayers and preached in Llantwit Major church to a very numerous congregation. I have not seen either so large or so handsome a church since I left England. It was sixty yards long, but one end of it is now in ruins. I suppose it has been abundantly the most beautiful as well as the most spacious church in Wales.'[25]

LLANRHAEADR-YNG-NGHINMEIRCH, Denbighshire: St Dyfnog's church and well

Nothing is known about the monk Dyfnog, to whom Llanrhaeadr is dedicated. The village is three miles south-east of Denbigh in north Wales. Rhaeadr means 'cascade', and describes the water that gushes from the hillside into Dyfnog's pool in the woodland above the church. This was a healing well visited by many pilgrims, and so the church was endowed generously. The chancel has a fine fifteenth-century barrel-vaulted roof, carved with vines and with angels holding the instruments of Christ's passion. The porch is decorated with carved oak taken from the former rood screen.

There is a magnificent Jesse window dating from 1533, paid for by pilgrims; it is one of the finest in Britain. It represents the family tree of Christ; the tree springs from the loins of Jesse, the father of King David, using an image taken from the prophet Isaiah: 'A shoot shall spring from the stock of Jesse' (Is. 11.1). In the Civil War of 1642, the Jesse window was removed and hidden; it was replaced at the Restoration of the Monarchy in 1661.

Beyond the churchyard are almshouses, still in use. A path in front of them leads under an archway into a wood. Turn right and follow the path along the stream. Soon, a large stone-edged pool is visible ahead, fed by streams from the rock face. A medieval Welsh poet wrote that he 'reveres Dyfnog's effigy, accepts his miracles, praises his wonder-working well, which gives grace to all nations ... indeed there was none like it.'

Successive antiquarians described how the pool was once covered by a roofed building where pilgrims bathed, hoping to be cured of skin diseases, 'scabs and the itch, and some said it cured pox' (Edward Lhuyd, seventeenth century). It was 'provided with all conveniences of rooms etc for bathing built about it' (Browne Willis, eighteenth century). It was 'arched over, from which the water used to fall through a pipe in the wall into a bath, whose bottom was paved with marble, with a building round it and roofed, but now exhibiting one shapeless ruin' (Richard Fenton, 1800s). 'The fountain was enclosed in an angular well, decorated with small human figures, and before, the well for the use of pious bathers' (Thomas Pennant, nineteenth century).[26] As one wanders around the edges of the marble-paved pool, it is not difficult to imagine its former state.

LLANSTINAN, Pembrokeshire: St Justinian's church

This is an early church dedicated to Justinian, a hermit who lived on Ramsey Island and was a friend of David. The church is in the valley of the river Cleddau, 10 miles north-east of St David's. It is built inside an ancient stone circle. Seven springs rise near the site, which was once beside a lake. The village of Scleddau, which surrounded the church, has now disappeared, although rambler roses from cottage gardens still grow in the hedgerows. The medieval church is built on Celtic foundations and has a 'squinch' or small triangular room between the nave and the chancel, on the site where a hermit's cell adjoined the church. By living in a hut built against the church wall, a medieval hermit could retain his privacy yet also be present at church services. A squinch is a feature of a number of early Pembrokeshire churches.

Llanstinan is 2 miles south-east of Fishguard, near the A40. After leaving Fishguard, watch for a sign to Llanstinan on the left, beside a disused quarry. Park in the lay-by, then walk for ten minutes along the signed footpath, through the Cleddau valley. Turn left through a farmyard. The church is on low ground in front of you.

LLANTWIT MAJOR: see LLANILLTUD FAWR

MATHERN, Monmouthshire:
St Tewdric's church and well

Mathern is a village a mile south of Chepstow, beside the M48 near the Welsh end of the Severn Bridge. The river reached Mathern in early times; a former harbour is now covered by low-lying fields. The area was ruled by the family of Tewdric, and Mathern's former name was *Merthyr Tewdric*, 'Tewdric's burial place'. The name *Ma Teyrn* ('the place of a king') first appears in the thirteenth century.

According to the twelfth-century *Book of Llandaff*, Tewdric transferred the crown to his son and became a hermit at Tintern. In the early seventh century he was recalled to fight the Saxons from over the River Wye. He won but was mortally wounded. He was brought to Mathern to be taken to the island of Flat Holm in the Bristol Channel, where he had asked to be buried, but he died at Mathern. He is said to be interred beneath the chancel of the church. The present church is Norman and Early English. As one drives along the lane that leads to the church, one passes Tewdric's well in a square pool, to the right of the road. According to legend, this is where his wounds were washed after his fatal battle.

MEIFOD, Powys: St Tysilio's church

The church of Meifod, six miles north-west of present-day Welshpool, is named after the Welsh prince-monk, Tysilio. According to his fifteenth-century Breton Life, he was sent to study at a monastery in Meifod, under a hermit named Gwyddfarch. Today's churchyard of nine acres may indicate the extent of the monastery, which in time contained three churches, one named after its founder (its remains were still visible in the seventeenth century), one named after Tysilio, and a third that was a pre-Norman dedication to Our Lady. The monastery became the mother church of Powys and the burial place of its kings. A fine Celtic tombstone in the church may mark a royal burial. It represents the triumph of God over evil. It is bordered by serpents and asymmetrical interlacing patterns. In the centre is a Latin cross and above it a Greek crucifix, on which hangs Jesus with pierced hands.

Tysilio's Life relates that he later returned to Meifod and became abbot in place of the now elderly Gwyddfarch. When Gwyddfarch died, he was buried outside the village, at the top of *Allt-y-Ancr* ('anchorite's hill'). Tysilio rebuilt the monastery church, and the twelfth-century poet Cynddelw described this achievement:

He raised a church with fostering hand;
a church with bright lights,
and a chancel for offerings,
a church above the stream, by the glassy waters,
a church of Powys, paradise most fair.[27]

The present Norman church was built in 1154 by Madoc ap Meredydd, prince of Powys, the last ruler under whom Powys experienced political unity and independence. The Norman arches are constructed of red sandstone, which was little used in the area and was probably expensive and difficult to obtain. Prince Madoc rebuilt the shrine at Pennant Melangell, using the same school of craftsmen.

NEVERN, Pembrokeshire: St Brynach's church

Nevern is eight miles east of Fishguard, near the Pembrokeshire coast. Brynach's church is at the foot of an Iron Age hill fort. Built on the slopes of Carn Ingli, the crumbling walls and towers of the stronghold dominate the village; the fort is one of the best-preserved in Wales. Its chieftain gave Brynach land for a church, with the Caman brook as a boundary between them. This was an important religious centre in early times, with a collection of carved crosses dating from about 400, at the end of the Roman occupation, onward.

There are two fifth-century gravestones with inscriptions both in Latin and in Irish ogham (see ARDFERT in Part One). Set into a windowsill in the nave, one of the bilingual tombstones bears the following inscription: '[the monument] of Maglocunus, son of Clutorius'. The slab was erected to the memory of the Welsh chieftain Maelgwyn. Outside the church to the east of the porch, a second bilingual stone commemorates a Christian named Vitalianus. Beyond the south transept stands a great cross, 4 metres high, carved in the tenth or eleventh century, covered with elaborate knotwork panels; it is one of the finest in Wales.

PENMACHNO, Gwynedd: inscribed crosses

Situated in the heart of Snowdonia National Park, Penmachno is three miles south of Betws-y-Coed. It is signposted south from the A5, and is at the end of the B4406. The church is locked; the key is held at the nearby farmhouse.

Penmachno church boasts three fine pillar stones. The first dates from the fifth century, and is carved with a *chi–rho* symbol for Christ, above an inscription that reads in translation, 'Carausius lies here in this heap of stones.' Carausius is an uncommon name; it may have become fashionable in the late third century when an emperor of that name ruled Britain as a breakaway state from Rome. The self-styled emperor was prominent in Wales, with which he may have had some link. Hoards containing coins bearing his name are common in Wales.

A second stone dates from the fifth century. Its inscription runs, 'Cantiorix lies here. He was a citizen of Venedos, cousin of Maglos the Magistrate.' The term *Venedos* is a Latin form of Gwynedd. It demonstrates that this area was recognized as a region by the fifth century. The typically Roman terms *civis* and *magistratus* occur in no other British Christian inscription. They imply that there was a formal Roman system of government in this area. Perhaps administration in the Roman style continued in fifth-century Gwynedd, possibly based on the Roman fort at Caernarfon.

The third slab is inscribed: 'The stone of ... , son of Avitorius. Set up in the time of the consul Justinus.' This consul held office in 540; he can be identified from inscriptions in the Lyons district of France. The tombstone suggests a link between Gaul and Gwynedd in the sixth century.

PENMON, Anglesey: St Seiriol's cell, church, and well

The monastery of Penmon is at the north-eastern tip of Anglesey, three miles north-north-east of Beaumaris. As with many early Christian sites, the isolation of its idyllic setting is misleading, as the monastery is surrounded by four clusters of hut circles, the remains of a large Celtic village of at least 300 inhabitants. Between the groups of homes, terraces survive to show that farming was practised.[28] The circular stone wall of Seiriol's hut rests snugly against a sheltering cliff. Beside its remains are the foundations of his well and its antechamber, where several people could sit. The brickwork over the well is eighteenth-century; the red bricks do not blend with the solid stones that surround the pool below. The well was revered through the centuries, and the well-keeper lived in a house nearby until relatively recently.

The present church was built in the twelfth century to replace a wooden one burned by the Danes in 971. Two fine tenth-century carved crosses are preserved inside the church. They show both Irish and Scandinavian influence and are thought to originate from a school of sculptors based in Cheshire.[29] From the monastery there is a magnificent view across Conwy Bay toward the mountains on the mainland, where Seiriol was said to have had a hermitage at Penmaenmawr.

Another group of monks lived on Ynys Seiriol (now Puffin Island), half a mile offshore. The monastic cemetery was also on the island, and many monks and rulers were buried here, including Seiriol and his cousin Maelgwyn, King of Gwynedd. The island was not always a safe haven: in 632 King Cadwallon took refuge there while King Edwin of Northumbria laid siege to the tiny island before capturing Anglesey. Norse settlers named the island 'Priestholm' after the priests who lived there. In medieval times, Seiriol's body was brought back from Priestholm to Penmon and buried in a shrine in the church crypt, beneath the chancel. Pilgrims descended a stone staircase to visit it.

Writing in the twelfth century, Gerald of Wales informs us that Penmon was one of three reformed Culdee monasteries in north Wales. This was a movement that originated in Ireland in the ninth century. Groups of monks who called themselves *Céli Dé* ('Servants of God') encouraged a return to solitude and the rigorous ideals followed by monks of earlier times. If Penmon became a Culdee community, this suggests Irish influence and a strong commitment to religious life. The community on Priestholm must also have flourished, for in 1237 King Lliwelyn the Great granted the monastery of Penmon to the prior of Priestholm.

Later in the century Penmon became an Augustinian friary. Dominating the site today is the friars' thirteenth-century refectory, with a dormitory above and cellars below. The men ate in silence while one of them read aloud. There is a corner seat beside a window, where the reader could take advantage of the natural light. The friars' main source of protein was fish: their fishpond survives, fed from Seiriol's well.[30] The Augustinians were responsible for a fine stained-glass window above Seiriol's shrine in the church. Only two fragments of the great east window remain: they depict Sts Christopher and

Seiriol, and are now combined in a small window in the south transept. Seiriol is dressed as a medieval friar in brown and white robes, with a cap and a curly beard.

PENNANT MELANGELL, Powys:
St Melangell's shrine

The church of Melangell is at the head of a remote valley in the Berwyn Mountains of mid-Wales. It is situated twenty miles west of Oswestry and two miles west of Llangynog. The churchyard had long been a holy place and may be the burial site of a Bronze Age chieftain. It is encircled by ancient yew trees, the oldest perhaps dating to 400 BC. A cist grave (one lined with slabs, like a coffin) lies beneath the stone floor of the tiny twelfth-century apse of Melangell's chapel; she may have been buried here before her remains were exhumed for veneration. A solid Norman font survives, as does Melangell's finely carved shrine, built in about 1164 but largely restored. Carved on the fifteenth-century rood screen, the prince, with his huntsman and hounds that feature in her story, chase a hare into Melangell's lap. A quarter of a mile south of her chapel, rock steps in the valley side lead to a ledge known as 'Melangell's Bed'. To find Pennant Melangell, drive to Llangynog. As the B4391 passes the church, turn sharply up a signed single track road to the head of the valley, until the road ends at the shrine. The church is open daily.

PISTYLL, Gwynedd: St Beuno's church and pool

Beuno's tiny church at Pistyll is set in a sheltered hollow by the sea, halfway along the Lleyn peninsula, six miles north-west of Pwllheli. At the east end of the hamlet of Pistyll, a steep track leads down from the main road to the church. The track is signed 'church', but the sign is only visible if you are travelling from the direction of Nefyn. The church is set inside an oval Celtic enclosure, and built around the great boulder which was its original cornerstone. Ancient fruit bushes still grow in the churchyard, successors of those once tended by medieval monks: gooseberry, daneberry and sloes, and also hops and medicinal herbs.

One enters the church at Pistyll through a Romanesque arch, crossing the threshold, a corruption of 'the rush-hold', since it held the rushes inside the church. Local Celtic craftsmen carved Pistyll's twelfth-century font, with its circular interweaving patterns. The church roof was thatched until the 1850s. In earlier times, the earthen floor of the church was spread with rushes and sweet-smelling herbs, as most churches were, and parishioners have revived this tradition. It is freshly strewn three times a year, at Christmas, Easter and Lammas Day. This is the Sunday nearest 1 August; its name derives from the Anglo-Saxon *hlafmaesse*, or 'loaf Mass'. Lammas was the feast on which the bread of the Eucharist could first be made from the year's new corn, and loaves were offered in thanksgiving.

Pistyll is Welsh for 'waterfall', and beside the churchyard, a fast-flowing stream tumbles into a large pool. This was the fishpond of the monastery that once stood on the site of Pistyll Farm, opposite the church. Pilgrims could rest at the monastery or at nearby farms, and many would sleep in shelters in the hospice field that adjoined the churchyard. There are similar hospice fields beside other churches on the Saints' Way that led along the Lleyn peninsula to Bardsey Island. At Pistyll, travellers could buy food and firewood from the villagers. They were entitled to ask for shelter, bread and cheese, in return for which the local inhabitants were excused from paying rent to their monastic landowners.

ST ASAPH, Denbighshire: St Asaph's cathedral

At a time when waterways were as important as roads, St Asaph was in a key position, at the junction of the rivers Elwy and Clwyd. St Asaph is near the north Welsh coast, five miles south of Rhyl, and was therefore also easily accessible from the sea. According to Kentigern's twelfth-century biographer, Jocelyn of Furness, the bishop founded a monastery here, which he later handed over to his disciple, Asaph. Jocelyn tells us how Kentigern 'went through the area, exploring different places, bearing in mind the air quality, the fertility of the soil, the suitability of the fields, pasture and woodland, and the other requirements for a monastic site'. Once the location was chosen, 'some cleared the ground and levelled it, while others dug the foundations. They chopped down trees, transported them and hammered planks together to build a church following Kentigern's plan, and made wooden polished furniture, for the British did not yet build in stone'.[31] The present cathedral dates mainly from the thirteenth century; it is set on the hillside above the river valley.

ST DAVID'S, Pembrokeshire: St David's cathedral

David established a monastery on the Pembrokeshire coast, around which developed the later town of St David's. He chose a site in the narrow valley of the River Alun, hidden from pirates by a bend in the river. In his eleventh-century *Life of David*, Rhigyfarch relates that the land belonged to an Irish chieftain named Baia, who occupied an earlier hill fort above the site. Baia and his wife noticed smoke rising from the monks' settlement, and challenged David in various ways, until Baia was killed by another Irish raider named Liski, who arrived in the night.

Rhigyfarch draws on an early source to describe how the monks spent their days in hard physical labour, followed by reading, writing and praying. In the evening they gathered in the church for vespers, after which they prayed silently until night fell. Only then would they eat a simple meal together. The brothers returned to the chapel to pray for another few hours. After a short night's sleep, they woke at cock-crow to sing matins and to 'spend the rest of the night until morning without sleep'. This harsh pattern of life may reflect the influence of the Irish *Céli Dé*, or 'Servants of God'. This was a movement of monks who urged a return to a stricter lifestyle and a more austere diet.[32]

Anyone seeking to join the community was to be kept waiting outside the door for ten days, to test his desire for monastic life. The candidate was then welcomed by the doorkeeper, and put to work alongside the monks for many months, 'until the natural stubbornness of his heart was broken'. When the abbot judged that he was well prepared, the novice was eventually invited to join the community.[33] This unusually severe style of life was designed to imitate that of the monks of the Near Eastern deserts.

St David's cathedral was rebuilt in 1275, largely from offerings at his shrine. The English kings William I and Henry II made the long journey to the cathedral. During William the Conqueror's visit in 1081, the Welsh princes probably appealed to the king to uphold the Welsh Church against the increasing power of Rome.[34] A modern oak casket in the cathedral was thought to contain relics of David and of a hermit named Justinian, who lived on nearby Ramsey Island and became a friend of David. However, radiocarbon dating in 2002 has established that the bones in the casket are likely to be only 700 years old; David's relics were probably destroyed at the Reformation. The thirteenth-century stone shrine survives; it formerly had a wooden canopy, and painted panels depicting Sts David, Patrick and Dennis. The shrine contains apertures in which pilgrims' offerings could be placed; it stood in the sanctuary, before the high altar.

ST GOVAN'S HEAD, Pembrokeshire:
St Govan's chapel

St Govan's chapel is on a cliff a mile south of Bosherston and seven miles south of Pembroke, on the south Welsh coast. To find the chapel, drive past St Govan's Inn, Bosherston. Continue along the Range Road to St Govan's. It is closed when there is firing on the range. Park at the top of the cliffs. The chapel is soon visible down the cliff path.

The tiny oratory is wedged in a narrow cleft halfway down the cliff, and is reached by 52 steps. It may date from the eleventh century, but its foundations are probably much earlier. The building consists of a simple nave with a stone altar, benches, a *piscina* (or water stoup), a shelf, and a well in the floor, adjoining the north wall. Its water is said to cure eye diseases, skin complaints and rheumatism. The chapel's arched roof with its stone vault is typical of early medieval churches in Pembrokeshire, and probably dates from the thirteenth century. The chapel opens into a hermit's cave. There is a second well, now dry, in a stone well house below the chapel. Govan may have been Gobham, an early Irish monk. According to tradition, he is buried near the chapel.

ST NON'S BAY, Pembrokeshire:
St Non's chapel and well

A mile south of St David's cathedral, the medieval chapel of his mother stands on a cliff top in St Non's Bay. It is built on Celtic foundations: the giant stones near the base of the building may date from this time. The building is oriented north to south, which would have been unusual for a chapel. Excavations carried out in the nineteenth century revealed slab-lined or 'cist' graves, probably dating from between the seventh and ninth centuries, to the east and south of the oratory. Inside, a gravestone carved with a simple ringed cross dates from the same period. Surrounding the chapel are giant boulders, which probably mark pre-Christian graves. Tradition relates that here Non gave birth to her son: a storm was raging, but around the mother and her child it was calm and sunny!

Close to Non's chapel is her holy well. This is one of the chief holy wells of Wales; it was famous for curing eye diseases. In the early eighteenth century, Browne Willis wrote: 'There is a fine well... covered with a stone roof and enclosed within a wall, with benches to sit upon round the well. Some old, simple people go still to visit this saint ... especially upon St Nun's day (2 March), which they keep holy and offer pins, pebbles etc. at this well.' A century later, the well was still popular, as Fenton reported: 'The fame this consecrated spring had obtained is incredible, and still it is resorted to for many complaints. In my infancy... I was often dipped in it, and offerings, however trifling, even a farthing or a pin, were made after each ablution, and the bottom of the well shone with votive brass.'[35] In the field leading to the chapel, there was a house for the well's caretaker. The well house was restored in 1951. There is a modern retreat house nearby, and a chapel dedicated to Our Lady and St Non, built in 1934 in the medieval style.

TRELLECK, Monmouthshire: the Virtuous Well

Trelleck is a village in the Forest of Dean, five miles south of Monmouth. Its name means 'three stones' in Welsh, referring to three Bronze Age standing stones, not far from the well. They are arranged in a line pointing to the well, and were later named 'Harold's Stones'. The Virtuous Well, or St Anne's well, lies on the edge of the village. To find it, on approaching the village from the south on the B4293, turn sharp right along a minor road signed Llandogo. The well is just inside a field on the left, and is signed from the road. The stone well house stands within a semicircular walled enclosure with stone seats. There is a niche for offerings on each side of the well.

There were said to be four springs rising at the site, three containing iron. Each was said to cure a different illness. The well was visited by many pilgrims until as late as the seventeenth century. Clouties, or prayer rags, are still tied to the nearby trees. At the centre of the village, Trelleck churchyard is believed to be the site of a Roman settlement. There is a pre-Norman preaching cross south of the church entrance, and south of the churchyard is a so-called 'Druid altar', a raised stone slab possibly dating from pre-Christian times. In a farmyard to the south of the church is *Tump Terrett*, a large mound which is possibly prehistoric, or may be a Norman motte, or castle mound. According to tradition it is the burial place of the warriors commemorated by Harold's Stones.

TYWYN, Gwynedd: St Cadfan's church and well

The coastal town of Tywyn is halfway between Barmouth and Aberystwyth, and is said to be the site of Cadfan's first monastery. Near the shore, toward the northern end of the town, the solid, yet spacious, church dates from the late eleventh and early twelfth centuries. A chapel dedicated to Cadfan stood at the north-east end of the churchyard until 1620; it may have contained his shrine. Cadfan's holy well is north-west of the church, and can be found in the grounds of the NatWest Bank. The spring was visited for healing until long after the Reformation. Baths and changing rooms were built alongside it; they were pulled down in 1894, by which time they had fallen into disuse.[36]

Inside the church, an eighth-century grave marker commemorates two women from leading families; another may indicate the burial place of Cadfan, since it reads in translation: 'Beneath a similar mound lies Cadfan; sad that it should enclose the praise of the earth. May he rest without blemish.' This is one of the earliest examples of written Welsh; until this point, inscriptions were normally in Latin. The inscribed panels are set low down on the shaft, perhaps to be read while kneeling. Two successive wooden churches were burnt by the Vikings. By the mid-tenth century, St Cadfan's had become the mother church of the area.

VALLE CRUCIS, Denbighshire: Eliseg's Pillar

Two miles north of Llangollen in mid-Wales, Valle Crucis, or 'valley of the cross' is named after a ninth-century high cross, dedicated to Eliseg, King of Powys. It is visible from the road, just north of Valle Crucis abbey. The pillar stands on a barrow; beneath it there may have been a cist grave or small cairn; remains were found which were thought to be those of a chieftain. His skull was gilded before reburial, as a sign of respect to an ancestor of the Powys line. The cross was thrown down in the seventeenth century, during the Civil War: only its plinth remains. Its worn inscription was recorded by the antiquarian Edward Lhuyd in 1696 and tells us valuable information about the kings of Powys. Selections from the lengthy inscription read: '+ Concenn, great-grandson of Eliseg, erected this stone to his great-grandfather, Eliseg. + It is Eliseg who annexed the inheritance of Powys through nine years from the power of the English, which he made into a sword-land by fire... + Conmarch painted this writing at the command of his king, Concenn. + The blessing of the Lord be upon Concenn and all members of his family, and upon all the land of Powys, until the Day of Judgement. Amen.' King Concenn died in 854.[37]

To the south of Eliseg's Pillar, Valle Crucis abbey was built by the Cistercians in 1201. The church, with its plain lancet windows, dates from this time. The more luxurious living quarters of the monks date from 1300. The chapter house is elegantly vaulted, and contains an elaborately screened library cupboard, a reminder of the abbey's role as a focus for Welsh culture and poetry. The extensive monastery fishpond survives; the monks' well is in a roofed well house, in a bank below the road.

Part Four
Cornwall

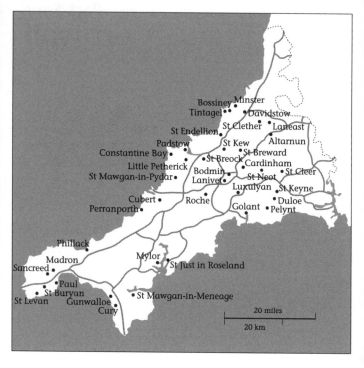

Saints of Cornwall

ALTARNUN: St Non's church and well

Non, the mother of David, is honoured at Altarnun, or 'altar of Non', seven miles south-west of Launceston. This beautiful village grew up around a fast-flowing stream, a tributary of the river Inney, on the north-east side of Bodmin Moor. The church is on high ground above the medieval bridge; there is a solid Cornish cross in the churchyard. The church contains a fine twelfth-century font; there are traces of original painting on its carved faces. The four heads facing four directions symbolize, among other things, the four evangelists taking the good news of the gospel to the ends of the earth. Above the altar, medieval glass fragments may depict Non. There is a fine wooden rood screen; the 79 bench ends were carved between 1510 and 1531 by Robart Daye. They include musicians playing the medieval fiddle and the Cornish bagpipes and some of the earliest carvings of corn dollies.

Non's holy well is in a field above the church, beside an ancient hawthorn tree. The well feeds a 'bowssening pool', which was used to cure insanity by a primitive form of shock therapy. Until the eighteenth century, deranged people were tumbled into the pool by a sudden blow to the chest. They were tossed up and down, accompanied by the chanting of prayers, until they were exhausted. The patients were then taken down to the church, where Masses were sung for their recovery. There used to be a similar bowssening pool at St Cleer, eight miles south of Altarnun. To find St Non's well, walk uphill, with the churchyard wall on your left, along the road leading north-east out of Altarnun. Enter the second field on your right, by way of a track. The bowssening pool and hawthorn tree beside Non's well are now visible in a small enclosure on the right, across the corner of the field.[1]

BODMIN: St Petroc's church; St Guron's well

According to the late twelfth-century *Life of Petroc* written by a canon of Bodmin, Petroc travelled inland with his companions to a remote location where a hermit named Guron lived. The writer is describing his own priory of Bodmin. Although Guron is more likely to have been a chieftain than a hermit, medieval tradition incorporated him into Petroc's story.[2] Dwarfed by the splendid minster church of Bodmin is the hermit's well in a sixteenth-century well house. Above its entrance is a relief of Guron kneeling beneath a tree. He prays before a crucifix carved over the door of his cell. The well is now dry; the spring has been channelled through pipes, and a great volume of water now pours into a trough beside the main street, below the well.

The Bodmin canon relates that Petroc ended his days as a hermit on the bleak open spaces of Bodmin Moor. He was buried in Padstow, but when the monastery was burned by the Danes in 981, the monks moved inland to Bodmin for safety, taking with them Petroc's relics, his staff, and his hand bell. His head reliquary can be seen in Bodmin church: it was constructed by Arab craftsmen in Sicily in the twelfth century. It is a small, house-shaped casket made of ivory plates bound with brass strips and decorated with delicately carved medallions. In the ninth or tenth century, the monks of Padstow annotated a copy of the Gospels from Brittany: this is the only surviving manuscript from a Cornish monastery. On its spare leaves and in its margins the monks recorded the liberation of slaves; most of the slaves were Cornish, while most of their owners were Saxon. The Padstow community brought the book to Bodmin when they fled the Viking raids; it is known as the *Bodmin Gospels* and is now in the British Museum.[3] The monastery at Bodmin flourished during the Saxon period and its monks spread throughout the south-west. The impressive church contains an elaborately decorated late Norman font, dating from the twelfth century.

CARDINHAM: St Meubred's church and well

Situated on the south-western edge of Bodmin Moor, Cardinham takes its name from the Celtic words *caer* (meaning 'castle') and *dinan* ('fortress'). The two-thousand-year-old camp can be seen on the moorland skyline from the north side of the churchyard. There were Christians here in early times. Beside the gate of the ancient raised churchyard, a cross head dating from around 900 has been attached to a sixth-century gravestone, inscribed to 'Ranocurus, son of Mesgus'. The stone is 3.3 metres long, of which 1.9 metres is visible above ground level. A second gravestone from the same period stands against a crossroads hedge at Welltown, a mile to the south-east.

A hermit named Meubred was said to have lived here, but nothing is recorded about him until the fifteenth century, when he is described as an Irish prince and a martyr. His body was enshrined in the church until the fifteenth century. Outside the church porch is a finely ornamented cross in Scandinavian style, dating from about 800, with the (incomplete) name of the person commemorated, ARTHI ..., carved below the cross head. The church contains a Norman font and 69 carved bench ends, dating from the fifteenth century. On a wooden chest brought from Carblake in the parish there is a carving of St Sidwell, with her sword and a sheaf of corn. The chest was probably made from the rood screen, stolen from the church at the Reformation. Meubred's holy well can be found by following the road north from Cardinham to Millpool for half a mile. The stone well house stands behind a bank adjoining the entrance to Trezance Farm. Beside it are the stones of a ruined chapel.

CONSTANTINE, Harlyn Bay: St Constantine's church and well

The author of the eleventh-century *Life of Petroc* describes a wealthy man named Constantine hunting deer at Little Petherick. Petroc interrupted the hunt, saved the stag, and converted Constantine. The author was weaving local traditions into his story, for on the coast three miles north-west of Little Petherick lay St Constantine's chapel and holy well. The saint was believed to have been a converted chieftain. The ancient well chapel is 3 metres long and 1.5 metres wide. The corbelled slate building has stone benches along either side and a water channel in the floor between them. There is a niche above the well at the south end.

The well was still much visited in the eighteenth century. The antiquarian William Hals says it was 'stronge built of stone and arched over; on the inner part whereof are places or seates for people to sitt and wash themselves in the stream thereof'.[4] Over time, the well house became buried by sand dunes; it was rediscovered and excavated in 1911. The tiny chapel can be seen, protected beneath a shelter, on the golf course in Harlyn Bay. On rising ground 50 metres away are the ruins of Constantine church, with its tower, chancel, nave, and south aisle. It was rebuilt in the fifteenth century but suppressed in about 1540, after which the church became buried by sand. At one time it was surrounded by a graveyard and houses. Its fine Norman font was taken two miles inland to its mother church of St Merryn. It is carved from local catacleuse stone, which resembles black marble.

CUBERT: St Gwbert's church and wells

We know little about Cubert, or Gwbert, who gave his name to a village three miles south-west of Newquay and two miles from the sea. An inscribed gravestone set into the outer wall of the tower indicates an early Christian presence. A Celtic cross shaft is built into the outer wall of the porch of the small, solid church. By the fourteenth century, it was believed that the parish was named after the northern saint, Cuthbert, but thirteenth-century documents name the parish saint as Cubert.[5]

Two miles to the north-west, Cubert is honoured at a freshwater well in a sea cave, beyond the sand dunes in Holywell Bay. There are three caves, and in the farthest of these a series of steps against the cave wall leads up to four or five shallow pools, formed by condensation dripping from the cave roof. The rock is pink and white from calcareous deposits, and the cave is accessible for only an hour each day, at low tide. In wet weather, the rocks are too slippery to climb, but in drier conditions one can clamber past the pools into a chamber in the cave roof. In earlier times pilgrims flocked to the well; this suggests that sea level has altered since then, as the cave is now so rarely above water level.

There is a second well in Holywell Bay, in the sand dunes. It is enclosed in a medieval chapel, with a surrounding wall. To visit it, park where the road ends. Take the track leading to the bay but turn right through the dunes, roughly following the stream. Keep to its left bank. Enter the golf course and at once bear right, downhill. Pick up the track through a copse beside the stream. After five minutes' walk through the copse, the well chapel is on the left, before a flight of steps that leads up to the golf course again.

CURY: St Corentin's church

Corentin was a Breton bishop; the name Cury probably preserves a pet form of his name. The village is near the west coast of the Lizard, four miles south of Helston. There is a Celtic cross in the churchyard and a decorated Norman arch over the south door. Inside, on a ledge, a modern statue depicts

Corentin with his bishop's mitre and staff and the fish of which he was said to have eaten a slice each day.

DAVIDSTOW: St David's church and well

The bleak moorland hamlet of Davidstow stands on high ground on the northern edge of Bodmin Moor, twelve miles west of Launceston. Its former name was Dewstow: St David's name is *Dewi Sant* in Welsh. There are some fine thirteenth-century bench ends in the church, including a rare depiction of a minstrel blowing the Cornish bagpipes. These instruments were played in Celtic times. In a field to the east of the church, clearly signed from the road, lies David's holy well. The rectangular pool is protected by a well house, whose stones were brought from the well of St Austen at nearby Lesnewth. The spring water is so pure that it is used by the local creamery, whose mild Davidstow cheese is widely sold.

DULOE: St Cybi's church and well

Cybi has dedications in Wales; in Cornwall, the churches of Tregony and Duloe are named after him. Duloe is four miles south of Liskeard, on an exposed site. It was already a holy place: on the edge of the village is Cornwall's smallest stone circle, consisting of eight large white quartz stones. It may encircle a chieftain's burial mound, since a Late Bronze Age burial urn was found at the base of one of the stones, and a golden torc, or neck ornament, was found here.

Cybi's church stands on high ground, perhaps inside an Iron Age fort, 300 metres south-west of the stone circle. A massive stone font inside the church dates from early times. It is decorated with a gryphon on one side and a fish on the other, to symbolize evil and the Christian's rebirth into goodness, the fish being an early Christian symbol for Christ. Cybi's well is half a mile east of the church, beside the road to Looe. It is set in a clump of laurels, on the opposite side of the road to West North Farm, a little lower down the hill. The outer chamber of the well contains a stone bench, and inside the well's inner chamber, ancient steps lead down into a pool of clear water. The well house was restored by a former rector of the church.

GOLANT: St Samson's church, well and cave; Castle Dore hill fort

Near the south Cornish coast, two miles north of Fowey,

Golant features in the story of Samson because, at the request of the local chieftain, Samson drove an evil serpent out of a cave from which it had been terrorizing the neighbourhood. We learn from Samson's seventh-century Life that after he had killed the serpent the grateful chief and his followers asked Samson to become their bishop. He refused but accepted the offer of the cave as a retreat. Samson's cave can be seen at Golant, down by the harbour. It is beside the railway, behind the third telegraph pole alongside the track. It is a long cavern and can be explored only with wellingtons and a torch. Samson's biographer has an explanation for the water that floods the cave: 'One day he was thirsty .... After he had prayed, he saw water dripping in a continuous shower from the rocky roof of the cave ... and to this day that water does not cease flowing, day or night.'[6]

Golant church is high above the harbour and the cave. It contains a fine wooden pulpit dating from the fifteenth century. One of its panels depicts Samson as a bishop; this may once have formed part of the rood screen. He is a solid figure whose furrowed brow reflects the cares of his office. He stands with dignity, his head framed in a recess that also forms his halo. At the west end of the church a modern stained-glass window depicts scenes from Samson's life, including his encounter with the 'poisonous and most evil serpent'. Beside the church porch is Samson's holy well in a medieval well house.

Half a mile to the west is Castle Dore hill fort, where the chieftain and his followers may have lived. It was defended by two circular ramparts, which are well-preserved; inside, there were many round houses. The fortress can best be approached from the B3269, by walking along the track to Lawhibbet Farm. The fort is in the first field to the right. Paul Aurelian, another early monk, is described as visiting a ruler named Mark and styled Cunomorus (or Sea Dog), probably at Castle Dore. Cunomorus is named on a sixth-century pillar stone that was found nearby; it can be seen beside the road as it leads into Fowey, in a lay-by on the left. The son of Cunomorus was named Drustan: the two men may have become King Mark and his nephew Tristan in the later legend of King Arthur.

GUNWALLOE: St Winwaloe's church
Set in Church Cove, above a sandy beach, this little church is

on the west coast of the Lizard, three miles south of Helston. It commemorates Winwaloe, who worked in Brittany. Its freestanding tower is built into the cliff. A wooden panel survives from the fifteenth-century rood screen, with painted figures of the apostles. Winwaloe's well could formerly be found between the church and the beach, but the sea has now engulfed it. It was still in use in the nineteenth century, but it filled with sand and pebbles at each high tide. Quiller Couch describes how one day each year was set aside for cleaning out the well; it was called Gunwalloe day, and was celebrated 'with much merriment'.[7]

LANEAST: St Sidwell's church and well
Laneast, six miles west of Launceston, is a quiet hamlet on the north-eastern edge of Bodmin Moor, above the River Inney. A Celtic cross stands outside the church porch, which has fine carved medieval roof beams. Elaborate porch roofs are a feature of a number of churches in this area. There is a Norman font decorated with wheel crosses and carvings of four human heads. There are medieval carved bench ends, including a fine representation of a green man.

To find the well, walk out of the churchyard and continue for 100 metres east-south-east along the road to the triangle of waste ground beside the farm. To the right of the white house opposite the farm, a signed track leads into a field and down to the well, which is about 300 metres from the road. It is housed in a fine granite-roofed building, perhaps dating from the sixteenth century. Its water flows downhill to join the river Inney. It was formerly used for christenings and is also called Jordan Well, to recall the baptism of Jesus. For the same reason, church fonts were sometimes called Jordans.

LANIVET: church and crosses
Halfway between Padstow and Fowey, Lanivet lay on the medieval pilgrim route from Ireland and Wales, across Cornwall, to Brittany and the great shrines of France and Spain. It is not known to whom the church was originally dedicated, but the prefix *lan* indicates an early church site. A sixth-century gravestone is a memorial to 'Annicu, son of ...' Annicu is a Roman name; it may commemorate a settler from Wales.[8] There is a tall early tenth-century wheel cross in the churchyard and a fine thirteenth-century four-holed cross.

LITTLE PETHERICK: St Petroc's church and well

The canon of Bodmin priory who wrote the late twelfth-century *Life of Petroc* describes the abbot appointing a deputy to take charge of his monastery in Padstow and then leaving with twelve companions to live in a nearby wilderness – a tidal creek in the estuary of the River Camel, named Nansfonteyn, or 'valley with a spring'. Also known as Little Petherick (or 'little Petroc's settlement'), the creek, two miles south of the busy town of Padstow, is still a tranquil place. Here, according to the Bodmin canon, Petroc built a chapel and a mill. He lived on 'bread and water, with porridge on Sundays'. The author describes Petroc practising the austere life traditional among Irish monks: he immerses himself in the creek up to his neck, chanting the psalms. Petroc's church is built into the hillside. Four pinnacles that decorate its tower were brought from a ruined chapel dedicated to Cadoc, in nearby Harlyn Bay. A short walk along the tributary of the Camel leads to Petroc's well, in a garden to the left of the track. The spring's course has altered; the water now tumbles past the dry well house.

LUXULYAN: St Sulien's church and St Cyr's well

Originally dedicated to Sulien, Luxulyan is in moorland four miles north-east of St Austell, in mid-Cornwall. Its church is built over what was probably a large pre-Christian burial mound. A Cornish cross is set in the wall outside the west door. Inside the church is a fine late Norman twelfth-century font. Carved around its bowl are monsters and a tree of life. The heads of the four evangelists are carved on supporting pillars at each corner. Nothing is known about Cyr, whose well is built into the wall below a house on the main street, on the hill below the church. It is halfway between the church and the post office, on the same side of the road as the church. The tall well house with its elegant doorway dates from the fifteenth century. The well ran dry when the railway was built and the spring line was cut. The village pump was beside it, and the water was collected in a granite trough, part of which is now built into the wall surrounding the well.

MADRON: St Madern's church, holy well, and baptistery

We know nothing about Madern, who gave his name to a hamlet in the moorland, a mile north-west of Penzance. Even today, Maddern is a common surname in the village. Madern's well is one of Cornwall's most ancient and famous holy wells. It can be found by driving north through the village. Turn right after half a mile. The well is ten minutes' walk along a signed track to the right. It is a small rectangular basin at ground level, overhung by ancient sallow willow trees. Tied to their branches are hundreds of *clouties*, or pieces of cloth. This pre-Christian custom, still practised across Europe, Asia, Africa, and South America, is a way of praying for healing or giving thanks for a cure.[9]

The water flows into Madern's baptistery, 75 metres further along the track. There are the foundations of a solid twelfth-century building with a granite altar and a baptismal basin built into its south-west corner. It was partially demolished at the time of the Reformation, and seventeenth-century observers noted a great thorn tree, whose branches formed a leafy roof over the chapel. Each year, parishioners used turf to repair a green bank alongside the altar, which they called 'St Madern's Bed'. Sick people came to bathe in the well and sleep on the bed, and many of them were cured, including a cripple who recovered so completely that he later enlisted in the Royalist army and was killed in action at Lyme Regis in Dorset in 1644.[10]

In 1750 the water from Madron well was channelled down the long hill to form the first water supply for Penzance. Although it is only a village today, Madron was the mother church of Penzance. An inscribed stone of fine whitish granite in the church vestry provides a glimpse of the early community who worshipped here. Originally a pre-Christian standing stone, it was reused in the sixth or seventh century to mark a Christian burial. Its inscription suggests that a warrior or nobleman's widow commissioned it for her late husband, who was named 'Fair Slayer'. Above the inscription, the stonemason carved a simple trefoil cross.[11] Displayed on a wall inside the church is a collection of tin marks, dating from 1189 onwards, carved with the Agnus Dei and seals of local families. In the churchyard are two small granite crosses, one bearing a simple figure of Christ.

MINSTER: St Materiana's church
The mother church of Boscastle, on the north Cornish coast, Minster church contained the shrine of Materiana in medieval

times; she may have been a Welsh princess. An earlier name for Minster was Tolcarne or Talkarn, meaning a rock chapel or cell. Minster is set deep in a secluded wooded valley. A church was built here in 1150 by William de Bottreaux, Lord of the Manor of Boscastle (or 'Bottreaux Castle'). The Norman tub font dates from this time; it is carved from porphyry stone and decorated with diagonal patterns. The church was given to Benedictine monks from Anjou in William's native France. A priory adjoined the church to the north; it is now destroyed. The monks lived here until about 1402, when King Henry IV closed all 'foreign' monasteries. The church was restored in the sixteenth century and again in the nineteenth. On the terrace below the church there is a holy well, now dry. Minster was also the mother church of St Materiana's church in Tintagel. Minster is not marked on most maps; to find it, take the Tintagel road from the centre of Boscastle. At the top of the hill, bear left past the garage. Then take the second left. The church is a mile further on, in the valley below, on the left.

MYLOR: St Mylor's church and well

Mylor, two miles north of Falmouth as the crow flies, is one of a number of Celtic sites around the Fal estuary that are most easily reached from the sea. The church stands above the harbour, on an early site. As with other Celtic foundations, such as Golant and St Just in Roseland, the church is situated just above the main seaway, out of sight from pirates. The farmhouse beside the vicarage is called Lawithick, or 'church site among the trees'; the use of the (abbreviated) prefix *lan* denotes an early foundation. East of the south porch, a unique granite cross stands 5 metres high. This was a pre-Christian monolith, with a sun-symbol consisting of three concentric circles carved at its top. The stone is longer than it appears, as it is planted two metres deep. It was later capped with a Christian cross. Water from the well in the churchyard is still used for christenings; the spring flows into a small brook.

NECTAN'S KIEVE, BOSSINEY: St Nectan's chapel and waterfall

A mile north-east of Tintagel on the north Cornish coast, the river Trevillitt flows through woodland toward the sea at Bossiney. Half an hour's walk upstream leads to a waterfall known as Nectan's (or Nighton's) Kieve. Nectan was said to be the eldest son of Brychan, and 'kieve' is Cornish for 'bowl'; it describes the pool enclosed by rocks beneath the waterfall. At the top of the falls are the lower courses of what may have been a medieval chapel dedicated to Nectan. Its walls are a metre thick; the timber superstructure was added in 1860. The local story is that Nectan lived as a hermit here, at the head of the glen.

PADSTOW: St Petroc's church

The eleventh-century biographer of Petroc relates how he sailed to Padstow on the north Cornish coast. The parish church was believed to be the site of his burial. Set into the wall to the right of the altar in the late medieval church, there is a carving of a monk, which possibly represents Petroc or may be St Antony. He is bearded and holds a walking stick and a hand bell, with which to summon people to pray. He also holds a book of the Gospels, to show that he preaches the Word of God. The statue was probably preserved from an earlier church on the site, where it might have stood in a niche above the church porch for worshippers to see as they entered the building. Outside the porch is a tall Celtic cross. In the church there is a fine fourteenth-century font, carved in black catacleuse stone (see CONSTANTINE, above) from the nearby quarry between Mother Ivey's and Harlyn Bay. Round the bowl of the font, twelve apostles are depicted, with an angel at each corner.

PAUL: St Paul Aurelian's church

The parish of Paul is near the coast, two miles south of Penzance. The church is at an ancient holy site: built into the churchyard wall near the main gate is a large Neolithic standing stone, perhaps 4,000 years old, capped with a Celtic cross. It stands beside the old road leading down to Mousehole harbour, which was an embarkation point for Brittany in early times. The large church at Paul was rebuilt in granite in the fifteenth century.

PELYNT: St Non's church and well

The church at Pelynt, three miles west of Looe, may stand within an Iron Age round (a circular settlement site). The Norman church was rebuilt in the fifteenth century. Non's well is a mile down the valley in Hobb Park, where a spring emerges from the hillside. Although restored, the well house retains its original shape, with a curved roof, a stone lintel, and walls of flat, unmortared stones. On either side of the entrance is a stone bench where pilgrims could sit and pray. Inside the well house, water trickles into a heavy bowl of pink granite, incised with wheel crosses; it dates from Celtic times. A hundred years ago the outline of a mound and wall could still be traced above the well; this appears to have been a chapel. The site may be linked with an Iron Age encampment farther up the hill. To find the well, take either minor road east from Pelynt, down a steep hill to Watergate. Turn left into the road for Duloe. Before crossing the bridge over the West Looe River, bear left up a road signed 'Hobb Park'. Continue for a mile and park at the cattle grid at the top of the hill. The well is signed in the first field on the right, down a flight of steps.

PERRANPORTH: St Piran's church

One of Cornwall's chief medieval shrines was that of Piran at Perranporth, seven miles north-west of Truro. All that remains today is a fine Celtic cross, beside a ruined medieval church. The outline of the churchyard, still partly visible in the sand dunes, probably delineates the boundary wall of the Celtic monastery, which was called Lanpiran. The wall enclosed both the cross and the church. Four hundred metres to the west is the site of a pre-Norman chapel, buried beneath the sand; the site is marked by a tall wooden cross. This was Piran's shrine; it has been excavated several times and was last buried in 1981. There are now plans to excavate the chapel once again. Its walls are of unhewn, cemented stones, leaning inward to minimize roof stress. The chapel's east wall may date from Piran's time.

Before the dunes encroached, Piran's oratory stood at the head of a small valley. Pilgrims drank from a spring that rose beside the chapel and flowed down to the sea. In the eleventh or twelfth century a north door was constructed to ease the flow of pilgrims, so they could pass through the chapel to venerate Piran's relics, allowing them to leave by the door on the opposite side. A thirteenth-century document describes a reliquary containing Piran's skull, which was placed in a niche above the altar, and a shrine containing his body, which rested on the chancel floor. Piran's small copper bell and his pectoral cross carved out of bone were also preserved, together with his pastoral staff, which was decorated with gold, silver, and precious stones. These disappeared in the seventeenth century. Piran's shrine was overwhelmed by the sand in medieval times. In the seventeenth century, mining caused the Penwortha stream to go underground. Drifting sand does not cross running water, and until this time the Penwortha had protected the parish church from the encroaching dunes, but with the disappearance of the stream, the parish church too was gradually engulfed in sand; it was abandoned in 1804.

To find the site, take the B3285 from Goonhavern in the direction of Perranporth. The 'lost church' is signed to the right, at a sharp bend in the road. Turn right here and park in a lay-by opposite the first road to the right. Take the footpath left across Penhale Sands, then bear right, following some of the many white marker-posts. After fifteen minutes, look for a tall Celtic cross, or ask a fellow-walker. The ruined church is visible in the sand beyond the cross.

PHILLACK: Felec's church

The village of Phillack is in the mouth of the River Hayle, three miles south-east of St Ives, in southern Cornwall. An early fourth-century stone carved with the *chi–rho* symbol for Christ was found here: it can be seen above the church entrance, set into the outside wall. This suggests that there were Christians in the Hayle estuary, as a result either of Mediterranean trade or of Romano-British Christians coming from farther north. An early grave marker stands against the outer wall of the church vestry. The inscription on the large, coarse granite slab may be translated as 'Clotual, great in judgement'. The stone may commemorate someone important in the tribe. It hints that Phillack with its harbour was an important place in post-Roman Cornwall. In the tenth century the settlement was named Felec: this is a British name meaning a chieftain or governor.[12] In medieval times, Felec was thought to be a female saint. There is a fine wheel cross just inside the churchyard, dating from about 1000. It depicts the crucified Christ and is decorated with plaitwork.

ROCHE: St Gonand's church; St Gundred's well

Nothing is known about Gonand, the patron of Roche, five miles north of St Austell, in mid-Cornwall. An unusual cross stands in the churchyard near the porch; it has a primitive head and is decorated with many irregular pockmarks and some incised serpentine lines. Roche takes its name from Roche Rocks; *roche* is French for 'rock'. These are a group of granite tors rising to a height of 30 metres, south of the village. To reach them, take the road opposite the churchyard gate, past the school, and after five minutes' walk the Rocks will be visible on your right. On top of the largest, reached by iron ladders, is a chapel of St Michael, with a priest's room below, licensed in 1409. Hermits lived here in medieval times, and there is a local tradition of a leper living in a cell on the Rock.

The holy well is on the other side of the town of Roche. It is named after Gundred, who may be the same person as Gonand. Over the spring is a fourteenth-century well house, with remains of a granite surrounding wall. There are stones from a chapel beside it. The spring has altered its course and now flows outside the well, where the ground is very muddy. The well is in a copse above a stream. Its water cured eye diseases and children's illnesses. It is off the busy A30: 400 metres west of the Victoria Inn, turn right (north) along a lane, over a level crossing. Continue to Holy Well Cottage. With permission, turn right down a narrow, rocky footpath. The well is at the bottom, to the left.[13]

ST BREOCK: St Brioc's church

In a deep, narrow valley a mile west of Wadebridge, Brioc's church is set in a lovely, wild churchyard, beside a fast-flowing stream. The valley is named Nansent (Cornish for 'holy valley'). The church, with its thirteenth-century tower, is normally locked, but the key can be obtained from the house at the far end of the churchyard by ringing the bell at the gate.

ST BREWARD: St Breward's church; St James's well

On the western side of Bodmin Moor, four miles south of Camelford, St Breward is a hill-top settlement, 200 metres above sea level. An unusual tenth-century wheel cross, decorated with trefoil shapes carved out between each arm, stands in the lower churchyard. The church contains solid Norman pillars, with fluted capitals, and a Norman font. The village was on a pilgrim route across Bodmin Moor: pilgrims travelled south to Lostwithiel and embarked at Fowey for Europe. Since many of them were making for Compostela, a chapel and holy well below St Breward were dedicated to St James. To find the well, take the track toward Combe. Fork right, signed 'Aviary'. eighty metres before Chapel Barn, turn right up a signed footpath to the well. 'Chapel Barn' refers to St James's Chapel, which formerly stood on the site. Granite mining has altered the course of the stream, which now emerges to the right of the well house. There used to be a hawthorn growing above it. Hawthorns were considered to be holy trees in Celtic times. The spring water was held to cure sore eyes.[14]

ST BURYAN: Buryana's church and holy well

Nothing is known about Buryan, but her Cornish name, 'hi beriona' means 'the Irish lady'. Her church site, five miles south-west of Penzance, is an ancient one. Excavation has shown that the circular churchyard lies within a Romano-British earthwork, probably an enclosed farm.[15] The twelfth-century martyrology of Exeter Cathedral states that the son of the eighth-century Cornish king Gereint was cured of paralysis at Buryana's intercession. According to traditions collected by John Leland in the sixteenth century, the Saxon king Athelstan of Wessex founded a collegiate church here as the result of a vow. In 930, on his way to the Scillies to conquer its inhabitants, he vowed that if he were successful, he would build a new church in Buryana's honour.[16] The stone arches of a magnificent tenth-century church can be seen in the north wall of the chancel. Athelstan may have commissioned the fine cross in St Buryan churchyard. Above a panel of decorated knotwork, Christ reigns from the cross, a triumphant warrior, clothed and booted, with arms outstretched to save. The Saxons held fighting in high regard, and according to their theology, Christ was a young warrior hero. The sculptor carved two similar crosses, one at nearby Sancreed, two miles north of St Buryan, and another now at Lanherne, near St Mawgan-in-Pydar, five miles north-east of Newquay. On these he inscribed his name, Runhol.

St Buryana's holy well is in a field a mile north-west of St Buryan, in the hamlet of Alsia. It provided the village with drinking water and was also a healing well. Mothers came from far and near with weak and rickety children, to bathe them in the well: rickets is a bone disease found in malnourished children. A nineteenth-century miller's daughter from Alsia recalled that village women fought with the pilgrims to prevent them from dipping their babies into the well and contaminating the water.[17] The well is on Lower Alsia Farm, whose owner welcomes visitors to the well. As the road runs through the hamlet, a flight of steep stone steps leads up through the hedge. Cross two fields, diagonally to the right, and the well is now visible, above a small stream. It is contained in a simple stone well house.

ST CLEER: St Cleer's church and holy well; Doniert's Stone

Several male saints named Clarus (or Clair in French) were venerated in medieval Europe, and it is not known which of them was honoured at St Cleer. The settlement is two miles north of Liskeard, on the south-eastern edge of Bodmin Moor. The church is in the centre of the village: the upper half of an early cross stands outside the porch. The earliest features of the building are the granite bowl of a Norman font and an elaborate Norman arch in the exterior north wall. There is a fourteenth-century squint from the Lady Chapel into the chancel. The church is normally locked; the key is kept at the vicarage across the road.

Down the hill, 300 metres north-west of the church, is a fifteenth-century granite baptistery, restored in the nineteenth century. The water used to flow out under the east wall into a bowssening pool, in which the insane were cured (see ALTARNUN). An early cross stands beside the baptistery. Less than a mile from St Cleer, beside the road to St Neot, are two late ninth-century stone cross shafts. They have rectangular sockets on top, and probably carried wooden crosses. The larger shaft is decorated with knotwork and a Latin inscription, *Doniert rogavit pro anima*, meaning 'Doniert has requested [prayers] for [?his] soul.' He is likely to have been a king of Cornwall who was drowned in 878.

ST CLETHER: St Clether's church, chapel, and well

St Clether, 8 miles west of Launceston, is a village on the north-eastern edge of Bodmin Moor. The settlement is on a valley slope above the river Inney. The Norman church stands beside the road above the village. The oval churchyard is surrounded by an embankment and dates from early times; in the spring it is carpeted with wild daffodils. To visit the chapel and holy well, walk through the churchyard and continue for half a mile along a signed track that leads through rough pasture and gorse, with a delightful view of the river below. The chapel is built into the rocky hillside, a little below a solid well house constructed over a spring. Its water flows down into the chapel, past three massive granite slabs that form its altar.

Clether's shrine was much visited by medieval pilgrims. In the fifteenth century, the building was altered: an oblong cavity was made in the east wall beside the altar, so that Clether's relics could be housed for veneration. The floor was lowered so that the water could flow out through the chapel into a second pool. A shelf for pilgrims' offerings was constructed above the pool. Behind the shelf was a small wooden door, which enabled a priest inside the building to retrieve the offerings. With these ingenious facilities, St Clether is the most complete medieval Cornish well and chapel. It was restored in 1895.[18]

ST ENDELLION: St Endellion's church; Brocagnus Stone

The village of St Endellion, eight miles north of Wadebridge, is named after one of the supposed daughters of Brychan. The settlement is one and a half miles from the north Cornish coast, and is one of a cluster of parishes named after the sons, or more often the daughters, of Brychan. Twenty early Christian graves were discovered near the church, on the opposite side of the B3314. A sixth-century pillar stone, 1.5 metres high, stands at the first crossroads on the minor road from St Endellion church to Portquin. Coincidentally, it is dedicated to a Christian named Brychan (the name means 'little badger'). Beneath a *chi–rho* symbol for Christ, its worn inscription reads: 'Brocagnus lies here, the son of Nadottus'. The dead man would not have been Endellion's father, but it indicates that the name Brychan was current in early times.

By the thirteenth century, St Endellion housed a college of priests. The church contains a Norman font and a fine barrel roof. The present church dates from the fifteenth century and is built of moor stone; the tower was constructed of stone from Lundy Island, 40 miles to the north. Lundy is visible from the churchyard on a clear day. Endellion's shrine survives at the east end of the south aisle of the church. It was carved of black catacleuse stone (see CONSTANTINE, above) in the fourteenth century. It contains eight deep niches; the tomb now serves as an altar.

ST JUST IN ROSELAND: St Just's church and well

This church and its beautifully tended grounds are above a sheltered cove in the Fal estuary on the south Cornish coast. We do not know who Just was, or where his cult began. The Latin name 'Justus' was used in the early British Church, and meant 'a just man'. 'Roseland' derives from the Celtic word *rhos*, meaning a promontory. St Just in Roseland was served by Celtic monks from nearby Lanzeague until the Saxon bishops of Cornwall, Crediton, and Exeter took it over. St Just in Roseland was the mother church of St Mawes, lower down the estuary. The holy well is east of the church, on the estuary path; its water is still used for christenings. To find it, walk through the lower lych gate above the creek and continue 50 metres along the track. A footpath on the right soon brings you to St Just's well. There is another well in the churchyard.

ST KEW: St Docco's church and well

St Kew, five miles north-east of Wadebridge near the north Cornish coast, is the site of the earliest named Cornish monastery. The seventh-century *Life of Samson* describes the bishop asking in vain to stay at the monastery, which was then known as the church of Docco. A bilingual grave marker has survived from its cemetery, a rounded pillow stone that marked the head of a grave. The mason carved the name of the dead man in Latin, writing IUSTI, which means '[the stone of] Justus', and enclosed the name within a roughly carved cartouche. Along the edge of the gravestone, the sculptor inscribed the man's name in Irish ogham, a stroke alphabet that was used frequently in south-east Ireland but rarely in Cornwall. The pillow stone can be seen inside the church, in a corner to the left of the door.

There is some medieval stained glass in the windows, and a tall Celtic cross stands in the churchyard. A holy well in the grounds of Trescobel, the former vicarage, was probably the monks' water supply. It was much visited by pilgrims; its well house was restored in 1890. To visit the well, park beside the church. With the church and a telephone kiosk to your left, walk along the road out of the village for five minutes, following the high wall of the former vicarage. With permission, walk round to the front of the house and along the drive to the gate. The well is just inside the front gate, along a path to the right.

ST KEYNE: St Keyne's church and well

St Keyne is a village near the south Cornish coast, two miles south of Liskeard. Keyne's medieval church stands on high ground above the village. Her holy well is in a valley a mile south-east of the church, down a narrow road. It is clearly signed from the road beside the church. The stone well house was restored in 1932. Above the well there used to be four holy trees, which were described by various antiquarians. In 1602, Richard Carew wrote:

> Four trees of divers kinde,
> Withy, Oke, Elme and Ash,
> Make with their roots an archèd roofe,
> Whose floore this spring doth wash.

The trees died and were replaced in the early eighteenth century. These trees have also gone. The church of St Martin-by-Looe was formerly dedicated to Keyne, and Kenwyn, on the north-western edge of Truro, may also be named after her.

ST LEVAN: St Selevan's church, baptistery and cell

The hamlet of St Levan is three miles south-east of Land's End. It overlooks the sea, which turns turquoise and azure as it pounds the white shingle of Porthgwarra Cove. The church is set in a sheltered hollow above the cliffs; it is dedicated to Selevan, who may have been a local hermit. His church was built beside a pre-Christian holy stone: a large fissured rock in the churchyard. Perhaps to counteract its power, six tall, elegant crosses were erected, three at either door of the church. One still stands, almost 3 metres high, and the heads of two others can be seen in the churchyard. The church contains fine medieval bench ends, with lively representations of a shepherd, a jester, and a pilgrim who has visited Compostela and wears a cockle shell in his hat as a token from the Spanish shrine.

Across the road, a track leads down to Selevan's ancient baptistery, above the cove. This is a small building, 1.5 by 2.1 metres, constructed of giant granite slabs; it was roofed until the eighteenth century. Adjoining it is Selevan's holy well, which was known for curing eye diseases and toothache. People bathed in the well and then slept on the stone floor of the baptistery. Farther down the path to the cove, a hermit's two-roomed cell can be seen, also edged with granite boulders. Excavation carried out in 1931 revealed a roughly flagged stone floor. It was built on an east–west axis, so one room may have been a chapel. This was a sheltered spot for a hermit, with easy fishing in the cove below.

ST MAWGAN-IN-MENEAGE: St Mawgan's church; Mawgan cross

The village of St Mawgan-in-Meneage is at the northern tip of the Lizard, four miles south-east of Helston. 'Meneage' means 'land of the monks'. Mawgan cross is an early grave marker on the village green, at a point where three roads meet. The stone dates from about 600, and is inscribed to 'Cnegumus, son of Genaius'. It stands 1.9 metres high. A cross head was later added to it; the head no longer exists. A medieval squint in the church is also a feature of several other churches on the Lizard.

ST MAWGAN-IN-PYDAR: St Mawgan's church and well; Runhol's cross

Pydar is a Cornish word meaning 'hundred'. It denotes one of the six land divisions or 'hundreds' of Cornwall, and was an area that could produce a hundred fighting men. The Welsh monk Mawgan gave his name to the beautiful Vale of Mawgan, five miles north-east of Newquay, with its ancient harbour of Mawgan Porth, and its inland settlement of St Mawgan-in-Pydar. Excavations at Mawgan Porth from 1950 to 1954 revealed three or four clusters of rectangular buildings, dating from about 850 to around 1050. Their occupants were farmers and fishermen with no metal implements. They kept sheep, goats, horses, oxen, dogs, cats, and poultry. There was evidence of some contact with Anglo-Saxons: a coin from the time of Ethelred II (*c.* 1000) has been found. Above the village was a cemetery of slate cists (slab-lined tombs), the western part set aside for many child burials.[19] The site has been preserved on the sloping green opposite the beach: the outline of some of the homes can be seen.

The soil near the shore was probably too barren to sustain a community of monks, but two miles up the river, where the land is more fertile, there was a Celtic monastery at St Mawgan-in-Pydar. The large parish church contains a fine Norman font. In the churchyard are two Cornish crosses, brought from elsewhere. Immediately inside the lych gate is the well, now dry, where Mawgan is said to have preached and to have baptized converts. Over the churchyard wall, outside the convent church of Lanherne, is a fine tenth-century cross carved by Runhol, who inscribed his name at its base. His name can be found on a similar cross at Sancreed, and he was also the sculptor of a cross at St Buryan.

ST NEOT: St Neot's church and well

The village of St Neot is on the southern edge of Bodmin Moor, five miles north-west of Liskeard. It is mentioned in Domesday Book (1086), at which time there was a small community of monks at St Neot. The churchyard contains one of the finest Celtic crosses in Cornwall, carved of granite and richly ornamented with interlacing. It probably dates from the late ninth century; its style resembles that of King Doniert's Stone at St Cleer and others at Lanivet, Sancreed, and Cardinham. Nearby are three wayside crosses, brought in from elsewhere in the parish, and a fifteenth-century lantern cross from St Kew. The church contains magnificent stained-glass windows dating from the fifteenth and sixteenth centuries. They tell the stories of saints and angels, the Creation, the Flood, and the life of St Neot. One window portrays a crowned figure with children in his lap. The nineteenth-century restorer has inserted an inscription that describes the figure as Brychan, although it is more likely to represent God the Father or Abraham with the souls of the righteous in his bosom.

St Neot's holy well is 400 metres from the church, near the St Neot River. To find it, leave the church and turn right along the main road. Turn right again along a signed track, following the river. The well is in a field at the foot of a scarp. According to legend, Neot was a small man, who used to chant the psalms while standing in the well. Michell in his *Parochial History of St Neots* (1833) states that 'there was an arch of stones over it, with a large oak springing from the arch, and with doors to the entrance. [It] was remembered by some old inhabitants of the village lately deceased. ... Weakly children used within living memory to be brought here.' The well house was rebuilt in 1862. The name of the early settlement of Menheniot, three miles south-east of Liskeard, may mean 'sanctuary of Neot'.

SANCREED: St Sancred's church and St Euny's well

Almost nothing is known about either Sancred or Euny, although Euny was a popular saint in western Cornwall. Outside Sancreed church, four miles west of Penzance, is a fine tenth-century cross, inscribed by the sculptor with his name, Runhol. Spelling was evidently less important at this time, since the carver spelt his name as RUNHO at Sancreed and as RUHOL on the cross now in Lanherne (see ST MAWGAN-IN-PYDAR). Sancreed is a Celtic foundation, with a circular churchyard. An early inscribed stone was turned upside-down in the thirteenth century and carved to resemble the Runhol cross.

Euny's holy well is 300 metres south-west of the church. To find it, cross the road that runs past the church and take the footpath signed 'holy well'. A small working garage is ahead of you. As you pass it you will see a stile to the right, beside a gate. Climb the stile and continue to walk along the lane for five minutes, past a concrete pump house. Wellingtons are useful here, where the ground floods. The well is now ahead of you, in an enclosure, down a steep flight of nine granite steps. Beside the well is an ancient thorn bush hung with clouties, or rags that represent prayers (see MADRON). Close by are the walls of a small rectangular chapel. Nearby, massive granite blocks form the wall of an earlier building, perhaps a monk's cell.

SANCREED: Carn Euny, and Chapel Euny well

Two miles west of Sancreed is the ancient British village of Carn Euny. This hamlet was occupied from the fifth century BC to the fourth century AD. In the fourth century it consisted of three interlocking courtyard houses, with a well-preserved *fougou*, which may have been used for storage and for hiding, if necessary. The copious well of Chapel Euny, half a mile away, was probably the water supply for this Romano-British village. There are actually two wells and the remains of a ruined chapel. To find the twin wells, park in the small car park, as if visiting Carn Euny. Consult the site plan and follow the longer track, labelled 'Route 2, 450 metres'. Where the track veers to the right for Carn Euny, continue instead for a short distance up the hill and take the muddy track to the left.

After five minutes, you will see the wells, surrounded by giant stone slabs. An ancient thorn tree, now adorned with clouties, is down a path to the left, beside the stream flowing from the wells.

TINTAGEL: fortress; St Juliet's chapel and wells; St Materiana's church

In the sixth century, the rocky headland of Tintagel was a chieftain's stronghold. Situated three miles south-west of Boscastle, it is almost an island; its Celtic name probably means 'narrow-necked fortress'. It is likely that Celtic chieftains moved frequently, for their entourage required more food than any district could supply for long. Tintagel may therefore have been occupied for only a few months each year. However, its rulers lived in style, and more imported Mediterranean pottery has been found here than at any other sixth-century British or Irish site: pieces of huge oil containers from Tunisia, smaller handled jars from Byzantium, and fine red dishes from Carthage. In 1998 fragments of a sixth-century Spanish glass flagon were also found. Some of the red dishes at Tintagel are stamped with a cross.[20]

Near the top of the fortress are the remains of Juliet's chapel. It was built in about 1000, and the east end was added around 1230, when a medieval castle was built on the site. The chapel's Norman font can be seen in the parish church of St Materiana, on the mainland below the fort. This church is set within what was perhaps the royal burial ground for the chieftains who lived in the stronghold above. A fourth-century Roman milestone preserved in the church was brought here from the Roman campsite on the cliff. Nothing is known about Materiana: she was possibly a Welsh princess. Her shrine was at Minster, outside Boscastle.

The fortress of Tintagel was abandoned from the sixth century to the twelfth; Juliet's chapel, however, remained in use. Unexpectedly, there are three wells on the rocky outcrop: a supply of fresh water was vital for a fort. Juliet's twin wells are just beyond her chapel; since they are fenced in, they can easily be spotted. There is a magnificent view from the chapel along the coast in both directions.

Part Five

Southern England

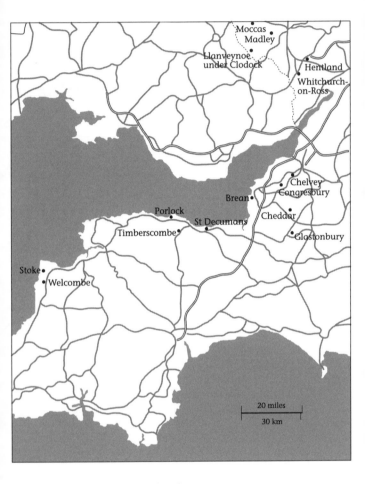

Saints of Southern England

BRADWELL-ON-SEA, Essex: chapel of St Peter-on-the-Wall

In Roman times Bradwell-on-Sea was probably Othona, one of the Forts of the Saxon Shore, built by the Romans to defend the coastline against the Saxons. The walls of the fort were 4 metres thick; its eastern front was probably a quay. This stretch of coast is intersected by many creeks inviting to invaders, and this is one of the few points along the shoreline where the mainland meets the open sea without intervening marshes. A road led to the sea at this point, which probably attracted St Cedd to the site in the seventh century, by which time the Roman fort lay in ruins. Cedd built a church across the chief entrance to the fortress, making use of its stone foundations. The Saxons settled mainly toward the quay to the east, beyond the ruined chapel, which was surrounded by a graveyard. Domesday Book (1086) records a fishery and salt pans here.

The chapel is perhaps the oldest church in England of which so much remains. It is the only surviving monument of the short-lived Anglo-Celtic Church of the East Saxons. Aidan of Lindisfarne trained as missionaries twelve young Englishmen, one of whom was Cedd. After preaching successfully in the Midlands, Cedd was sent south in response to a request from King Sigbert. He arrived in 653, probably landing at the quay of the old Roman fort of Othona, and travelled through the kingdom of the East Saxons. He returned north to be consecrated bishop and then came south again, building churches at Bradwell, Tilbury, and other sites. He was bishop of the area from 654 to 664.[1]

St Peter's is one of six seventh-century churches in the Kent region, all built on Roman sites and constructed largely out of recycled Roman material; each had an apse in the Continental style. On his arrival as bishop, Cedd probably built a small wooden chapel. He perhaps replaced it with the present church as his acquaintance with Kent developed. The church is 15 metres long and 6.5 metres wide. Its semicircular apse no longer survives, but it probably contained a cube-shaped altar and a bench round the wall for clergy, with the bishop's throne in the middle.

It appears that there was a double chancel arch, which suggests the existence of a double monastery at Bradwell, in which case the nave would have been divided by a screen or curtain to separate the men from the women. The monks and nuns would have lived in separate buildings under the same superior, as at Whitby, and would have worshipped in separate parts of the same church. There was a sacristy on the north side in which the clergy could vest; it was entered from the apse. A similar room on the south side was used to contain the people's offerings in kind; it was entered from the nave. This asymmetrical though logical arrangement was known in the East and in North Africa but rarely in the West.[2]

BREAN, Somerset: St Bridget's church

There are two early church dedications to Brigit near the Somerset coast; at these sites, the goddess Brígh may formerly have been honoured. One of these is on a low hill at Chelvey, eight miles south-west of Bristol. Another is St Bridget's church at the foot of Brean Down, two miles south of Weston-super-Mare. The goddess Brígh appears to have been the titular deity of the Brigantes, the largest confederacy of tribes in Britain, who dominated northern England before the arrival of the Romans. The Brigantes were also found in Switzerland near Lake Constance, where the town of Bregenz is named after them.[3] The Celtic word *brigā* means 'high one' or 'high place'. Living in their hill forts, the Brigantes were successful warriors, and those whom they defeated coined the word 'brigand' to describe their unwelcome presence.

Brean is another name derived from the Celtic word *brigā*. Until medieval times Brean Down was an island; people lived, farmed, and worshipped on the Down for four thousand years. A Romano-Celtic temple was built here in about 340; it appears to have been used for only thirty years. It may be that Brígh was honoured on Brean Down before Brigit was commemorated in the church below. There is an extensive sub-Roman Christian cemetery on the shoulder of Brean Down, one of six so far discovered in Somerset. Its graves appear from time to time in the eroding sand cliff. Remains from the tombs were carbon-dated to around 410. The temple on the Down above was partly demolished to build a structure on an east–west axis, possibly a Christian place of worship. Coins found here indicate that this building was in use in the fifth century.[4] On top of the Down, a further five graves dating from the fifth to the seventh centuries were discovered. These too were oriented east–west in the Christian manner.

In 1976 Dr Martin Bell of Lampeter University found the footings of round stone houses and bones and pottery dating from the Bronze Age, out in the flat land 100–200 metres offshore, showing that sea level was lower in earlier times than it is today. Perhaps this was the site of the original village of Brean.[5] St Bridget's church in Brean is one of a series of possible Celtic foundations along the Somerset shoreline. The church dates from the thirteenth century. It contains some fine stone carvings, including that of a woman's head: she wears a headdress popular in the time of Richard II (1377–99). A row of carved wooden angels supports the roof beams.

CHEDDAR, Somerset: chapel of St Columbanus

Set beside the River Yeo, the minster church at Cheddar stands on the site of a Roman villa. The church was built long after the villa was ruined, but the site may have been chosen because Christians had owned the villa and were buried there.[6] The church is now dedicated to St Andrew; it contains a finely-decorated fifteenth-century stone pulpit. St Thomas More asked to be buried in this church, in the fifteenth-century chapel of St Nectan, off the south aisle. Not far from the church, in Station Road, the Kings of Wessex Community School is the site of an early medieval settlement and possibly also of a Celtic one.[7] In 1960 Philip Rahtz discovered the remains of an Anglo-Saxon palace in the grounds of the school. The building was made of wood and had a thatched roof. According to the Anglo-Saxon Chronicle, the Kings of Wessex met here in 942, 956, and 968. The site can be visited: outlined in the grass are the positions of a twelfth- to fourteenth-century great hall and a twelfth-century *witan*, or council chamber.

There are substantial remains of a tenth-century chapel, dedicated to Columbanus. It was rebuilt in the eleventh century and again in the thirteenth, when the bishops of Wells restored both the chapel and the east hall. By then, the complex was probably no more than a royal hunting lodge with a hall, a chapel, and a domestic annexe. The chancel of the chapel was widened to the same span as the nave. A lime kiln alongside it was used to provide mortar for its walls. It was roofed with wooden shingles or thatch. Later the chapel was used as a barn and then as a house for farm workers.

CHELVEY, Somerset: St Bridget's church

This is an early church site dedicated to Brigit, eight miles south-west of Bristol. It may originally have been dedicated to the goddess Brígh (see BREAN DOWN). Chelvey Manor is mentioned in Domesday Book (1086), so the adjacent church was probably also in existence. The north wall of the nave is Norman; so too is the arch over the south door and the font: these date from about 1140. In the thirteenth century the square corners of the bowl of the font were cut off to make it octagonal. The key to the church is obtainable from the rectory at Backwell, two miles to the east. The rectory and church in Backwell are opposite the Junior School in Church Lane.

CONGRESBURY, Somerset: Cadbury Camp and St Cyngar's church

The hill fort at Cadbury, three-quarters of a mile north of Congresbury, was probably occupied by members of the Dobuni tribe, who were based in the Cotswolds. It was abandoned during the Roman occupation, from AD 43 to 410, although the lowland region around it grew and flourished under stable Roman administration. North of the hill fort, in Henley Wood, a pagan Roman temple was built. After it fell into ruin in the third century, local Christians appear to have been buried at the site, over earlier pagan graves. The hill fort gained a new lease of life and was reoccupied from 410 to 700. It is one of five camps in the south-west to be named 'Cadbury' or 'Cada's fort'.

This is the only fortress in the region to have been lived in once again after the departure of the Romans. Amphorae have been found here, still imported from Mediterranean lands, as they had been in Roman times. The people living here were wealthy: the camp has produced the second largest collection of fragments of early medieval glass from any western site. There were at least sixty vessels; the only site that has so far produced more is Whithorn in Galloway, which yielded pieces of some eighty vessels.[8] There may be evidence of Christianity at Cadbury: a Latin cross is carved on a piece of African red slipware dating from the mid-sixth century.[9] It is possible that the monk Cyngar lived among his people in the fort, for on the neighbouring hilltop of Henley Hill (Yatton) is what appears to have been an early Christian cemetery. There was a pagan temple here, and later, perhaps in the sixth century, between 50 and 100 graves were dug through the site.

In Saxon times, the settlement of Congresbury grew beside the River Yeo that flows at the foot of the fort, a mile to the southwest. Here there was a minster and monastery. The large oblong site of 10 acres is bounded by deep ditches, and probably dates from the seventh century. There was a second church within the enclosure, dedicated to St Michael. Since the Archangel Michael is associated with the souls of the dead, this was probably a mortuary chapel.

In 1996, in the floor of a barn near Congresbury, stones were discovered which had formed part of Cyngar's eleventh-century shrine, including a piece of one of its corner pillars. The shrine probably stood near or behind the high altar of the minster church. However, Cyngar's cult may have waned, for in 1217/18 the church was rebuilt and rededicated to St Andrew. The great east window was constructed at this time. St Cyngar's shrine was now seen to be in the way, and his relics were relegated to a side chapel off the south aisle. Some of the stone foundations of his shrine were re-used in the new east wall of the church, which was rebuilt yet again in the fourteenth and fifteenth centuries.

In the churchyard, an ancient yew stump growing inside a beech tree is still known as 'Congar's Walking Stick'. He was said to have planted his staff here, where it took root. This miracle persuaded the Saxon king Ine of Wessex to grant land for a monastery here. Even today, yew is a traditional wood for making walking sticks. Next to the church there is a fine thirteenth-century priests' house, built to accommodate the clerics who ministered to the pilgrims visiting Cyngar's shrine.

GLASTONBURY, Somerset: Glastonbury Abbey

In Iron Age times Glastonbury was an island, at least in winter. Lake villages have been found in the marshland that surrounded it. The name Somerset indicates a region of summer pastures; in winter, when the land was flooded, the animals would have been slaughtered or moved to higher ground. There may have been a Celtic monastery at Glastonbury; it is more likely that early hermits lived on the Tor above the settlement. Excavations on the Tor from 1964 to 1966 revealed what may have been the remains of monks' cells, cut into the rock below the summit in the sixth century. Here sherds of amphorae were found, perhaps containers for wine or olive oil, imported from the Mediterranean. There were a great many animal bones, mostly of cattle, with a few sheep or pigs. These were the residue of joints brought to the site from animals butchered elsewhere. Two graves contained leg bones of young people, well under twenty years old, of undetermined sex. There was a medieval tradition of a monastic foundation on the Tor in early times with two hermits.[10]

There was no source of water on the Tor, but there was some arable land. The ridges round the Tor indicate that it continued to be farmed in medieval times, for there was little land available for agriculture except for that on the steep-sided hills, since all the low-lying land was marsh. The present tower on the Tor was built in about 1360, following an earthquake that took place around 1300. Carvings in its outer west wall represent the Archangel Michael weighing souls and Brigit milking a cow: she was a patroness of fertility and of cattle, as was her precursor, the Celtic goddess Brígh.

When the Anglo-Saxon king of Wessex conquered the area, a new settlement was developed on the land below the Tor. The present abbey ruins date from the eleventh century. The enormous church and its surrounding buildings housed up to sixty men. Celtic monks including Kea, Fili, Rumon, and Collen were honoured at Glastonbury, but many Somerset dedications to Celtic saints date from the eleventh century, when monks of Glastonbury abbey created a new interest in the lives of their Celtic predecessors.

In 1184 the great church was destroyed by fire. Glastonbury's superiority among English monasteries was threatened, and enterprising monastic historians developed a legend describing how Joseph of Arimathea, the disciple who buried Jesus in his family tomb, came to Glastonbury and built its first church. In 1191 the monks 'discovered' the tomb of King Arthur and his consort Guinevere beneath the floor of their church. The supposed relics of the royal couple were entombed in a shrine in the chancel in 1278.

The abbey was a great medieval centre of pilgrimage, and the town contains a number of buildings dating from this time. In the High Street, The George and Pilgrim's Hotel dates from the fifteenth century. The High Street continues eastwards into Bove Town. Jacobi Cottage in Bove Town, now a private house, was once a chapel, the last stopping-place on the Old Wells Road for pilgrims visiting the abbey. The outline of the chapel windows can be seen in its stone walls. The waters of a spring ran through the chapel, flowing along a channel in the paving slabs of the stone floor. This was known as the Slipper Chapel, and pilgrims removed their shoes here, and washed their feet before proceeding barefoot to the abbey. The chapel was dedicated to St James (or Jacobus in Latin) of Compostela, a great Spanish pilgrimage centre.

A few hundred metres higher up the hill, on the opposite side of the road, 82 Bove Town is now a guesthouse named 'The Lightship'. This is a fourteenth-century A-framed farmhouse, which became a hospice for pilgrims travelling from Wells to Glastonbury. Downstairs is a giant fireplace where the meat for hungry travellers was roasted on a spit. Unusually, on the first floor there is a smaller fireplace, with sockets in the walls on each side to contain a second spit, since so much food was needed. In Bove Town the road banks steeply at this point, and the earth is held firm behind enormous stone slabs taken from the abbey precincts.

On the south-western edge of the town, Wearyall Hill is, according to medieval legend, the place where Joseph of Arimathea planted his staff. It grew into the Glastonbury Thorn, a cutting of which can be seen on the hillside; the tree flowers at Christmas, and each year a sprig is presented to the Queen.

HENTLAND, Hereford and Worcester: St Dubricius' church

The name Hentland comes from the Welsh *hen llan* ('old, or former, church') and describes a church restored after a period of disuse. Hentland is at the end of a road half a mile south of Kynaston, four miles west-north-west of Ross-on-Wye. There was a Roman building on this site before the Romano-British bishop Dubricius made Hentland his headquarters and remained here for seven years, according to medieval legend. Part of the nave of the church dates from 1050, but most of the building is thirteenth-century. In the churchyard is a thirteenth-century lantern cross; its worn carvings include a crucifixion scene and the figure of a bishop, presumably Dubricius. Llanfrother, one and a half miles to the north, is said to be the site of a monastery established by Dubricius, on a bluff rising steeply above the River Wye, immediately south of the present village of Hoarwithy.

LLANVEYNOE UNDER CLODOCK, Hereford and Worcester: St Beuno's church

This remote settlement is on a shoulder of the Black Mountains, three miles north-west of Clodock. Continue north through Longtown and turn left at the sign for Llanveynoe. After a mile, the small church is visible along a track to the left of the road, opposite a telephone kiosk. The church is now dedicated to Sts Beuno and Peter: dedications to the apostles were introduced in Norman times. The earlier dedication to Beuno may reflect the tradition that Beuno trained in south-east Wales before returning north to his own territory. An ancient yew tree in the churchyard predates the church. Inside the church are two fine tenth-century stone slabs. One of them is engraved with a plain cross and the inscription *Haesdur fecit crucem* ('Haesdur made the cross'). On the other slab, a simple figure of Christ hangs from a cross; this may be the top of a coffin. The present church was built in the thirteenth century; its walls and roof are of local sandstone. South of the church is a slender sandstone preaching cross.

MADLEY, Hereford and Worcester: presumed birthplace of Dubricius

According to medieval legend, Dubricius cured Peipiau, the ruler of the small kingdom of Erging (now Archenfield) of a drivelling mouth, and Peipiau granted him Madley for a settlement. It is three miles west of Hereford, on the Roman road to Abergavenny, in a broad stretch of the Wye Valley. The original west door of the church survives from around 1250, decorated with ironwork. A record of 1318 at Hereford cathedral refers to a statue of Our Lady at Madley, visited by pilgrims. The church was re-dedicated at some point to the Nativity of the Blessed Virgin, rebuilt, and extended. Putlog holes for scaffolding are still in place in the nave. Unusually, the church has a polygonal apse, with thirteenth- and fourteenth-century stained-glass windows. Beneath the apse, the crypt probably contained the statue. There is a medieval yew tree in the churchyard.

MALMESBURY, Wiltshire: Malmesbury Abbey

According to medieval tradition, Malmesbury Abbey was founded by an Irish monk and hermit named Maildhub, who established a small monastery and a school for nobles' sons. Historians have cast doubt on Maildhub's existence, but the settlement is an ancient one. In 2000 a previously unknown Iron Age town was discovered beneath modern Malmesbury. It was 40 acres in size, encircled by stone ramparts over 3 metres wide. The town was built between the fifth and second centuries BC and was strongly fortified. The settlement was probably the main centre of a tribal group that eventually federated with its neighbours to become the kingdom of the Dobuni. It was built on high ground within a loop of the river Avon, with a few hundred inhabitants sheltering behind 1.5 metres of stone defences. They lived in round houses of stone or timber, with roofs of thatch. They farmed, and the settlement was perhaps the chief economic centre of the south-east Cotswolds. Radiating out from it is a 30-mile cluster of Iron Age farms and settlements, as aerial photography shows.[11]

The medieval town wall partly follows that of its Iron Age predecessor. Although Malmesbury stopped being a significant centre of population from about 100 BC to AD 800, it may have continued as a religious centre. There was possibly a Roman temple beneath the abbey, which may have been built on the site of a small Celtic temple dedicated to a local deity. The Saxons conquered this area in the sixth century after a victory at Dyrham near Bath. Malmesbury became part of the West Saxon kingdom, Wessex. Aldhelm became abbot of Malmesbury in about 675. The south porch of the abbey may survive from his seventh-century church. Over the door, the tympanum depicts Christ enthroned, with supporting angels. Each side wall contains a panel of six apostles with an angel flying overhead. The rest of the south porch, with its bands of stone carving, dates from the twelfth or thirteenth century and is one of the finest in Europe.

MOCCAS, Hereford and Worcester:
St Dubricius' church

Moccas, eight miles east of Hay-on-Wye, is off the B4352, a mile north of Blakemere. Its name comes from *Mochros*, meaning 'the place of pigs', as does that of Muckross Abbey in

Ireland. The twelfth-century *Book of Llandaff* describes Dubricius building a dwelling and a chapel here, dedicated to the Trinity. The Trinitarian dedication may indicate that the text was composed in an Anglo-Norman context. A white boar appears as a messenger from God, to show Dubricius the place where he is to build. In medieval hagiography, other Celtic saints who were shown the site of their chief monastery by a wild boar were Illtud and Cadoc, Brynach of Nevern, Cyngar, Kentigern, Paul Aurelian, and Ciarán of Saighir.

The text reads: '... and with his disciples [Dubricius] stayed [in the place] for many years. They named the place *Mochros* ...; fittingly "place of pigs", since on the preceding night an angel appeared to him [Dubricius] in a dream, saying to him: "The place which you have selected and chosen, in the next day, walk over the whole of it, and where you shall find a white sow lying with her piglets, there found and build your living place [*habitaculum*] and chapel [*oraculum*] in the name of the Holy Trinity."'

PORLOCK, Somerset: St Dubricius' church

This church was formerly closer to the sea, which has now receded. Its stocky tower, dating from around the thirteenth century, may have had a light on top of its spire to guide boats into the harbour. The church was restored in the fifteenth century and again in the nineteenth. In the church are two pieces of a pre-Norman cross, the earliest stone carving in west Somerset. It is not known how early this dedication to Dubricius may be. The church is called 'ecclesia S. Dubricii' in the foundation deed of the Harrington chantry in 1476. There is an ancient yew tree in the churchyard.

ST DECUMANS, Somerset: St Decuman's church and well

This settlement is a mile south-west of Watchet, on the north Somerset coast. The chancel floor of the church contains thirteenth-century tiles, probably made at Cleeve abbey. Like a number of other Celtic saints, Decuman was said to have picked up his head after being beheaded; he then walked to the spring that flows to the west of the church, and his life blood conferred healing properties on the water. This is a common medieval explanation for what contemporary science would ascribe to a well's chemical or mineral content. The spring is down a lane on the steeply sloping hillside. It is covered by a circular well house, and a little lower down the slope the water flowed, until recently, into two semicircular basins before going underground. A record from around 1100 states: 'The fountain of St Decumanus is sweet, healthful and necessary to the inhabitants for drinking purposes.'

SHAPWICK, Somerset: first shrine of St Indract.

Indract and his companions may well have been murdered at Shapwick.[12] The original site of the village is at Old Church Farm, half a mile out of Shapwick, on the right hand side of the road leading eastward from the present church. Excavation here has provided evidence of Roman settlement and of a large medieval building lower down the field from the site of the former church. A Roman road ran from the Fosse Way past Shapwick to the sea. There may have been a Romano-British villa at Shapwick; in 1988 Britain's largest hoard of early Roman coins was found here. It was buried around AD 230 and was the equivalent of about ten years' pay for a legionary soldier.[13] In medieval times the villagers moved to a new location, half a mile west of their original settlement. This is where the present fourteenth-century church can be found.

STOKE, Devon: St Nectan's church and well

The eleventh-century abbey of Hartland in north Devon claimed to possess the relics of Nectan, the eldest son of Brychan. Set in a wooded valley near the sea, the abbey was a centre of pilgrimage in medieval times. The large and impressive church of St Nectan was built beside the sea at Stoke, one and a half miles west of the abbey. The earliest feature of the church is a fine carved Norman font, with faces of the baptized at each corner, looking down on the piteous faces of the unbaptized who gaze up from below. The church contains a magnificent fourteenth-century rood screen: there was originally an organ and seating on top of the screen. Outside, on the east face of the tower, there is a fourteenth-century statue of Nectan; its head is modern. Just off Stoke's main street, down a steep path, alongside a garden, is Nectan's holy well. The path is clearly signed; the well is enclosed in an arched stone well house.

TIMBERSCOMBE, Somerset: St Petroc's church

Timberscombe, close to the north Somerset coast, adopted Petroc as its patron saint. It is one of a cluster of Somerset churches dedicated to early Welsh monks: nearby Carhampton is named after Carantoc, Porlock honours Dubricius, and a church and holy well outside Watchet are dedicated to Decuman. It is uncertain whether these were early or late medieval dedications. Timberscombe is one of several churches in this area with a magnificent rood screen. This is a wooden screen, once topped with a cross, or rood; it separated the priest in the chancel from the congregation, who stood in the nave. Wood was plentiful in the area, and there were skilled carvers at Dunster abbey. Petroc's church also contains a wall painting of King David chanting psalms while playing the harp, and medieval floor tiles brought from nearby Cleeve abbey.

WELCOMBE, Devon: St Nectan's church and holy well

The hamlet of Welcombe is four miles south-west of Hartland abbey, which contained Nectan's shrine in medieval times. The fourteenth-century church has subsequently been restored. It contains a Norman tub font. Near the church, at a junction of lanes, is Nectan's well, in a stone well house. A niche in its outer wall above the entrance arch was probably designed to contain a statue.

WHITCHURCH-ON-ROSS, Hereford and Worcester: St Dubricius' church

This is one of a cluster of churches associated with Dubricius. Its name means 'white' or 'stone' church, and dates from a time when most buildings were constructed of wood. A number of churches associated with Dubricius are beside a river bank, indicating that waterways were an important means of travel. At Whitchurch, we can imagine the early Christians arriving by coracle, as an ancient landing stage still survives in the churchyard, leading down to the broad River Wye. This has long been one of the traditional coracling rivers. The church contains a late twelfth-century font and there is a medieval preaching cross in the churchyard.

Part Six

Northern England

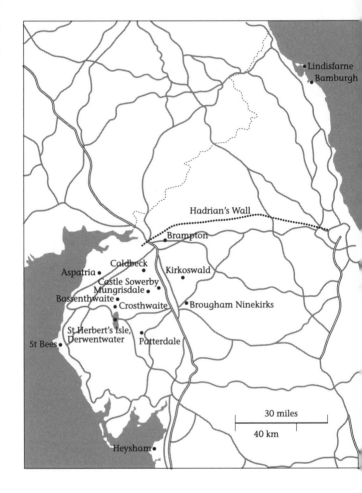

Saints of Northern England

ASPATRIA, Cumbria: St Kentigern's church and well

One of nine Cumbrian churches dedicated to Kentigern in medieval times, Aspatria is three miles from the coast, on the A596, eighteen miles south-west of Carlisle. An incised tomb slab carved with a swastika was found here, dating from around 430, a century before Kentigern's time. This indicates the presence of early British Christians in the area.

St Kentigern's well in the churchyard is now dry, but until recently it was fed from an underground spring and used for baptisms. Aspatria suffered from Norse–Irish coastal raids, and the remains of a Viking hogback tombstone, shaped to represent a house for the dead, mark a wealthy Norseman's burial.

BAMBURGH, Northumberland: King Oswald's fort and St Aidan's church

The rocky outcrop of Bamburgh is fifteen miles south-east of Berwick-upon-Tweed. There may have been a coastal fort on this site in Roman and pre-Roman times. In 547 the Anglian King Ida fought his way northward to become the first king of Northumbria. He seized the fortress and made it his capital. It is an ideal defensive site, commanding a view of attackers from either land or sea. King Oswald (604–42) lived in a fortress at Bamburgh. Three hundred years after Oswald's time the stronghold was captured by King Athelstan of Wessex, the grandson of Alfred the Great, when he was conquering England and Scotland. It was subsequently raided by the Vikings, who destroyed it in 993.

Oswald gave Aidan land for a church in Bamburgh, not far from the palace. Toward the end of the reign of King Oswin, Oswald's successor, Aidan fell ill at Bamburgh, and a shelter was made for him at the west end of the church. Aidan died while resting against a wooden beam for support. The plank survived when Penda, the pagan king of Mercia, burned the church; it is still preserved. The impressive church that exists today was built between 1170 and 1230 by a community of Augustinian canons. Its chancel is probably on the site of Aidan's church. A modern shrine commemorates the death of Aidan on 31 August 651. Aidan's monks took his body back to their monastery on Lindisfarne for burial.[1]

BASSENTHWAITE, Cumbria: St Bega's church

This little church is three miles south of Bassenthwaite village, along a signed track. It is probably earlier than the village and is situated on an ancient trackway leading from Little Crosthwaite to Bowness. It is possible that the church is built at a place where Bega once resided, but there is no evidence for this. A small community could have lived here beside the fast-flowing stream that flows from Skiddaw into the lake. In the north and east outer walls of the church, random courses of large stones, perhaps from a Roman building, indicate a Norse, or pre-Norman, style of building.

The present church is Norman, with a fourteenth-century chantry chapel. The octagonal font dates from around 1300. St Bega's was given to Jedburgh abbey in the eleventh century and to Carlisle cathedral in the thirteenth; both Jedburgh and Carlisle were then administered by the Augustinians. There is a wrought-iron hourglass-stand fixed to the south pillar of the chancel arch, dating from about 1600. It was positioned so that both the preacher and the congregation could time the sermon! William and Dorothy Wordsworth visited the church in about 1794; it features in Wordworth's *A Guide to the English Lakes*. Alfred Tennyson visited St Bega's in 1835, and probably chose it as the setting for the opening of his poem *Morte d'Arthur*. The church was extensively restored in 1874.

BRAMPTON, Cumbria: St Martin's church

This is an early church associated with St Ninian. Brampton is nine miles north-east of Carlisle, which was the centre of a diocese at this time. The tiny church is a mile and a half out of the town, at the end of a single-track road to the right of William Howard School. The road is signed 'Old Church Cemetery'; the church key is kept at the farmhouse next door. The church lies within the site of a Roman camp, one of a series of forts along the Stanegate, constructed before Hadrian's Wall was built. It is situated beside the river Irthing and was used by a Roman auxiliary unit for a brief period of twenty-five years; it was abandoned around AD 150. Amphorae and other artefacts were discovered at the site.

The church was probably built soon after the Romans withdrew in the first decade of the fifth century; it hugs the Roman rampart and is not aligned with the camp, but uses the Roman earthworks for shelter. There used to be a holy tree here named St Martin's Oak. At the foot of the esker, or ridge of gravel and sand, on which the fort was built is a well that may have been a shrine to the local water spirit, since there are signs of a Roman concrete surround. It was later known as Ninewells, which may mean 'Ninian's well' or may derive from the Celtic word *nyen*, meaning 'holy'. The first graveyard here was oval, following Celtic tradition. The church was rebuilt in Norman times, using some stone from the abandoned fort; only its chancel remains. This is one of the earliest Christian sites in Cumbria.[2]

BROUGHAM NINEKIRKS, Cumbria:
St Ninian's church; Brougham fort.

Brougham Ninekirks, or 'Ninian's church at Brougham', lies three and a half miles east of Penrith, beside the River Eamont. It can be reached by following a signed footpath from the A66. The path follows the winding river for about a mile, and the church is then visible in a hollow. This was the site of the *vicus* or civil settlement that served the Roman fort of Brocavum, two miles to the west. The fort guarded a bridge over the River Eamont, where the road from Carlisle to York met the road across the Lake District through Ambleside to Hardknott. Because of its strategic location, the emperor Hadrian came to Brocavum to inspect his northern defences.

Ninian's church is located in a more peaceful spot. A *vicus,* or urban community, where local people provided for the soldiers' needs, was normally situated near a Roman military establishment. The earliest material discovered at the site is eighth-century metalwork, so it is impossible to know whether Ninian's followers worked here. The church on the site is a long, low sandstone building; it was dedicated to the Saxon saint, Wilfrid. The Norman church was rebuilt in 1660 by Lady Anne Clifford, countess of Pembroke, who had inherited Brougham castle as part of her family's vast estates. She wrote: 'It would in all likelyhood have fallen down it was soe ruiness if it had not bin repaired by me.' Her restoration work is recorded above the altar, in a plaster wreath containing her intials AP (Anne Pembroke). The Earl of Pembroke was her second husband.

Inside the church, little has changed since the seventeenth century. The interior is whitewashed, with clear glass and a flagstone floor. All the furnishings are of finely-crafted oak. The family pews are panelled, and each has a wooden canopy with tall turned balusters and metal hat pegs. There is an elegant screen, a two-decker pulpit and a fine carved communion rail dating from about 1685. The communion table with its turned legs rests awkwardly on top of the fifteenth-century altar slab; Stuart theology called for a communion table rather than an altar of sacrifice. There is a plain medieval chest in the church; the socket of a preaching cross stands in the churchyard, and a medieval carving of a man's head survives in the porch.

Brougham castle is also worth a visit for it contains a Roman tombstone dating from around 400, built into the ceiling of the third floor of the keep of the medieval castle. It records the death of a soldier, and may indicate that he was a Christian. The inscription runs: 'Titus M ... lived 32 years more or less. M ... his brother set up this inscription.' The Latin phrase *plus minus* ('more or less') is a formula that may have been used by Christians to show that their belief in the resurrection made an exact record of age unimportant; your age at death hardly matters, they felt, when you expect to live for ever. There may therefore have been an early Christian presence in the Roman fort as well as at Brougham Ninekirks.

CALDBECK, Cumbria: St Kentigern's church and well

Caldbeck is situated in the moors 10 miles south-south-west of Carlisle. Here, according to tradition, Kentigern baptized converts at the spring in the river bank. The well is still used for christenings, and in the summer families watch from the medieval packhorse bridge that adjoins the churchyard. The first stone church was built here by the Normans in about 1118. When it was enlarged, the original chancel arch with its fine dog-tooth moulding was moved to its present location in the porch. There used to be a hospice for distressed travellers at Caldbeck.

CASTLE SOWERBY, Cumbria: St Kentigern's church and well

An ancient site dedicated to Kentigern, Castle Sowerby is not on most maps. There is no village here but only a country house. The church was built at a place where Kentigern was said to have baptized converts. The well, now dry, is in the churchyard wall, beside the track that leads to the church and the house. The church with its whitewashed walls is in a beautiful though isolated location, surrounded by farmland and bleak moors. There was originally a small twelfth-century church here, enlarged in the sixteenth century and repaired in the eighteenth. To find Castle Sowerby, leave the M6 at junction 41. Take the B5305 as if for Sebergham. After six miles, turn left for Lamonby. Castle Sowerby is then signed.

CROSTHWAITE, Cumbria: St Mungo's church

According to the twelfth-century monk Jocelyn of Furness, Kentigern came to the head of Derwentwater in about 553 and established a base at Crosthwaite, a mile north-west of Keswick. Jocelyn tells us that Kentigern 'spent some time in a forested area, strengthening the faith of those who lived there. He set up a cross there as a sign of faith, and so the place is named Crosthwaite.'[3] *Thwaite* is Norse for a clearing in a forest. The large church at Crosthwaite dates from 1525. The church is unique in possessing a complete set of consecration crosses: twelve are carved round its inside walls to dedicate the building to God. The church was blessed according to the English rite rather than the Roman rite, and so a further twelve crosses were carved on its outside walls.

DERWENTWATER, Cumbria: Friar's Crag and St Herbert's Isle

A seventh-century hermit named Herbert lived on an island in Derwentwater, which was then a marshy lake. Each year he used to travel 100 miles to Lindisfarne in order to visit Cuthbert. Their final meeting was in Carlisle in 686; both men died on 20 March the following year. Remains of a circular stone building at the centre of St Herbert's Isle may be those of the hermit's cell. Boats sail to the island in the summer, from the landing stage at the northern end of the lake. Contact Keswick Launch, tel. 01768 772263, for information. On the mainland a mile south of Keswick, a track leads to Friar's Crag from the B5289 at the northern end of the lake. From this point, monks set out to visit Herbert's island hermitage.

HEYSHAM, Lancashire: St Patrick's chapel

There is a tradition that when Patrick escaped from Ireland, he landed on the Lancashire coast at Heysham, which overlooks

Morecambe Bay, before travelling north to rejoin his family. It is more likely, however, that monks came here after Patrick's death. No evidence of a monastery has been found on the headland, but carved into the rock at each end of the oratory are sixth-century repositories for bones, six in a row on one side, with others lower down the slope. The cavities are too small for graves. Each has a rim to take a lid, and a socket at its head, into which a cross would have been inserted. In the eighth century a tiny chapel dedicated to Patrick was built on the headland. Others brought their dead for burial in this holy place. The bodies of 90 Vikings and later Christians have been found in and around the chapel, near the shrines of the monks.

The chapel on the headland was decorated with yellow, red, white and green-brown wall plaster. Traces of both paintings and lettering have been found. In the chapel was a ceremonial stone chair or throne. One of its arms has been discovered, shaped like a bird's head, with prominent eyes and a hooked beak; this can be seen in the museum at Lancaster. The stone blocks that form the chapel walls are held together by mortar made with burnt sea shells for lime, poured between the stones while it was still hot. This was a style used by the Romans. The tall, narrow building was extended by the Saxons in the tenth century. Its new doorway was decorated with a ribbed arch.

A stone passage leads downhill from St Patrick's chapel and its graveyard to a flat, sheltered spot where the parish church of St Peter stands. If there was a monastery, it may have been here. The base of an elaborate Anglian cross can be seen in the churchyard; carved on its north face is a roofed structure with windows framing the heads of saints. Anglians settled in this area of Britain in the sixth and seventh centuries. The church was rebuilt in the mid-tenth century as a barn-like building with small stone doorways, two of which survive. A fine Viking hogback tombstone also dates from this time. It is shaped like a feasting-hall, with an animal's head at each end of its gabled roof. Along each side is a procession of creatures and people.

KIRKOSWALD, Cumbria: St Oswald's church
The name of Kirkoswald, six miles north of Penrith, commemorates King Oswald and Bishop Aidan of Lindisfarne. Aidan could not speak English when he arrived in

Northumbria from Iona, so King Oswald accompanied him on his missionary journeys, acting as his interpreter. They travelled great distances together, preaching the gospel. Across the Pennines, 80 miles south-west of Oswald's fortress in Bamburgh, the village of Kirkoswald preserves a tradition that the two men found the people worshipping the spirit of a spring that flows out from the hillside.

Aidan introduced the people to Christianity and built a church over the spring. Its water flows under the nave and emerges outside the west wall of the church. There are foundations of Saxon pillars in the chancel, and, outside the church, a Saxon ribbed gravestone leans against the wall to the left of the porch. The body of the church is Norman; its wooden porch dates from 1523. Since the church is in a hollow, its bell tower was built on the hillside above so that its bells could be heard. The present belfry dates from the nineteenth century.

LINDISFARNE, Northumberland: St Aidan's monastery

In 835 the Irish monk Aidan came from Iona and established a community on Lindisfarne. Little remains of Aidan's monastery, since a large twelfth-century priory was built over it. The name Lindisfarne is Celtic and means 'the land by the Lindis', a small stream, now called the Low, which is visible only at low tide. Until recently, residents and visitors had to walk across the sand to Lindisfarne, like their Celtic predecessors, passing the curlew, redshank, and other wading birds that comb the shallow waters for food. Aidan's monastery probably consisted of small, simple huts housing one or two monks, perhaps a master and a novice. They would be grouped irregularly round the church. This area may have been divided off from the guesthouse and other more public buildings. The whole complex would have been enclosed by a bank and ditch. Aidan's successor, Bishop Finán, built a church in the Irish style, of hewn oak covered with reed thatch.

As in other Celtic monasteries, there were outlying hermitages, and 400 metres south-west of Lindisfarne, St Cuthbert's Isle contains the remains of a seventh-century cell and a later medieval chapel; a tall wooden cross marks the site of its altar. At low tide the island can be reached on foot from Lindisfarne, and Cuthbert used the rocky islet as a place of retreat. Aidan's monastery was destroyed by the Vikings in 793, and the monks left Lindisfarne a generation later, dismantling their wooden church and taking its timbers with them.[4] Close to the present ruined priory, the parish church of St Mary may stand on the site of a second Anglo-Saxon church. The Priory Museum contains a fine collection of early grave slabs and crosses excavated at the site. A guidebook is also available.

MUNGRISDALE, Cumbria: St Mungo's church

The church of Mungrisdale, ten miles west of Penrith, is dedicated to Kentigern under his pet name of Mungo (meaning 'my dear one'). It is uncertain whether the hamlet's name means 'valley of Mungo's pigs' or 'valley of the monks' pigs'.[5] *Gris* is Old Norse for pig and also for wild boar. The present single-chambered church was built in 1750. The porch still retains its original cobbled floor. Inside is a fine three-decker pulpit, dating from 1679. The priest could stand and preach from the upper deck; he and his clerk would sit in the two lower decks. The church also contains a King James Bible dating from 1617 and an early Prayer Book.

PATTERDALE, Cumbria: St Patrick's church and well

Patterdale is at the southern end of Ullswater; its name means 'Patrick's Dale'. The medieval church has been heavily restored. The well is beside the A592, in a stone well house, near the boat landings at Glenridding, a mile north of the church, to the left of the road if one is travelling north. According to legend, Patrick was shipwrecked on Duddon Sands, north of Barrow in Furness, and made his way to Ullswater, where he baptized at the well.

ST BEES, Cumbria: St Bega's priory and cave

The Norman priory of St Bees on the Cumbrian coast was founded by monks from the great Benedictine abbey of St Mary's, York. Norsemen arrived here in the eleventh century and called the settlement *Kirkeby Begoc* ('the village near Bega's church'). The fine west door of St Bees Priory is decorated with chevrons and beak-heads of grotesque birds or beasts; it was built in about 1160. Inside, the nave pillars date from around 1220. There is an early Christian cross in the graveyard, opposite the great west door, and inside is the stump of a fine carved cross dating from the tenth or eleventh century. A bracelet that belonged to Bega, said to have healing properties, was kept at St Bees Priory until the twelfth century. An hour's walk westward around the cliffs to St Bees Head brings one to Smuggler's Cave in Fleswick Bay. According to legend, this is where Bega took shelter after reaching the Cumbrian coast in her flight from an arranged marriage in Ireland.

WOOLSTON, Shropshire: St Winifred's well

The story of the Norman monks who took Winifred's relics from her monastery in the remote Welsh settlement of Gwytherin to Shrewsbury abbey has been reworked by Ellis Peters in the first of her Cadfael Chronicles, entitled *A Morbid Taste for Bones*.

Woolston is a small village four miles south-east of Oswestry, and it has been suggested that Winifred's well commemorates a stage in the progress of her relics from Gwytherin to Shrewsbury. From Woolston, it would have been a day's journey to Shrewsbury. However, the well is likely to be much older. The water flows through stone troughs, to create pools for bathing. The water healed wounds, bruises, and broken bones. People with eye diseases visited a spring lower down the water course.

The site may have been a medieval moot, where people gathered to administer justice; a 'moot point' is a subject requiring judgement at such a site. A courthouse is built over the well, dating from the sixteenth or seventeenth century. It is a charming, half-timbered building in a secluded copse at the end of a leafy lane. In early times, gatherings to enact laws were held at significant sites such as a mound or a group of standing stones, a holy well, or an ancient oak tree. To find the well, coming from Oswestry, turn left into the village and, as the road bends right, walk left down a lane marked 'access to houses only'. At the end of the track, the footpath to the well is through a gate on the right.

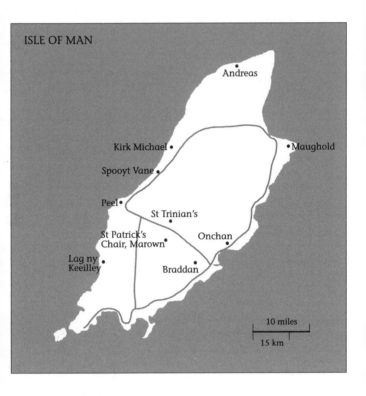

The Isle of Man

THE ISLE OF MAN

ANDREAS PARISH: Kirk Andreas; Knock-y-Dooney

This parish on the north-west coast of the island shows evidence of several early strands of Christianity. Kirk Andreas is built over a *keeill*, or chapel, dedicated to Columba. It may have been founded by monks from his monastery of Iona. A mile away, the *keeill* site of Knock-y-Dooney is one of three whose names incorporate the Manx word *doonee*, meaning 'that pertaining to the Lord'. It is an early term deriving from the Latin *dominica* and was in use only from about 430 to 550. It is likely that its usage spread to Man from Ireland, and that the Manx *doonee* churches were founded by Irish missionaries or emigrants.[6]

Preserved in Andreas church is an early sixth-century pillar stone from Knock-y-Dooney, with an inscription in Irish ogham on one side. The same text is carved in Latin, in rustic Roman capitals, on the broad face of the stone. It reads 'Ammecatus, son of Rocatus, lies here.' These are names of Irish warriors, so the chapel may have been attached to the fort of a local chieftain. The stone resembles those found in north Wales; the *keeill* was perhaps founded by missionaries from the well-established Romano-British Church in the Conwy valley.[7] One of the finest Manx collections of tenth-century Norse cross slabs can also be seen in Kirk Andreas.

BRADDAN PARISH: Old Kirk Braddan

Braddan is just outside Douglas on the A1; its church is dedicated to Brendan. In 1291, Bishop Mark of Galloway held a synod here and enacted 35 canons concerning Church life on Man. Among the carved stones in the church are a Celtic wheel-headed cross slab with a carving that may represent Daniel in the lions' den (no. 72) and Thorliefr Hnakki's pillar cross (no. 135). This is the only Scandinavian pillar with a Celtic cross head. Runes carved up the side read 'Thorliefr Hnakki erected this cross to the memory of Fiacc, his son, brother's son to Hafr.' The dead boy's father and his uncle have Norse names, but Fiacc is a Celtic name. This indicates a mixed-race marriage: presumably Fiacc's mother was a Celt.[8]

GERMAN PARISH: St Patrick's Isle, Peel

St Patrick's Isle is situated halfway along the west coast of Man. Until the eighteenth century, it was accessible only on foot at low tide. There is now a causeway leading to the island, which is dominated by the medieval cathedral of St German and a later castle. The island was inhabited from early times, and a number of large round-houses dating from around 400 BC have been excavated. Later there was a Christian community on St Patrick's Isle. Its first buildings have not survived: they would have been small cells of wattle and daub, with a church of heavier timber and a few more communal buildings. From the seventh century onward there was an extensive cemetery at the southern end of the island, close to where the medieval cathedral now stands.

The ruins of a church, a chapel and a round tower survive from the Celtic monastery, each dating in part from the tenth century. St Patrick's church was constructed of roughly dressed local sandstone. It had *antae*, or side walls projecting beyond the line of the gables; this style of building was common in Ireland. St Patrick's chapel is smaller but of similar construction. An altar slab was found when the two buildings were restored in 1873; it can now be seen in the Manx Museum, Douglas. It is decorated with five small crosses set within a larger one and formed the front panel of a stone altar.

Near St Patrick's church is a squat round tower, 15 metres high. Four windows facing the compass points near the top indicate that this was its original height. It, too, is built of red sandstone; its battlemented parapet was added in about 1600. Lintel graves and crosses dating from the seventh and eighth centuries were found beneath the south transept of St German's cathedral. A lintel grave is one that is closely lined with upright slabs and covered with other stones (lintels) resting on the side slabs. The monastery was ravaged by Viking raiders, and the little island became a base for Norse settlers. They built a fort of timber or pile, which gave Peel its name.

MAROWN PARISH: St Patrick's Chair

Near the centre of the southern half of Man, in the parish of Marown, is St Patrick's Chair. To find it, take the A1 out of Douglas and turn south on the B35. After a mile, a farm track leads east to the site. Walk along this path for about ten minutes, and the monument will now be visible in the middle of a field to your left.

It is thought to be an early Christian preaching station: a site where the gospel was proclaimed before churches were established. Three slabs are set in a cairn of stones: they may originally have formed a pre-Christian dolmen. At some time between 400 and 700, simple crosses were carved on two of the slabs. The site acquired its name much later: dedications on Man are Norse or medieval. However, missionaries may have come to the island from the time of Ninian onward.

MAROWN PARISH: St Trinian's chapel

Trinian is a Manx and Scots Gaelic form of Ninian. Monks from Ninian's monastery of Whithorn in south-west Scotland settled on the Isle of Man, where the ruins of St Trinian's chapel can be seen beside the road from Douglas to Peel, south-east of Greeba. Whithorn was granted land near Greeba in the twelfth century, and the chapel's south door dates from this time. There was an earlier building on the site: a sixth- or seventh-century cross slab survives, while to the right of the altar paving stones form a plain cross within a circle and may mark the site of the founder's shrine.

MAUGHOLD PARISH: St Maughold's monastery, Maughold

Kirk Maughold is on the north-east coast of the island, on a hillside above the sea. The present church dates from the twelfth century, but within the graveyard are the remains of three *keeills*, and the sites of three more, including two beneath the medieval church. Each had a window of red sandstone and was surrounded by a small cemetery. Maughold was the principal monastery on Man. Its first monks appear to have originated from Northumbria and from Galloway in south-west Scotland. The buildings were probably of timber, like those of Northumbrian monasteries. Many of its monuments were carved by itinerant Anglian stonemasons. Iron ore was mined at Maughold, allowing metalworking to take place. By 795 the Vikings had begun to rob exposed places on the coast, and Maughold was an easy target. By about 830, colonists arrived and took possession of the arable land. Without land, the monastery could not continue.

It is considered unlikely that there was a Manx saint named Maughold, but glimpses of the monks who lived at the monastery are afforded by its fine collection of carved stone slabs. The oldest is a memorial to Irneit, a seventh-century monastic bishop. His name is inscribed in a circle surrounding a hexafoil cross. This design, resembling a six-petalled flower, is found in sub-Roman Britain and Gaul, so the stonemason had probably learned his skill abroad. A pair of eighth-century stones coming from the head and foot of a grave commemorate someone named Blakman. His name is Saxon, but the style of the cross is Celtic. It shows how Teutonic settlers spread across northern Britain and adopted Celtic culture.

Another slab is inscribed (in Latin): 'Branhui led off water to this place'. Branhui was a monk with a Welsh name who provided the monastery with its water supply in about 800. Traces of his stone-lined conduit have been found. A ninth-century cross depicts two desert Fathers who inspired Celtic monks: Sts Antony and Paul the Hermit. They sit on solid chairs on either side of a ringed cross, each bearded and dressed in a monk's cowl and hood.

MICHAEL PARISH: Kirk Michael

The parish church of Kirk Michael on the north-west coast contains a fine collection of Norse crosses with Celtic features. A wheel-headed cross slab (no. 101), decorated on each side with interlaced patterns, bears a long inscription carved in Old Norse runes. We learn that it was commissioned by a Celt for his father, who bore a Norse name. Presumably the father, a metalworker, had married a local Celtic woman. The inscription reads 'Melbrigdi, son of Athakan the smith, erected this cross for his soul, [saved from] sin.' The runes continue: 'but Gaut made this and all in Man'. This refers to a Viking immigrant named Gaut who founded a school of sculpture on the island. Gaut signed himself on another grave slab as 'Gaut, son of Bjorn, from Kuli', so he may have come from the Isle of Coll in the Hebrides, where Columba's monks once grew grain to feed the community on Iona.[9]

Gaut's simple, attractive style is evident on other crosses around the island. His claim to have created all the crosses in Man refers to the tenth-century runic crosses in the style of the Norse settlers; there are many earlier Celtic cross slabs on the island. Gaut drew on the Celtic artistic tradition and also used interlacing patterns found on Scandinavian monuments. He probably learned his trade as a sculptor in the north-west of

England, which was colonized by Norsemen from Ireland and the Scottish islands in the early tenth century. The crosses in Kirk Michael show figures from both Norse mythology and the Christian story. A fine decorated cross slab from the late tenth or early eleventh century (no. 129) depicts the crucifixion. Christ on the cross is portrayed as a triumphant warrior, wearing a pleated kilt. In the upper corners of the slab are a cock, symbolizing the resurrection, and a winged angel.

MICHAEL PARISH: Patrick's Chapel, Spooyt Vane

Cabbal Pherick (or 'Patrick's Chapel') is on the west coast. To find it, take the A3 southward from Kirk Michael for one and a quarter miles. To the south-east of the road, a wicket gate leads to Glen Mooar, and a footpath follows a stream. Follow the path for half a mile; the foundations of the *keeill* are now visible on your left inside an enclosing bank.

The chapel was built on a timber frame supported by slate walls; its roof was probably thatched. The altar under the east window was outlined with small stones set on edge and faced with larger stones. A partial reconstruction of the *keeill* can be seen in The House of Manannan at Peel. Outside the enclosure are the foundations of a cell where the priest lived. To the west there is a small well. *Spooyt Vane* is Manx for 'white waterspout', and beyond the *keeill* is the high waterfall that gave the settlement its name. Converts could be baptized beneath its white water

ONCHAN PARISH: Old Kirk Lonan

Lonan Old Church, on the east coast of Man, is dedicated to Adomnán. In Ireland and Scotland his name was shortened to 'Onan', and the name Lonan is a shortened form of 'Keeill Onan'. However, dedications on Man are unlikely to predate the Middle Ages. There are some early grave markers in a shelter in the churchyard, and an impressive Celtic wheel-headed cross stands in its socket stone, probably in its original position. It is decorated entirely with interlacing, knots and plaitwork. It stands 1.5 metres high and measures 1 metre across; it dates from the ninth or tenth century. To find Old Kirk Lonan, take the A2 out of Douglas and turn south at Ballamenaugh. The old church is about a mile from the main road.

PATRICK PARISH: Lag ny Keeilley, 'Hollow of the Chapel'

This site is on the south-west coast of Man. It is in an attractive location, on a cliff overlooking the Irish Sea. The *keeill* can be reached by following the A275 south from Dalby for one and a half miles, until one comes to the Manx National Trust property of Eary Cushlin on the west. The chapel is signed from Eary Cushlin car park. A path leads through beautiful scenery to the site; the walk is about one and a quarter miles. In earlier times, this was the packhorse road to the south of the island. People continued to bring their dead along the track for burial at Lag ny Keeilley until about 1800.

The solitary monk who founded the *keeill* had levelled the enclosure with considerable effort by digging into the hillside and building up a horizontal platform. Within a retaining embankment he constructed his chapel and his cell. The *keeill*, or chapel, is 4 metres long and 2.65 metres wide. Its altar survives; a pear-shaped stone that had been brought up the steep track from the beach formed one of its supporting pillars. Above the altar was a window with a carved sandstone frame. A slab of local slate with a hollow in one corner was probably a cresset, containing oil and a wick for a lamp. Some flat stones survive from the original pavement, as does the stone socket for a door in the west wall. This is a unique feature: there is no sign of a door at other *keeills*.

Nearby are the remains of a rectangular stone dwelling for the priest, with a small garden plot. A piece of a granite quern found near the *keeill* may indicate that the priest baked bread. In Ireland, however, those caught grinding corn on a Sunday brought their quern to the church and smashed it as part of their penance. The same may have been true on Man, since quern fragments are common at *keeill* sites. The burial ground contains stone-lined lintel graves and some simple slate crosses. About 600 white quartz pebbles were found in and near the *keeill*, suggesting that it continued as a place of pilgrimage. People left a white stone at the chapel much as they light candles in churches today, as a form of prayer. Near the end of the packhorse road, almost within site of the keeill, is a well known as *Chibbyr ny Vashtey* in Manx, meaning 'the well of baptism'. It was visited for healing until recent times.[10]

Part Seven
The Saints

ADOMNÁN

The ninth abbot of Iona, Adomnán (624–704) was born in his father's homeland of Donegal and came from the royal family of the northern Uí Néill. He first trained as a monk under Columba's nephew, Ernán. We know little about him until he became abbot of Iona in 679 at the age of 55. In his early years as abbot, a bishop from Gaul named Arculf visited Iona when he was shipwrecked off the British coast on his way home from a pilgrimage to Jerusalem. Adomnán welcomed him and wrote a book about the Holy Places, using information from Arculf and other sources. Adomnán presented a copy of his book to the king of Northumbria. Bede drew upon this guidebook, which became widely used throughout Europe.[1]

In 688 Adomnán went to the monastery of Jarrow in Northumbria, where he spent at least a year and would have met Bede. In the four years after his return to Iona from Northumbria Adomnán worked on his *Life of Columba*. In 692 he went back to Ireland, where he challenged his former friend, King Finnachta, over an annual payment of cattle tribute. Adomnán cursed King Finnachta, who died three years later. As the ruler of Columba's monasteries in northern Ireland, Adomnán returned in 697 to take part in the Synod of Birr. He proposed a law to exempt women, children, and clergy from taking part in warfare; his new law also applied in Scotland. Penalties for transgressing it were to be paid to the Columban monasteries.

Adomnán was responsible for the oversight of all the Columban foundations and travelled extensively. On the Scottish west coast, he is honoured on North Uist in the Outer Hebrides, and he had a chapel on the Isle of Bute, at Kildavanan. Adomnán spent much time among the Picts, east of the Grampian Mountains. He maintained a good relationship with the Pictish royal house, and is commemorated throughout Pictish lands, especially in Aberdeenshire, Banff, and Forfar. Kirk Lonan on the east coast of the Isle of Man is also named after him.

In his old age Adomnán is said to have worked among the Picts in Glen Lyon, one of the highland routes leading east toward Loch Tay. Beside the River Lyon, near the Bridge of Balgie, is Milton Eonan ('mill town of Adomnán'). The church at Innerwick, on the other side of the bridge, contains a bronze bell said to be his. Eight miles to the east, where the valley broadens, the church of Dull is dedicated to him. There was a famous monastery here, possibly founded from Iona; it remained a centre of learning for many centuries.[2] Closer to Innerwick is a small hill named Camusvrachan, traditionally the place where, when plague struck, Adomnán prayed with the people and sent them up to their summer shielings, away from the polluted river.[3] Adomnán returned to Iona, and died shortly after his final visit to Ireland.

AIDAN

Aidan of Lindisfarne (d. 651) was largely responsible for introducing Christianity to Northumbria. Our chief source of information about him is Bede's *Ecclesiastical History of the English People*. Writing in about 731, Bede was able to draw on the knowledge of elderly monks in his community when he describes Aidan's work. Bede tells us how he arrived from Iona at the king's request to convert his subjects: 'When King Oswald asked for a Scottish bishop to preach the gospel to himself and his people, first another man was sent, an austere man who was unsuccessful. The English people ignored him, so he returned home, and reported to the assembled council that he had been unable to do any good among the people to whom he was sent to preach. They were uncivilised, stubborn and barbarous.'[4] The monks gathered on Iona discussed what to do, and an Irishman named Aidan suggested that the previous missionary bishop might have been too severe. The community therefore decided to consecrate Aidan as bishop and sent him to Northumbria instead.

Aidan arrived with twelve companions in 635. Bede describes Aidan with affection and admiration. He did not approve of the Irish bishop's method of calculating Easter, but he praised his love of prayer and study, his gentleness and humility, and his care for the sick and the poor. Bede's unusually lavish words may have been intended as a reproof for the lax bishops of his own time. He relates: 'When [Aidan] arrived, at his request the king gave him the island of Lindisfarne for his bishop's seat. Here the tide ebbs and flows twice a day, so the place is surrounded by the sea and becomes an island. Again twice a day, the shore becomes dry and is joined to the land.... The bishop was not skilled at speaking English, and when he preached the gospel, it was most delightful to see the king himself interpreting God's word to his commanders and ministers, for he had learnt to speak fluent Gaelic during his lengthy exile.'[5] Oswald had spent his youth on Iona, after his uncle had seized the throne in 616. King Oswald lived in a fortress on a rocky outcrop at Bamburgh, fifteen miles south-east of the present town of Berwick-upon-Tweed. From Bamburgh, Aidan's island monastery of Lindisfarne was just visible, six miles up the coast. Oswald ruled for only eight years: at the age of 38 he was killed in battle by the pagan King Penda of Mercia.

Bede tells us how Bishop Aidan lived: he preferred to travel on foot rather than on horseback, to enable him to engage people in conversation. If they were pagan, he taught them about Christianity; if they were believers, he encouraged them.[6] Aidan spent each Lent on the Farne Islands, about two miles offshore, for forty days of solitude. He was on Farne when King Penda ravaged Northumbria and reached the royal stronghold at Bamburgh. His soldiers set fire to the fortress, and Aidan, seeing the flames from his cell on Farne, prayed until the wind changed direction and the flames engulfed Penda's troops, who were forced to retreat. Among Aidan's friends and followers were a number of women, including Oswald's half-sister, Princess Ebbe, who became a nun at the double monastery for both men and women at Coldingham. Another of Aidan's friends was Hilda, who became abbess at Whitby, where her double monastery became a centre of learning and the arts. Aidan became ill and died in his church at Bamburgh. He had been bishop of Northumbria for sixteen years.

ASAPH: see KENTIGERN

BEGA

Bega was a legendary seventh-century Irish nun. St Bees on the Cumbrian coast is named after her. Her cult may have arisen from the bracelet kept at her shrine in St Bees, which was said to have healing properties. Its Old English name, *beag*, may have suggested the saint's name. She may or may not be the nun Begu (d. 660) of Hackness in North Yorkshire who, according to Bede, saw in a vision the death of Hilda, who founded the communities of both Hackness and Whitby. A hymn in a fifteenth-century Book of Hours in the Bodleian Library, Oxford, describes Bega as an Irish chieftain's daughter who vowed chastity. She escaped before an arranged marriage and fled across the sea, landing at St Bees, where she founded a convent.[7] There is a church dedicated to Bega beside Lake Bassenthwaite, at the foot of Skiddaw, and a church and holy well are named after her at Kilbucho in the upper Tweed Valley. She is also honoured at Dunbar on the coast east of Edinburgh. Bega is the subject of the novel *Credo* by Melvyn Bragg, which conveys a lively impression of the society in which the Celtic saints lived and worked.[8]

BEUNO

Beuno is one of the few known Celtic monks who lived and worked in north Wales. His Life survives only in a fourteenth-century translation of a lost Latin original, but some elements in it appear to be genuine. Beuno was born of a noble family in mid-Wales in the second half of the sixth century. He was said to have trained for the priesthood in one of the great monasteries of south Wales, and then returned to his father's territory of Powys, where he was given Berriew as a site for his first monastery. Berriew is beside a tributary of the River Severn, and his Life describes how Beuno remained here for some years until he was frightened by the sight of a Saxon warrior patrolling on the far side of the Severn. In the face of the advancing English, he decided to move to safety and travelled north-west through the Berwyn Mountains into the valley of the River Dee. Here there is a cluster of dedications to him around the village of Gwyddelwern, where he is said to have founded a community.[9]

There is a group of churches and holy wells named after Beuno near the Flint coast. Beuno was said to be the uncle of Winifred, and according to her Life, he obtained land from her parents at Holywell, near the sea, where he also built a church. His Life recounts how he later travelled fifty miles west along the coast to Caernarfon, where he asked the chieftain, Cadwallon, for a site on which to build a church. Cadwallon offered him land that belonged to someone else, after which Beuno cursed him angrily. Cadwallon's cousin, Gwyddaint, then gave him part of his own township of Clynnog, ten miles farther along the coast. Around 616 Beuno established a monastery here, where he spent the last phase of his life. From here Beuno or his followers travelled along the Lleyn peninsula and visited Anglesey, where a number of churches are named after Beuno and his disciples. He is said to have died in Clynnog at the end of Easter week in 642.[10]

BLANE

Blane was a British monk from the kingdom of Strathclyde who lived in the late sixth century. He is said to have been brought up on the Isle of Bute, where his uncle, Catán, established a monastery at Kingarth. Catán sent Blane to Ireland to train as a monk. He later succeeded his uncle as abbot of Kingarth and bishop of the surrounding area. A number of early churches in western Scotland are named after Blane; he established his chief monastery at Dunblane, where his hand bell is preserved in the cathedral.

BRANWALADER: see BREWARD

BRENDAN

Brendan (d. *c.*575) is one of the most popular Irish monks, although we know little about him. His family name, *moccu Altai*, indicates that he belonged to the Alltraige, a tribe who lived in north Kerry. Brendan was said to have been tutored by Bishop Erc of Kerry and to have been one of the 'twelve apostles' who followed the leadership of Finnian of Clonard. He seems to have been one of the many monks who chose the ocean as a focus for their monastic exile. Writing in the seventh century, Adomnán says that Brendan visited Columba on the island of Hinba, off the Scottish west coast.

Brendan established a monastery at Ardfert in his own tribal territory, 3 miles from the Kerry coast. He made his principal foundation at Clonfert on the west bank of the River Shannon in about 550. He established a community at Annaghdown in Galway; an island chapel on Inisglora, off the west coast of County Mayo, is also dedicated to him. Throughout medieval times, Brendan was considered a patron of sailors, and churches in a number of coastal settlements in Ireland and Scotland are named after him.[11] Brandon Mountain at the western end of the Dingle peninsula was the centre of his cult. The mountain became a centre for pilgrimage perhaps as early as the eighth century, and each July pilgrims climb the mountain to visit the shrine at its summit, where there are remains of cells, a chapel and a holy well.

Brendan owed his popularity largely to a medieval monastic

romance, written in about 780, named *The Voyage of St Brendan*. In the story, he chooses fourteen monks from his community at Clonfert and takes them to his native Kerry, to set sail in search of the Promised Land of the Saints.[12] The legend is set in the context of real expeditions beyond the Faeroes to Iceland, where glaciers and volcanoes are described. In the story, Brendan eventually reaches the Promised Land. He returns home with some of its heavenly fruit and precious stones, then dies peacefully among his brother monks.

BREWARD

Little is known about Breward, or Branwalader, a name that means 'raven lord'. He was perhaps a Breton saint, where he is named in a tenth-century litany. The Saxon King Athelstan founded Milton Abbey in Dorset in about 933 in honour of Our Lady, Samson, and Branwalader and gave it the arm of Bishop Branwalader, together with relics of Samson, perhaps obtained from Brittany. Breward's cult was well established in medieval times. He is the patron saint of St Breward in Cornwall, of Broladre and Brelade in Jersey, and perhaps of St Briavels in Gloucestershire.

BRIGIT

Many traditions but few certain facts have come down to us about the life of Brigit. She lived two generations after Patrick and died around 525. She is believed to have been born some 30 miles west of the present city of Dublin, near Kildare. In about 480 or 490 the King of Leinster gave her land at Kildare (meaning 'church of the oak'), where she built a monastery beneath an ancient holy tree, which survived until the tenth century. Brigit had a reputation for generosity, and Kildare came to be known as 'the city of the poor'. An early Irish *Life of Brigit* describes her travelling around the countryside in a chariot. Its driver was a priest who could baptize the people to whom they preached.

Brigit owes her name to Brígh, a Celtic goddess of fire and light, and inherited some of her attributes. When Gerald of Wales visited her monastery in the twelfth century, he saw a fire which her nuns carefully tended. He wrote: 'The fire is surrounded by a circular withy hedge, which men are not allowed to enter.' The communal hearth was a central feature of ancient rural communities, and was held to be holy. In monasteries, the fire lit on Easter night might be kept alive for the following year. Of the many legends about Brigit, one describes how she was called to the bedside of a dying pagan chieftain. As she sat beside him, she picked up some rushes from the floor, weaving them into a cross, and explained the story of the crucifixion to him. Brigit's crosses are still made, although the tradition probably pre-dates Brigit, since their most ancient form has three arms, not four.

In the National Museum, Dublin, there is a shrine made of silver and brass, set with jewels, containing a relic of Brigit's shoe. 'St Brigit's mantle' is found in Belgium, in Bruges cathedral; it is said to have been brought there by the Saxon King Harold of England's sister after the Norman invasion of 1066. It is a small square of red woollen cloth with curly tufts. Such shag-rug mantles were woven in Ireland from Bronze Age times until the sixteenth century.[13] Brigit was invoked for healing and fertility; she protected cattle and blessed their milk. She inherited these powers from the goddess Brígh, whose festival was celebrated on 1 February, at the beginning of springtime. This became Brigit's feast day.

Since Brigit was a popular saint, she has many dedications across the Celtic world, including various Scottish Kilbrides and numerous Welsh Llansanffraids ('church of St Bride'). There are a few foundations connected with her early followers, such as Abernethy in Perthshire, and some early dedications at places where Brígh may once have been revered, such as Chelvey, Brean Down, and Brent Knoll, three sites on or near the Somerset coast.[14]

BRIOC

According to a Breton Life of this monk, written in about the eleventh century, Brioc was of a noble family from Ceredigion. He studied in Paris under Germanus, and returned to Ceredigion to convert his parents and his native people. He built a church and established a community before departing for Brittany, where he founded two monasteries, including Saint-Brieuc, where he became the first bishop. He died in old age, and was buried there. He was patron of Llandyfriog in Ceredigion, of St Breock in Cornwall, and perhaps of St Briavels in Gloucestershire.

BRYCHAN

In Celtic times, Irish families emigrated to south Wales in search of land. In the fifth century, the family of Brychan landed in south-west Wales and travelled east along ancient routes to the hilly region of Brecon, where they settled. The name Brecon is derived from Brychan. We hear about his life in a document possibly dating from early times that tells how his mother, Marcella, returned to Ireland during a severe winter in order to marry an Irish prince. The frost killed many of the warriors who accompanied Marcella, but her father had a fur cloak made for her, and she arrived safely. She gave birth to a son before returning home and named him Brychan, which means 'little badger'.[15]

In time, Brychan became the ruler of Brecon. He was said to have married three times and had many children. Ancient lists record twelve sons and twelve daughters, although different versions include different names. Churches dedicated to Brychan's children are found in Wales, south-east Ireland, Devon, Cornwall, and Brittany. Some of these may date from early times, but Brychan was popular in the Middle Ages, and many more churches were then named after his family. Traditions about Brychan in south-west England are contained in a *Life of Nectan*, written in the twelfth century at Hartland Abbey, close to Barnstaple Bay in north Devon. The Life portrays Nectan as Brychan's eldest son, although Welsh traditions are different.[16]

BRYNACH

According to his Life, Brynach was Brychan's chaplain or 'soul-friend' and married one of his daughters. His chief church is at Nevern, near the north Pembrokeshire coast. Another twelve churches are dedicated to him, situated along the ancient routes from Brecon to Ireland, concentrated at the western end, near the embarkation points for Ireland. His title, *Brynach Wyddel*, means 'Brynach the Irishman'. In later life, Brynach is said to have become a hermit in the mountains above Nevern, from where Ireland can be seen on a clear day.

BUITE

Little is known about Buite mac Brunaigh who founded the monastery of Monasterboice in County Louth, near the east coast of Ireland, in about 500. The name Monasterboice means

'Buite's monastery'. He was described as a bishop, a follower of St Patrick, who healed many people. After his death in about 521, the monastery became a significant centre of learning. Three magnificent high crosses survive at the site, dating from the ninth century.

CADFAN

The twelfth-century *Book of Llandaff* describes a Breton monk named Cadfan, who sailed to mid-Wales in the sixth century with twelve followers and settled beside a spring on the seashore at Tywyn, half way between Barmouth and Aberystwyth. Here they founded a monastery and were joined by many brothers. Twenty miles to the east, Cadfan is honoured at Llangadfan, a small church high above the river Banwy. A number of churches in mid-Wales are named after his followers.[17] Cadfan is said to have established a monastery on Bardsey Island, beyond the tip of the Lleyn peninsula.

CADOC

Cadoc was a leading figure among the monks of south Wales in the early sixth century. The two earliest biographies of him, written 500 years after his death, are unreliable collections of legends. We are told that Cadoc was of noble birth: his father, to whom Newport Cathedral is dedicated, was a prince of Gwent in south-east Wales. Cadoc's mother, Gwladys, was said to be a daughter of Brychan, the ruler of Brecon, which lies to the north-east of Gwent. Cadoc worked among the descendants of Romano-British Christians. The twelfth-century *Life of Cadoc* describes him as coming from an imperial Roman family, loving the works of Virgil, and regretting that, as a Christian, he would be unable to meet the pagan poet in heaven!

There is a cluster of churches dedicated to Cadoc in the upper Usk Valley, centred on Llangattock-nigh-Usk ('church of Cadoc near the Usk') in his father's territory, five miles north-west of Abergavenny. Caerleon's church is also named after Cadoc. As a youth, Cadoc is said to have studied at Caerwent, nine miles east of Caerleon, in a monastery founded by an Irish monk named Tathan. Cadoc later established a monastery of his own at Llancarfan, four miles north-west of Barry, and a group of monks from Caerwent was said to have joined him. According to his twelfth-century *Life*, Cadoc was martyred in the late sixth century. While he was celebrating the Eucharist in his old age, in his monastery at Llancarfan, a Saxon warrior entered the church on horseback and pierced him with a lance.

CATÁN

A sixth-century Irish monk who migrated to the Clyde area, Catán founded a monastery on the Isle of Bute. A number of churches in the Western Isles are named after him, and he is honoured at Ardchattan on the shore of Lake Etive. Catán is said eventually to have returned to Ireland, where he died and was buried.

CEDD

The short-lived Anglo-Celtic Church of the East Saxons was established by Cedd (d. 664). Bede, our chief source of information about Cedd, tells us that he came from an Anglian family who took their four sons to Lindisfarne to be educated.[18] They became monks under Aidan, who sent them to Ireland for further training. Two became priests and, at the request of Peada, King of Mercia, the other two, Cedd and Chad, came south to be monk-bishops. In 653 Cedd began to preach in Mercia, and then continued to Essex, where Sigbert, king of the West Saxons, had recently become Christian. Cedd built churches including those at Tilbury and at Bradwell-on-Sea. Bede describes him 'ordaining priests and deacons to assist him in the work of faith, and the ministry of baptizing.... Gathering a flock of servants of Christ, he taught them to observe the discipline of regular life, as far as those rude people were then capable.'[19]

On one of Cedd's visits to Northumbria in 658, the king offered him land for a monastery. Bede tells us that the bishop 'chose himself a place to build a monastery among remote and craggy mountains, which looked more like hiding places for robbers and lairs for wild animals than places fit for people to live in.'[20] The site selected by Cedd was Lastingham, eighteen miles west of present-day Scarborough. He prayed and fasted there for the forty days of Lent, before beginning to build. On another visit to the north, Cedd acted as interpreter at the Council of Whitby. Bede informs us that although Cedd followed Celtic customs rather than those of Rome, 'he was in that council a most careful interpreter for both parties.'[21] After the synod, Cedd introduced Roman customs in his diocese. He died of the plague at Lastingham soon afterwards. When his people at Bradwell in Essex heard of this, thirty of them travelled up the coast to pay their respects. All but one, a boy, died of the plague like Cedd.[22]

CIARÁN OF CLONMACNOISE

A man of great promise who died young, Ciarán was described by his medieval biographers as the son of an Ulsterman who had settled in Connacht. They record that, unlike many Irish abbots, Ciarán was not of noble birth. They indicate that he was a holy man by stating that, like Jesus, Ciarán was a carpenter's son and died at the age of 33. He was said to have studied under Finnian of Clonard, with Enda on the Aran Islands, and later still with Senan on Scattery Island in the mouth of the Shannon. Ciarán founded a community on an island in Lough Ree, and later continued downstream along the Shannon, settling at Clonmacnoise. Annals compiled at Clonmacnoise record that this took place in the 540s. The rich pasture land was given to Ciarán by Diarmaid Mac Cerbhaill of the royal house of Uí Néill. Diarmaid helped to build the first wooden church with his own hands and became high king soon afterwards. Within a year Ciarán had died of the Yellow Plague, which swept through Ireland and decimated many communities.

Some of the finest scholars of Ireland and Europe studied at Clonmacnoise, including Alcuin, bishop of Tours. The monastery was in a central position and came to rival Armagh in importance. It became the burial place of the kings of Tara and Connaght. The Clonmacnoise crosier, now in the National Museum, Dublin, is believed to have belonged to Ciarán. The ornate metalwork shrine of the *Stowe Missal* (c.1030) bears an inscription stating that it was crafted by a monk of Clonmacnoise. Some secular texts written by the monks have also survived, including *The Book of the Dun Cow*, which contains the earliest known version of *The Cattle Raid of Cooley* (or *Táin Bó Cuailnge*), a popular Irish saga.[23]

CIARÁN OF SAIGHIR

Ciarán was one of the early monks who worked in south-east Ireland before the arrival of St Patrick. Little is known about him. He was born on or near Clear Island, off the south-western tip of County Cork, where he is said to have become a hermit, after being baptized and ordained abroad. He later built a large monastery at Saighir, which is now known as Seirkieran, in County Offaly. Here, the kings of Ossory, his family tribe, were buried. The monastery became the seat of the bishops of Ossory. Ciarán is a much-loved local saint and on his feast day, 5 March, pilgrims flock to Seirkieran. In medieval times, Piran of Cornwall was wrongly identified with Ciarán.

CLETHER

Listed as one of the sons of Brychan in the twelfth-century *Life of Nectan* written at Hartland abbey, Clether is also mentioned in Welsh traditions. Brychan had a chaplain or 'soul-friend' named Brynach, and a twelfth-century *Life of Brynach* describes a chieftain in Pembrokeshire named Clether, who had twenty sons and offered them to Brynach as servants. We are told that the 'righteous old man' then went to Cornwall, where he served God until his death.[24] St Clether, on the edge of Bodmin Moor in Cornwall, is a village where in medieval times pilgrims visited the hermit's remote chapel and well, and they still do so today.

COLMÁN OF KILMACDUAGH

Colmán is the Gaelic for 'little dove', and there were some three hundred Celtic saints named Colmán.[25] The popularity of this name among Irish monks was a standing joke. In one saint's Life, a group of monks were working beside a stream when their leader shouted, 'Colmán, get into the water!' and twelve men jumped in. Colmán of Kilmacduagh (d. *c.*632) was born in the mid-sixth century. He became a monk on Aran Island, off Ireland's north-west coast, and then returned to the mainland, where he settled in the Burren, County Clare. He lived here with a disciple on an austere diet of vegetables and water. Colmán later founded the monastery of Kilmacduagh and was consecrated as a bishop. Part of his crozier is preserved in the National Museum of Ireland, Dublin.

COLUMBA

Perhaps the most outstanding of the Celtic monks, Columba (521–97) was a warrior and politician, a scholar, priest, and poet who played an important role in both Irish and Scottish history. Columba, whose name means 'dove', was born into the royal family of the Northern Uí Néill at Gartan in Donegal and studied under a Christian bard in his mother's country of Leinster. He became a monk at an early age and was ordained deacon in the monastery of Finnian at Moville. Later he was ordained priest, and in about 556 he founded his first monastery, at Derry in his family's territory, on land given to him by his tribe. He established various other communities, including that of Durrow, in central Ireland. Irish accounts of Columba relate how on a visit to his former abbot, Finnian of Moville, Columba borrowed a book from the library and secretly copied it at night. He was discovered when he had almost finished, and Finnian demanded the copy. This first recorded breach of copyright was brought to trial before the High King, who ruled in Finnian's favour.

Columba sailed to Scotland as a 'pilgrim for Christ'. As a successful warrior-prince, politician, and abbot, Columba may also have been invited by his relative Conall, the new king of Dalriada (Argyll), to help him repel the Picts.[26] Columba settled on the isle of Iona, to the west of the larger island of Mull. We know a considerable amount about life in his monastery, thanks to his biographer, Adomnán, who was abbot of Iona only a century later. Columba acquired neighbouring islands to provide necessary resources for the monastery. The monks grew grain on the islands of Coll and Tiree ('Barley Island'). His uncle, Ernán, was prior of a community on the island of Jura to the south-east, where his mother, Eithne, is also said to have established a convent.[27]

Columba lived on Iona for 35 years. He returned to Ireland in 575 after an absence of twelve years, to attend an assembly of the Uí Néill clan at Druimm-Cete in Derry, as adviser to Áedán, the new king of Dalriada. The assembly agreed to Dalriada's independence from Ireland. The standing of the Irish bards was also discussed, and Columba argued in their favour. Columba returned to Ireland ten years later to visit his own monastery at Durrow and that of Ciarán at Clonmacnoise. He died on Whitsun Eve in his monastery on Iona.

From Columba's time onward, Iona was considered to be the centre of Celtic learning. Irish monks came to Iona to study and pray, as did Irish-trained monks from across Europe. Meanwhile brothers from Iona played a leading part in the spread of Christianity among the Picts of eastern Scotland and the Anglo-Saxons of Northumbria. The Columban monastery of Lindisfarne was founded by Aidan, a monk from Iona, and these two communities became focal points of the Columban family, its cultural traditions, and its manuscript art.

COLUMBANUS

Columbanus (c.540–615) was the most influential of the Irish missionaries to Europe. He was born in Leinster, probably of a noble family, and was well educated. He was a monk in Congal's monastery of Bangor at the head of Belfast Lough in north-east Ireland until he was about fifty, when he sailed to Gaul with twelve companions. He landed in Burgundy, where the king gave him a ruined Roman fort for a monastery at Annegray in the Vosges mountains. The community grew, and Columbanus then established Fontaines and Luxeuil, which became one of the leading monasteries in Europe, sending monks as far as Bavaria.

His monks followed Celtic customs and calculated the date of Easter according to the Celtic calender. A lengthy letter to Pope Gregory the Great survives, in which Columbanus explains his position. The Roman bishops of Gaul summoned Columbanus to a council, where he defended his views. He also challenged the royal family by refusing to bless the illegitimate sons of the new king, and in 610, together with his monks, he was taken under armed escort to Nantes, to be deported back to Ireland. While waiting to set sail, he wrote a touching letter to the new monks, urging them to make foundations, encouraging their new abbot, and telling them of his sorrow at leaving them.

A storm prevented the ship from setting out, so Columbanus re-crossed France and, with some of his monks from Luxeuil, rowed up the Rhine, hoping to settle beside Lake Constance, but he encountered opposition and decided to cross the Alps into Italy. His companion Gall (d. c.630), who had come from Bangor with him, remained in Switzerland, living as a hermit. A century later a community was established on the site of Gall's hermitage, and the town of St Gall grew around it. In around 613 Columbanus settled at Bobbio in northern Italy, where he and his followers built a monastery on the site of a ruined church. He died two years later; he was buried in Bobbio, while his pastoral staff was taken back across the Alps to his friend Gall in Switzerland. Because of his example, his inspiration, and his pioneering achievements Columbanus is considered to be the greatest of Ireland's missionaries to Europe. The chapel of the Saxon palace at Cheddar in Somerset is dedicated to him.

CONSTANTINE

There are traditions about a Constantine who became a holy man in Brittany, Scotland, Wales, and Cornwall, but they may not all refer to the same person. In the sixth century, Gildas censured Constantine, King of Dumnonia, for adultery and the murder of two princes, but promised God's forgiveness if he repented. Later writers went further, and described Constantine's conversion.[28] Two places are named after Constantine in Cornwall: one near Padstow, whose holy well was visited as late as the eighteenth century, and the other on the banks of the River Helford in south-west Cornwall. The church at Govan, now part of Glasgow, is also dedicated to a chieftain named Constantine who became a monk.

CORENTIN

An important Breton saint, Corentin is first mentioned in a late ninth-century *Life of Winwaloe* written by Abbot Wrdisten of Landévennec. Because of his holiness, local people chose him to be first bishop of the Breton diocese of Cornouaille. He was consecrated by Martin of Tours. Quimper cathedral and five other Breton churches are dedicated to him. The Cornish village of Cury, on the Lizard, is named after him, and there is a medieval painting of him dressed as a bishop with a mitre, a staff, and a fish, in Breage church, of which Cury was a dependency. Corentin carries a fish because his thirteenth-century Breton Life describes him as a hermit who took a slice of the same fish each day for his meal.

CUBERT: see GWBERT

CWYFAN

The medieval *Life of Beuno* describes him gathering a band of followers, one of whom was Cwyfan. Of the four settlements dedicated to Cwyfan, one is a chapel on a tidal islet off the Anglesey coast at Llangwyfan near Aberffraw. Another is at Tudweiliog on the Lleyn peninsula, where pilgrims visited his holy well in order to be cured of sore eyes, ague and warts. Cwyfan is also honoured at Dyserth, south-east of Rhyl, near the north Welsh coast.

CYBI

The earliest surviving Life of Cybi, dating from around 1200, states that he was born in Cornwall, the son of a military leader. Two churches in Cornwall are dedicated to him. One is at Tregony on the south coast: this was formerly a port in the tidal estuary of the River Fal. Cybi's other Cornish church is at Duloe, near Looe, north-east of Tregony. It is possible that Cybi travelled from Cornwall to Wales: here he has dedications at Llangibby-on-Usk north-east of Newport, at Llangybi north-east of Lampeter in Ceredigion, where a healing well is named after him, and at Llangybi at the neck of the Lleyn peninsula, where a remarkable early medieval well house survives. According to his Life, Cybi later established a monastery on the island of Anglesey at Caergybi (Holyhead), where he subsequently died.

CYNGAR

Congresbury in Somerset is named after this saint, who may have been a missionary from Wales. Congresbury is first mentioned in Asser's *Life of Alfred* as a derelict Celtic monastery that Alfred assigned to Asser, bishop of Crediton. Cyngar's shrine in Congresbury church was a centre of pilgrimage throughout medieval times. Eleventh- and fourteenth-century pilgrim guides describe Cyngar's body enshrined in the church. The improbable *Life of Cyngar* tells of a dream in which a wild boar shows Cyngar where he should live. On waking, he sees a boar in a reed bed and builds an oratory on the site. A wild boar features in a number of Celtic saints' Lives, such as those of Cadoc and Ciarán of Saighir: often a white sow indicates where the monk's chief monastery should be built. Swineherds lived on the edge of settlements, where a monk could combine solitude with accessibility to local people. Medieval Christians familiar with the classics would recall that a huge white sow showed Aeneas where the great city of Alba Longa, the precursor of Rome, was to be founded.

DAVID

The patron saint of Wales, David (d. *c.*589) lived and worked in what is now Pembrokeshire. Most of our knowledge about him comes from a *Life of David* written in about 1095 by a Norman cleric named Rhigyfarch, whose father had been bishop of St David's for ten years. According to his Life, David's father was Sant, King of Ceredigion, and his mother was named Non. David rose to a position of leadership at the Synod of Brefi (c.545). He wore rough clothes and carried a large branch rather than a crozier. He apparently went about bareheaded and barefoot, carrying a bell which he named *bangu*, or 'dear, loud one'.

David established a monastery at what is now St David's. Rhigyfarch relates how the monks grew their own food, working hard with mattocks, hoes, and axes. They ploughed the fields themselves instead of using oxen. The brothers ate frugally; according to the ninth-century *Life of Paul Aurelian*, David himself lived on bread, vegetables, and water. There was little emphasis on study, in contrast to the value placed on learning in the monasteries of south-east Wales. David's early followers may have worked in Cornwall and Brittany. Nine churches in Cornwall were named after him.

DÉCLÁN

Déclán was one of the monks who worked in south-east Ireland in the early fifth century before the arrival of Patrick. His Life relates that he came from the royal house of the Déisi, a tribe who had been expelled from Tara in Meath. Déclán was born in Lismore and established a monastery twenty miles farther south, on the coast at Ardmore, in about 416. According to his twelfth-century Life, the area was mainly pagan at Déclán's birth, but a priest named Colmán came to his home, introduced his parents to Christianity, and baptized Déclán. He went abroad to study and returned with his monk's bell and staff. He preached, baptized, and built churches among the Déisi. When he went further afield and preached to King Aongus of Cashel, the king refused baptism, since the clan of Aongus were not on good terms with the Déisi.

Déclán founded a monastery at Ardmore; a mile away, around the headland, is Déclán's 'Desert' or hermitage, where he went to pray and where he retired before his death. His Life describes how, when death approached, Déclán returned from the hermitage to his monastery, 'for at that time he lived in a narrow place beside the sea, where a shining stream flows down from the hillside above. It is surrounded by bushes and trees and is called Déclán's Desert. The city is a mile away, and Déclán came here to avoid being disturbed, in order to fast and pray. He was carried back to his town'.[29] Déclán is one of Ireland's most popular local saints.

DECUMAN

The patron saint of St Decumans outside Watchet on the north Somerset coast, Decuman may have been a Welsh monk. His name suggests that he was perhaps a Romanized Briton (*Decumanus* is Latin for 'tenth'). He is patron of Roscrowther parish (or Llanddegyman) in south Pembrokeshire, where his monastery is named in the *Laws of Howel the Good* as one of the 'seven bishop houses in Dyved', alongside St David's, Llandeilo, and others. Decuman's fifteenth-century Life was probably written at Wells cathedral, to which St Decumans belonged. It relates that he lived as a hermit near Dunster in north Somerset and was murdered one day while at prayer. Like St Nectan and others, he then carried his head to a nearby well. In Celtic thought the head, rather than the heart, was regarded as the seat of life. These stories were told to demonstrate the saints' power over death. Decuman also has dedications in Cornwall.

DEINIOL

The sixth-century Welsh monk-bishop Deiniol, or Daniel in English, was said to be a descendant of a northern British chieftain. His father, Dunawd, established a great monastery at Bangor-is-y-Coed beside the river Dee, four miles south-east of Wrexham. Deiniol spent time here as a monk, and a number of churches in the surrounding area are dedicated to him. Deiniol left his father's community to establish one of his own. He travelled west through the mountains and marked out a new site by driving posts into the ground and weaving branches between them. The noun *bangor* means 'the binding part of a wattle fence', and the monastery of Bangor beside the Menai Strait took its name from its surrounding palisade, as did his father's foundation.

DERFEL

A sixth-century missionary, possibly of Breton origin, Derfel Gadarn ('the Mighty') was said to have been a soldier before becoming a hermit at Llandderfel in mid-Wales. He was known for his skill in curing sick animals, and after his death pilgrims came to Llandderfel with their animals, to pray for a blessing from Derfel.

DUBRICIUS (DYFRIG)

An important Romano-British monk-bishop, Dubricius (d. *c*.550) has a number of dedications in Hereford and Gwent. His mother was a chieftain's daughter from the small territory of Erging in Herefordshire. He was said to have been born at Madley, near Hereford. His chief monastery was at Hentland, near Ross-on-Wye. The seventh-century *Life of Samson* presents Dubricius as a prominent figure among the Christians of south Wales. It relates that Dubricius appointed Samson abbot of the community on Caldey Island, a daughter house of the famous monastery at Llanilltud Fawr (Llantwit Major). His consecration as a bishop is described, as is his ordination of Samson as a deacon. Dubricius is said to have retired to Bardsey Island in old age and to have died there. His cult was taken farther afield: the church of Porlock on the north Somerset coast is dedicated to him.

EILIAN

Eilian was a monk from Anglesey who was said to have cured Maelgwyn Gwynedd's father, Cadwallon, of blindness. In return for being cured, Cadwallon gave Eilian a grant of land to build a church. According to the story, Cadwallon gave him as much as his tame doe could cross in a day, but a rich person's greyhound killed the doe and was cursed by Eilian. Until the mid-nineteenth century, pilgrims came from all parts of north Wales to Eilian's well for a blessing on cattle and corn and for the cure of ague, fits, scrofula, and other diseases. Their offerings, which were placed in a chest in the church, amounted to a very large sum. Eilian's well was also visited in order to curse enemies.[30]

ENDELLION

We first hear of Endellion, described as one of the twelve daughters of Brychan, in the twelfth-century *Life of Nectan,* written at Hartland Abbey in north Devon. The church of St Endellion is near the north Cornish coast. In the early seventeenth century the antiquarian Nicholas Roscarrock, who lived in the parish, believed that Endellion lived at Trentinny, a farm half a mile south of the church. The medieval tomb thought to have been her shrine survives in the church. Two nearby holy wells are also named after her.

ERC

Said to have been baptized by Patrick, Erc became bishop of Slane, near the ancient stronghold of Tara. He is mentioned in ninth-century Irish martyrologies. A saying attributed to Patrick runs:

> Bishop Erc,
> Whatever he judged was rightly judged:
> Whosoever gives a just judgement
> Shall receive the blessing of Bishop Erc.

EUNY

A widely revered Cornish saint venerated in at least five places in western Cornwall, Euny's earliest cult centre was probably Lelant, where he was said to be buried. He is also linked with Crowan, Merther Euny, Redruth, and Chapel Euny in Sancreed. He may have been a British monk, although in 1478 William of Worcester heard that he was an Irishman, the brother of Erth and Ia. In the sixteenth century boys were named Euny, particularly in Redruth.[31]

FÉCHÍN

A holy man from Sligo who travelled widely in Ireland, Féchín's first foundation was at Fore in Westmeath. He later established other communities including one at Cong, beside Lough Corrib, from which a fine cross survives. Carved in about 1123, the processional cross is made of oak decorated with metal filigree and was designed to enclose a relic of the cross of Christ at its centre. The earliest manuscript of Féchín's Life comes from his island settlement of Ard Oilean, off the coast of Connemara. There are monastic ruins at most of Féchín's foundations, a few dating from his lifetime. Féchín died of the Yellow Plague in the 660s. His followers took his cult to Scotland, where the monastery of St Vigeans at Arbroath near the Fife coast is named after him.

FERGUS

The *Aberdeen Breviary* tells us that Fergus was an Irish bishop who worked as a missionary in northern and eastern Scotland, where he has many dedications. Fergus may be the *Fergustus episcopus Scotiae Pictus* ('Fergus the Pict, bishop of Scotland') recorded as taking part in the Council of Rome in 721. This council condemned irregular marriages of various kinds, sorcerers, and clerics who grew their hair long in the Celtic tradition. Fergus died at Glamis in Angus. His relics were kept at Glamis for 700 years until an abbot of Scone removed them to his own church to inter them in a more splendid marble tomb. His arm was enshrined in Aberdeen.

FILLAN

The son of a Munster chieftain, Fillan became a monk and went to Scotland in the eighth century with his mother Kentigerna and her brother Comgan, who had been driven out of Leinster by a coalition of neighbouring rulers. The family settled on the Scottish west coast, where there are a number of dedications to Comgan and Kentigerna. Fillan travelled eastward and spent some time as a hermit in a cave at Pittenweem in Fife, before becoming abbot of a nearby monastery. Fillan is said to have retired to Glen Dochart, building a mill at Killin, at the head of Loch Tay. To the west of Glen Dochart, people bathed in Fillan's Pool, a shallow stretch of the River Dochart at Auchtertyre, as a cure for madness. Fillan died and was buried nearby. His hand bell survives, and his staff, encased in a delicate medieval reliquary, is now in the Royal Museum of Scotland, Edinburgh.

FINBARR

The patron of Cork, Finbarr lived in the second half of the sixth century. His name means 'white crown' or 'white head'. His father was said to be a smith who married a slave girl. Finbarr studied under Bishop MacCuirp at Macroom and later became a hermit at Gougane Barra. He established his chief monastery and school at Cork, at the mouth of the River Lee, which rises in Gougane Barra lake. He attracted followers, and Etargabail on the east bank of the lake became a famous school that drew students from southern Ireland. Gougane Barra was the centre of Finbarr's cult in earlier times, as it is today. The town of Cork grew around the monastery Finbarr founded there. He was consecrated a bishop in about 600 and buried in Cork. Finbarr probably remained in southern Ireland, but his followers travelled widely. Barra in the Scottish Hebrides is named after him.

FINNIAN OF CLONARD

The large and famous monastery of Clonard, 34 miles west of Dublin, was founded by Finnian (d. *c*.549). His tenth-century Life, preserved in the *Book of Lismore*, relates that he was born and educated in County Carlow in south-east Ireland, where he made his first three foundations. Finnian then travelled to south Wales, where he spent time in the great Welsh monasteries. He returned to Ireland and established two more communities before settling at Clonard in County Meath. Finnian's Life claims that three thousand monks studied at Clonard. So great was Finnian's reputation that he was nicknamed 'Teacher of the saints of Ireland'. When men left Clonard they took with them a Gospel book, a crozier, or a reliquary as they set out to establish their own communities.

Twelve leading Irish monks were known as Finnian's 'Twelve Apostles'. Among them were Ciarán of Clonmacnoise, Kevin of Glendalough, Brendan, and Columba. Several of Finnian's 'apostles' had died before his lifetime, or had not yet been born, but the list indicates Clonard's considerable influence. Finnian was a correspondent of the British monk Gildas. The *Penitential of Finnian* was probably written at Clonard. This is a manual of punishments for crimes, based partly on Irish and Welsh sources, and also on the writings of Jerome and Cassian. Much of it, however, is original. It is the oldest of the Irish Penitentials, which made an important contribution to the Church's understanding of pastoral care.[32] Like many other Irish monks, Finnian died of the plague.

GUNWALLOE; GUENOLÉ: see WINWALOE

GWBERT

A Welsh monk who gave his name to Gwbert-on-Sea, two miles north of Ceredigion, this may be the man after whom the Cornish village of Cubert is named. Other monks from Ceredigion are commemorated in nearby Cornish settlements. A farm named Lanlovey on land adjoining Cubert church suggests that this was a Celtic foundation,[33] since the prefix *lan* is the Celtic word for a church site. A healing well inside a cave in nearby Holywell Bay is named after Cubert. In earlier times, pilgrims flocked to the well, whose fresh water was good for bowel conditions and cured children's diseases. Mothers brought sick or deformed children here, and cripples left their crutches in the cave.[34]

HELEN (ELEN LUYDDOG)

The Celtic princess Helen was the wife of Magnus Maximus, the self-styled emperor of Britain, Gaul, and Spain from 383 to 388. She accompanied her husband to Europe, spending some time with him at Trier, before his death in Aquileia. Here she came to know Martin of Tours (c.316–97), a bishop who greatly influenced the development of monastic life in the West. She returned to Britain after her husband's defeat and death, with her sons, Publicus and Constantine (or Peblig and Cystennin in Welsh). Churches are dedicated to each of them in north and south Wales.

Helen is thought to be responsible for a network of ancient trackways near the Welsh coast, called Sarn Helen; in places they can still be seen. In *The Dream of Maxen Wledig*, a story chanted by medieval Welsh bards, Helen orders the roads to be constructed to improve travel between fortresses for the royal entourage: 'One day the emperor (Magnus Maximus) went to hunt at Carmarthen … and he built a castle there, with very many soldiers. Then Helen decided to have roads built between the castles throughout Britain. That is why they are called Helen Luyddoc's roads, because she was British-born, and Britons made these great roads only for her.'[35]

IA

One of Cornwall's female saints, Ia is the patron saint of St Ives on the north Cornish coast. The earliest traditions about Ia are found in the *Life of Gwinear,* written by the Breton cleric Anselm in about 1300. Here we read that Hya, a highborn Irish nun, arrived too late at the Irish coast to accompany Gwinear and his companions to Cornwall, but a leaf enlarged itself to the size of a boat and carried her there. From a cliff top, a curragh resembles a curled leaf. Ia's tomb was in St Ives church, and her holy well is in a stone building outside the lower wall of the cemetery. Other Cornish chapels and wells are named after her. In the region of Finistère in western Brittany is the settlement of Plouyé (meaning 'place of Ia'). This is a large and possibly early parish, suggesting that her cult may have originated in Brittany.

ILLTUD

The seventh-century *Life of Samson* tells us that Illtud (c.425–505) was a Breton soldier of fortune who came to Wales to fight under a Glamorgan chieftain. Dissatisfied with a soldier's life, he became a monk, and his wife became a nun. Illtud was ordained a priest by Germanus, bishop of Auxerre in about 445, and five years later he established a monastery at Llanilltud Fawr, meaning 'Illtud's great church' (in English, Llantwit Major), on the south coast of Wales. Illtud may have lived here first as a hermit before he attracted followers and built a church with a school and a monastery. Dubricius prepared Illtud as a monk and marked out the monastic enclosure. The author of Samson's *Life* describes how young Samson was taken by his parents to Illtud's famous school. He explains that Illtud combined Christian, classical, and Druidic learning: he was the most learned of all Britons in scripture and philosophy, poetry and rhetoric, grammar and arithmetic. He was of Druid descent, most wise, and able to foretell the future. The writer adds a personal comment: 'I have been in his magnificent monastery.'

Illtud's monastery was one of the most influential of its time. Famous monks and scholars studied there, including Samson, Gildas, and Paul Aurelian. Illtud is said to have drained land for cultivation and introduced an improved form of plough. He sailed back to Brittany with some shiploads of corn to relieve a famine. There are seven dedications to Illtud in Brittany. Monks set out from Llanilltud Fawr to preach: there are fourteen dedications to Illtud in south-east Wales. There is one in the north, on the coast two miles north-west of Dolgellau. It is named Llanelltyd, using the northern, Brittonic, spelling of his name, instead of the usual southern, Gaelic form.

INDRACT

Possibly a mid-ninth-century abbot of Iona or Kells, Indract is described by the Irish *Martyrology of Tallaght* (*c*.800) as a martyr for the faith at Glastonbury. According to his early twelfth-century Life, Indract was the son of an Irish prince. When he was a deacon he visited Rome with twelve companions. On the way home they stopped at Glastonbury, bringing with them sacks of celery seed. They stayed for the night near Shapwick. King Ine of Wessex (688–726) was at South Petherton with his entourage, and one of his thegns murdered Indract and his companions, thinking their sacks contained gold. Indract was buried at Shapwick, in the mother church of the area. The martyr's relics were taken by King Ine to Glastonbury Abbey, where they were buried beside the high altar of the old church, which was destroyed by fire in 1184. The author of Indract's Life says he has taken the story from an old English source. A holy well is dedicated to Indract in St Dominick parish in Cornwall, near Halton Quay, above the river Tamar.

JULIOT

Juliot was a woman saint with three dedications on the north Cornish coast. The name Juliot is a diminutive form of Juliana. The twelfth-century *Life of Nectan* from Hartland Abbey lists Juliana as one of the twelve daughters of Brychan, and the church on the rocky fortress on Tintagel may be dedicated to this person. She is also conflated with Julitta, who was supposedly martyred in Tarsus around 304 together with her son Cyricus. The mother and child have three dedications in Cornwall: the child martyr Cyricus was a patron of children, and there are further sites honouring the mother and child in Devon and Somerset.

KENTIGERN

A Briton who became bishop of Glasgow in the sixth century, Kentigern's name means 'chief prince'. We know little about him, but we do know that he existed, since his name appears in early texts. In the twelfth century a Cumbrian monk named Jocelyn, from Furness Abbey, wrote his Life. He relates that Kentigern was the illegitimate son of a British princess. Her angry father set her adrift in a coracle, and she floated across the Firth of Forth, landing on a beach at Culross on the Fife coast. Here, she lit a fire and gave birth to her son.[36] There was an early monastery at Culross, where Kentigern was said to have trained as a monk.

It appears that when an anti-Christian chieftain came to power, Kentigern fled south, first to Cumbria and then to Wales. Jocelyn describes Kentigern arriving at Carlisle and proceeding to Crosthwaite. A number of other churches in Cumbria are dedicated to Kentigern, some using his pet-name, Mungo (meaning 'my dear one'). Jocelyn recounts how Kentigern arrived in Wales and eventually gained permission from Maelgwyn Gwynedd to build a monastery at a site now named St Asaph. A wild white boar showed Kentigern where he should build his church, a feature in the stories of other Celtic saints, such as Ciarán of Saighir and Cyngar. Kentigern's ablest student was said to have been Asaph, the grandson of Pabo Post Pryden, king of north Britain. According to Jocelyn, when the political scene shifted in Strathclyde, Kentigern left Asaph in charge of his Welsh community, and returned to Glasgow with a large group of monks.[37] Kentigern is said to have died in his monastery, which stood on the site of Glasgow cathedral.

KESSÓG

One of the early Irish monks who settled in Strathclyde, Kessóg (d. *c.*520) was born at Cashel in southern Ireland, of the royal family of Munster. He travelled to Scotland, where he became a monk and, later, bishop of the ancient earldom of Lennox. Kessóg built a monastery on a small island in Loch Lomond named Inchtavannach. A church on the mainland a mile to the north-west, beside Luss Water, is also dedicated to Kessóg. He was known as a zealous preacher and was said to heal the sick with a herb named *lus* in Gaelic (similar to *fleur-de-lys* in French), which may be the yellow flag that grows near the mouth of Luss Water. Kessóg has other dedications in the region. At Callander there is a small hill known in Gaelic as *Tom mo Cheasaig* (Kessóg's Mound), where he is said to have preached. He was murdered by assassins at Bandry, within site of his island monastery. There are two sixteenth-century references to Kessóg's hand bell, and the Colquhoun family are hereditary keepers of his *bachuil*, or monk's staff.

KEVIN

Kevin (d. *c.*618) was born in the early sixth century of a noble Leinster family ousted from kingship. His name, *Cóemhghein*, means 'fairborn'. The surviving Lives of Kevin are late and unreliable: the earliest appears to have been written by a monk at Glendalough in the tenth or eleventh century. Kevin was said to have been trained by three wise old monks. While searching for a deserted place in which to live and pray, he came to Glendalough, where he lived in the hollow of a tree, beside the upper lake. Later he was ordained as a priest by a bishop named Lugidus, who sent him out with some monks to found a new church in an unidentified place. Here he spent a while 'gathering servants for Christ' before moving with them back to Glendalough, where he founded a monastery.

His Latin Life describes Kevin travelling west across Ireland to visit the young Ciarán of Clonmacnoise as he lay stricken with the plague, but Ciarán died before the older monk's arrival. After some years as a hermit, Kevin apparently returned to his monastery to die. He was succeeded as abbot by his nephew Molibba, who appears to have been the first bishop of Glendalough.

KEW

Nothing is known about this female saint, the patroness of the Cornish village of St Kew. Kewstoke in Somerset on the shore of the Bristol Channel may also be named after her. The settlement of St Kew was also named Lannow – '*lan* (church site) of Docco'. By the early eighteenth century the parish believed Kew and Docco to be brother and sister, but there is no early evidence for this. Docco established a monastery at Llandough in south-east Wales, and Lannow appears to have been its daughter house. Mentioned in the seventh-century *Life of Samson*, Lannow is the earliest named Cornish monastery.

KEYNE

Described in twelfth-century Welsh genealogies as one of the daughters of Brychan, Keyne has a number of dedications in Wales. A *Life of Keyne* was included in John of Tynmouth's fourteenth-century *Nova Legenda Angliae*. He probably took his information from a longer Welsh *Life of Keyne*, written after the late eleventh century. According to John of Tynmouth, Keyne refused marriage and became a nun. She left Wales and crossed the River Severn in search of solitude. She lived for a while at a place infested with serpents, which she turned into stone. This was probably Keynsham, four miles south-east of Bristol, a settlement at a crossing point of the river Avon. Ammonites, which are fossils shaped like coiled serpents, were found here and may have given rise to the legend. A similar miracle is attributed to Hilda of Whitby, where ammonites also abound. A village is named after Keyne near the south Cornish coast, two miles south of Liskeard.

MAEL: see SULIEN

MÁELRUBHA

An Irishman who worked among the northern Picts, Máelrubha (*c*.642–*c*.722) became a monk at Bangor in County Down. He sailed to Scotland and established a flourishing monastery at Applecross, on the mainland opposite the Isle of Skye. He built a church on an island in Loch Maree, 35 miles west of Inverness, where his spring was famous for its healing properties. Máelrubha was killed by Norsemen at Skail, near the north coast of Sutherland. His body was brought back to his community at Applecross, but within a century the monastery had been destroyed by Vikings.

MAILDHUB

The name Maildhub means 'black prince'. According to medieval tradition, Maildhub was an Irish monk who established a community and a school at Malmesbury. The Saxon monk Aldhelm was his most outstanding pupil and became his successor. However, Aldhelm makes no mention of Maildhub in his prose works or poetry, and we hear nothing of the Irish monk until 400 years after Aldhelm's death. The earliest histories of Malmesbury are by Faricius of Arezzo (d. 1117) who was at Malmesbury between 1080 and 1100, when he was appointed abbot of Abingdon, and by William of Malmesbury (*c*.1090–1143). William describes Maildhub as an 'Irishman by birth, a philosopher by erudition and a monk by profession,' who left Ireland in search of a solitary life.

MANCHÁN

Twelve miles east of the great monastery of Clonmacnoise, on a small island rising out of a bog, a monk named Manchán established a hermitage in the early seventh century. The site is named Lemanaghan, or 'Manchán's grey place'. In 645 Manchán's patron, Diarmuid, King of Ireland, passed through Clonmacnoise when he marched to battle against Guaire, King of Connacht. The congregation of Clonmacnoise prayed to St Ciarán for King Diarmuid's safe return, and when he won the battle he is said to have given the people Lemanaghan in memory of his victory. Manchán settled here with his mother, Mella; a small stone oratory on the site is known as her cell. Both Manchán and Diarmuid died in the great plague of

664–6. Part of an eleventh-century abbot's crozier was found in the bog at Lemanaghan, together with Manchán's magnificent shrine, which can be seen in the church at nearby Boher.

MAUGHOLD

Kirk Maughold on the north-east coast of the Isle of Man is named after this saint, whose existence is debated. In his *Life of Patrick* (c.1186), the monk Jocelyn of Furness describes a spring at Kirk Maughold as St Machaldus' well. He linked it with the story of an Irish adventurer told by the seventh-century biographer of Patrick, Muirchú, who described a cruel tyrant named Macc Cuill and his dramatic conversion to a holy life. Macc Cuill usually killed travellers passing through his territory, and when he heard that Patrick was coming, he planned to murder him. Patrick survived and restored a dead man to life. The tyrant was converted, declared his belief in God, confessed his sins, and asked to do penance. Patrick ordered him to abandon everything and set off in a small boat without oars or a rudder. Macc Cuill was set adrift and arrived at a distant land, where two holy bishops trained him. Eventually he too became a bishop. [38]

MAWGAN

Mawgan was a Welsh monk who is commemorated in a number of places, particularly in the Teifi valley, but no medieval Life of him survives. In his eleventh-century *Life of David*, Rhigyfarch mentions a 'monastery of Maucannus', but whether or where it existed is uncertain. In Cornwall, St Mawgan-in-Pydar, near the north coast, and St Mawgan-in-Meneage, on the Lizard peninsula, are early sites named after Mawgan. Setting sail from nearby Mawgan Creek, pilgrims could continue to north-east Brittany, where the saint is honoured in the region around St Malo.

MELANGELL

According to legend, Melangell was an Irish chieftain's daughter who fled to Wales to escape an arranged marriage. She settled as a hermit at Pennant Melangell. A local chieftain named Brochwel, King of Powys, who lived in Shrewsbury, was hare-coursing at Pennant Melangell. His hounds raised a hare, which fled to a thicket where Melangell was praying. The hare hid in the folds of her cloak, while the hounds ran away. The huntsman raised his horn to his lips, but was unable to remove it. Brochwel was so impressed that he gave Melangell the valley, where she established a community of nuns. The remains of her shrine can be seen in the small church at Pennant Melangell, near the site of her grave.

MIRRIN

In about 560 an Irish monk named Mirrin founded a community at Paisley on a tributary of the river Clyde, west of Glasgow. As a boy, Mirrin had been taken by his mother to Congal, the abbot of Bangor, a monastery at the head of Belfast Lough in Northern Ireland. After training as a monk, Mirrin became prior of Bangor and later went to Scotland, possibly as one of Columba's followers. On Inchmurrin ('Mirrin's Isle') in Loch Lomond, the largest island in the loch, a ruined chapel is dedicated to Mirrin.

MOLAISE

An Irish monk (d. *c*.639) about whom little is known, Molaise is venerated in Ireland and Scotland. His name is a diminutive or affectionate form of Laisrén (*mo Laisrén*, meaning 'my little Laisrén').[39] Molaise was abbot of Old Leighlin in County Carlow and established a community at Inishmurray in Sligo, where considerable remains of the monastery survive. It is still a centre for pilgrimage. Molaise was said to have promulgated the Roman system of calculating the date of Easter, rather than the Celtic method. A cave hermitage is named after Molaise on Holy Island in Lamlash Bay, off the south-east coast of Arran Island in south-west Scotland.

MOLING

The cult of Moling (d. 697) was early and widespread. Moling came from a noble Leinster family and became a monk at Glendalough. He later founded his own monastery at St Mullins, beside the River Barrow in County Carlow. Moling is said to have established a ferry across the Barrow; it is still in existence. He lived for a time in a hermitage near St Mullins, and later became bishop of Ferns, which lies to the east, over the Blackmore Mountains. Here he is said to have helped the people by obtaining the remission of a heavy tribute of oxen to the local king.

There is a small pocket Gospel book in Trinity College, Dublin, named the *Book of Mulling*. It is encased in an elaborate jewelled shrine of bronze with silver plates, and was probably written in the ninth century, copied from a manuscript written by Moling. It contains the Gospels, a Mass for the Sick, and a simplified plan of the monastery at St Mullins, whose boundary wall is indicated by two concentric circles. Twelve crosses are marked on the plan but no buildings. This indicates that, symbolically at least, high crosses were a significant feature of Irish monastic life.

MUNGO: see KENTIGERN

MYLOR
St Mylor in Cornwall is probably named after one of two or three Breton saints named Melor. The chief cult of Mylor or Melor centred on the church of Lanmeur near Morlaix in Finistère, an area of western Brittany. Here he was believed to have been a prince who was murdered. Mylor's cult probably spread to Cornwall from Brittany. Mylor churchyard contains a pre-Christian standing stone, indicating that this was an ancient holy site. Linkinhorne in eastern Cornwall is also dedicated to Mylor. Amesbury Abbey acquired his relics at the time of its foundation in about 979, and Mylor became a patron saint of the abbey.[40]

NECTAN
Claimed to be the eldest of Brychan's 24 children, Nectan is known from three twelfth-century documents written at Hartland Abbey in Devon: a short Life, an account of the rediscovery of his relics, and a list of his miracles. Nectan is not mentioned in Welsh accounts of Brychan, although a monk named Nectan occurs in medieval Welsh genealogies. The Life says that Nectan crossed the Bristol Channel and settled at Stoke in Hartland as a hermit. His brothers and sisters settled in Wales, Devon, and Cornwall and met together at his cell every New Year's Eve. He was beheaded by two robbers. Nectan was widely venerated in south-west Britain. At Nectan's Kieve, a waterfall near Tintagel, a medieval chapel may have been dedicated to him.

NEOT

In his *Life of Alfred*, Asser (d. 910) writes that the king visited a church in Cornwall 'in which St Guerin lies in peace (and now St Neot lies there as well)'. Neot appears to be a Celtic name, although later Lives claim that he was a Saxon or an East Anglian, to make his story more attractive to their respective readers.[41] As a young man, Neot joined the community in Glastonbury; he later settled as a hermit at St Neot, where he founded a small monastery. His relics were enshrined here, although most of them were later taken to St Neots in Huntingdon and to Crowland Abbey in Lincolnshire. Neot's legend is portrayed in twelve early sixteenth-century panels of stained glass in St Neot church. They present incidents from the twelfth-century *Life of Neot*, written at Bec, which borrows from other Lives of Irish saints.

NINIAN

We know very little about the early bishop Ninian except that he worked in Galloway, in south-west Scotland. Writing three hundred years later, Bede tells us that Ninian studied in Rome before founding a monastery,[42] which he dedicated to Martin of Tours.[43] It has been suggested that Ninian originated from Carlisle: this was the centre of an early bishopric, and Whithorn came within its ambit. A church probably existed in Carlisle from late Roman times onward, since fourth-century Christian artefacts have been found there. There are possible early dedications to Ninian in the area around Carlisle, at Brampton and Brougham Ninekirk. Bede tells us that Ninian preached among the southern Picts. In Stirling the church and well of St Ninian's may be an early foundation, while across the Firth of Forth, further into the territory of the southern Picts, there was a chapel dedicated to Ninian at Arbroath.

NON

In his *Life of David*, written around 1095, Rhigyfarch tells us that David's father was Sant, King of Ceredigion, and his mother, from the neighbouring kingdom of Dyfed, was called Non. According to Rhigyfarch, she was a virgin who conceived her son through being raped by Sant when he was passing through Dyfed (modern Pembrokeshire). After the rape, Non lived on bread and water. It was seen as fitting that David's parents should be named Sant (from the Latin word *sanctus* or 'holy') and Non, meaning 'nun'. On a cliff top in St Non's Bay, a mile south of St David's Cathedral, St Non's chapel is supposed to mark the spot where Non gave birth to David. Non's cult spread to Cornwall, where Pelynt and Altarnun may be named after her. Pelynt's name comes from *plou Nent*, which means 'parish of Non'. It is the only example of a Cornish church that incorporates the Breton word *plou*. In Brittany, Non is sometimes commemorated as a male companion of David. Non died in western Brittany and is buried at Dirinon, ten miles east of Brest.

PADARN

Padarn was an early Welsh monk whose seven known dedications are beside two Roman roads that run north and south, linking forts on either side of the Cambrian Mountains. This implies that Padarn's followers worked in the settlements around the ruined Roman garrisons. His name, Paternus, was a common Roman name. His chief monastery was at Llanbadarn Fawr, on the outskirts of Aberystwyth.

PATRICK

Patrick was a Briton who worked in Ireland in the fifth century; his father was a Roman *decurion* or civic official. In his remarkable autobiography, the *Confession*, Patrick tells us that his father was a deacon and his grandfather was a priest. Patrick does not tell us where he was born; one possibility among others is the area of western Scotland near Dumbarton, in the Romanized area south of the Antonine Wall. In his *Confession*, which he wrote in old age, Patrick tells us that when he was sixteen he was captured by Irish raiders and taken to Ireland as a slave. Put to work as a shepherd tending flocks, he began to pray and became converted to a monastic way of life. He recalls: 'I even remained in the wood and on the mountain to pray. And – come hail, rain or snow – I was up before dawn to pray.... I now understand this, that the Spirit was fervent in me.'[44]

After six years Patrick escaped, or was freed, and returned home to Britain. He trained as a priest, perhaps in Gaul. Patrick felt drawn to return to Ireland as a missionary and eventually did so. He tells us that he was a bishop, and he appears to have been based in the north-east, where he may have founded a settlement at Armagh. The later monks of Armagh claimed him as the founder of their cathedral, and they recorded stories about Patrick that may be based on fact or may simply be ecclesiastical propaganda to promote their patron saint.

In his *Confession*, Patrick tells us that he travelled to the far ends of the known world in order to bring Christianity to an alien people. He established Christian communities and trained others to lead them. Patrick appears to have worked in central and northern Ireland, while other early bishops were preaching in the south. A story relates how Patrick came to Cashel to visit Aongus, king of Munster, who agreed to be baptized. During the ceremony Patrick accidentally pierced the king's foot with his staff. The king made no complaint, thinking that this was part of the ritual. As an old man, Patrick wrote two letters to the soldiers of Coroticus, a chieftain living on Dumbarton Rock, capital of the British kingdom of Strathclyde. The second of these letters survives. The chieftain's soldiers had raided Ireland, captured some of Patrick's converts, and sold them to the Picts, and Patrick wrote demanding their release. We do not know where or how Patrick died. Many Irish churches claim to have been founded by Patrick and his followers.

PAUL AURELIAN

Paul Aurelian was a prominent figure in Celtic times. We learn about him from a Life written in 884 by a monk named Wrmonoc at the Breton monastery of Landévennec in Finistère. The biographer conflated his story with one or possibly two other Pauls, but it seems that Paul Aurelian was born in Wales into an important Romano-British family in the late fifth century. The author tells us that, as a young man, Paul studied alongside David and Samson in Illtud's famous monastery at Llanilltud Fawr in south Wales. According to his biographer, Paul left Illtud's community at the age of sixteen and became a hermit, living 'in the uninterrupted life of contemplation'. He founded a monastery at Llanddeusant near Llandovery and was ordained priest. He left with twelve monks, after which he may have established a community at Llangors, near Brecon.

In time, Paul's fame reached the court of King Mark, who may have lived in the hill fort of Castle Dore, near Fowey on the south Cornish coast. His biographer tells us that Mark ruled over a people who spoke four languages, and he wished to strengthen their Christian faith. At his invitation, Paul arrived with twelve priests. He spent some time working there, but when he was asked to become their bishop he left and sailed to Brittany. Paul founded a church on the Île-de-Batz, and agreed to become the first bishop of the settlement, which was later named St-Pol-de-Léon in his honour. He was widely venerated in this area of Brittany. We do not know whether Paul Aurelian worked in the parish of Paul on the south Cornish coast, or whether it was given its name later by Breton monks who brought his cult to Cornwall.[45]

PETROC

Petroc was one of Cornwall's most popular saints in medieval times; his name may mean 'little Peter'. The earliest *Life of Petroc* survives in Breton manuscripts, but it was probably written by a Cornish cleric, since the author was familiar with various locations in Cornwall associated with him. His eleventh-century biographer tells us that Petroc was a Welsh prince who became a monk and went to Ireland to study with his companions. They returned to mainland Britain and landed at Padstow in Cornwall; the town's name means 'Petroc's stow'.

In the late tenth century Petroc's shrine with his staff and his bell were taken inland to Bodmin, perhaps because of Viking raids around the coast. Augustinian canons encouraged Bodmin's development as a centre for pilgrimage to Petroc's shrine. In the late twelfth century, a canon of Bodmin priory wrote a longer *Life of Petroc*, linking him with Welsh traditions. He describes the monk's arrival at Bodmin, where a hermit named Guron welcomed Petroc and his three companions hospitably, setting out a table with white bread for them. Guron left them his hut and travelled a day's journey to Gorran near the Cornish coast, seven miles south of St Austell. This village was the centre of Guron's cult. At least eight Cornish chapels and wells are dedicated to Petroc, and he was even more popular beyond Cornwall. There are a number of churches dedicated to Petroc in Wales.

PIRAN

The earliest reference to Piran is the place-name Carnperan ('Rock of Piran'), recorded at Perranzabuloe in 960. Piran's surviving Life was probably written in the twelfth or thirteenth century in Cornwall or at Exeter Cathedral. It is an adaptation of the *Life of Ciarán of Saighir*, but Piran is more likely to have been Cornish than Irish. By 1086 a minster church with a large parish was dedicated to him at Perranzabuloe ('Piran in the sands'). Piran later became the patron saint of tin miners, who worked in the area. There are a number of other dedications to Piran on the north Cornish coast, and others on the south coast near the pilgrim routes from Brittany.

SAMSON

We know a considerable amount about Samson (*c*.490–*c*.565), because a long and interesting *Life of Samson* survives. It was written by a Breton monk, perhaps as early as the seventh century.[46] Samson was born of a wealthy family in south-west Wales. His parents took him to St Illtud's famous school at Llanilltud Fawr, in the Vale of Glamorgan, where Samson later became a monk. Samson was ordained priest and went to the monastery's daughter house on Caldey Island off the Pembrokeshire coast; in time he became its abbot. He later visited Ireland, where he acquired a chariot, or light cart, in which to travel. He put the cart on a boat and returned to Llanilltud Fawr, where he was invited to become abbot. He was consecrated bishop in about 521. With his father Amon and two companions, Samson then withdrew to a quieter place, a ruined fort near the Welsh bank of the River Severn.

Samson next decided to travel as a pilgrim for Christ. He sailed to Cornwall with a group of relatives, landing at Padstow and continuing up the Camel estuary until they came within two miles of the monastery of Docco, now named St Kew. They hoped to stay here, but the community sent one of their number, Juvanius, to dissuade Samson from doing so, since the community had grown lax. The group continued southward across Cornwall. As they travelled, they met a group of people with their chieftain, celebrating the mysteries of their ancestors. Samson carved a cross on a standing stone and healed a boy who had fallen unconscious from his horse. The ruler told his followers to come forward and reaffirm their baptism. He next asked Samson to drive an evil serpent from a cave, which the monk did. According to tradition, the cave can still be seen at Golant, north of Fowey, where a church and holy well are named after Samson.

He established a monastery, probably at Fowey, leaving his

father Amon in charge of the new community. Samson then sailed to Brittany with his followers. He founded Dol on the north coast and several other monasteries. He signed decrees of Church Councils in Paris in 553 and 557. On one of his journeys to Paris, a wheel fell off his much-used chariot. Samson took an active part in Breton politics and has dedications in eastern Brittany and Normandy. A town in Guernsey and one of the Scilly Isles are named after him.

SEIRIOL

A local Anglesey saint, Seiriol is honoured at Penmon near the eastern end of Anglesey and on nearby Puffin Island (Ynys Seiriol). The monastery at Penmon was said to have been founded by Einion, Prince of Lleyn, who appointed his nephew, Seiriol, as head of the community. Here can be found the most complete monk's hermitage to survive in Wales. A well and the stone foundation of a hermit's circular hut nestle beneath an overhanging rock. At Clorach, a mile east of Llanerchymedd, nearer the centre of Anglesey, twin wells on either side of the road were named after Seiriol and Cybi who, according to tradition, used to meet here. For both men, the journey was about ten miles each way. Since Cybi faced the sun in the morning and again in the evening, he was nicknamed 'the Tanned' while Seiriol was nicknamed 'the Pale'. The wells were visited for healing as late as the nineteenth century.[47]

SELEVAN

Perhaps the son of a Cornish chieftain named Gereint, Selevan may have been the father of Cybi, who has dedications in both Cornwall and Wales. The hamlet of St Levan near Land's End is called after Selevan, whose name comes from that of King Solomon. The Irish surname Sullivan is another form of Solomon. Celtic Christians liked to have biblical characters as their patrons: Samson, Daniel, David, and Asaph are other examples of this. Stories recorded at St Levan in the eighteenth century describe Selevan as a hermit and fisherman. Remains of a Celtic baptistery and holy well survive at Porthgwarra Cove half a mile from the parish church, and a hermit's cell was excavated nearby.

SENAN

Born near Kilrush in County Clare, Senan (d. *c.*544) tended his father's cattle before becoming a monk. He made a number of foundations, including Inniscarra (near Cork), Inis Mór (Canon Island), Mutton Island (County Clare), and Scattery Island near his birthplace, Kilrush. A number of medieval ruins survive on Scattery Island, although it is not certain whether any of them date from Senan's lifetime. The shrine of Senan's bell is preserved in the Royal Irish Academy, Dublin. The patron of Sennen in Cornwall is probably not Senan but a local female Cornish saint.

SERF

Serf was a native missionary who is said to have worked among the southern Picts in the district around Stirling; his mother may have been a local princess. It is not known whether Serf lived in the fifth or in the eighth century, or whether there were two men with the same name working in this area. The 'early' Serf was said to have been ordained by Palladius, a deacon from Auxerre who accompanied Germanus on a mission to Ireland in 431 to combat the Pelagian heresy. Serf's cult centre was at Culross, on the northern shore of the Firth of Forth, twelve miles south-east of Stirling. There are churches dedicated to him at Dunning, Alva, Tillicoultry, and Clackmannan. He is said to have lived as a hermit in a cave at Dysart, now a suburb of Kirkaldy. An island in Loch Leven, seven miles west of Glenrothes, is perhaps dedicated to the eighth-century Serf.

SIDWELL

The biographer of Paul Aurelian tells us that Paul had a sister named Sitofolla, a nun who lived near the seashore. She may be the saint named Sidwell whose relics were honoured in a church outside the east gate of Exeter by 1135, close to a well that bore her name. People came to her shrine for healing throughout medieval times. In the twelfth century the bishop of Exeter compiled a book of liturgical readings, for use in the cathedral, which records Sidwell's story as it was then told: her stepmother had her murdered by labourers reaping in the fields, who cut off her head with their scythes. This preserves a pre-Christian myth, in which the harvest goddess was said to die when reapers cut the last sheaf of corn. Sidwell is depicted with her scythe on rood screens, bench ends and windows in about twenty churches. The Cornish church of Laneast on the edge of Bodmin Moor is dedicated to her.

SULIEN

Said to be a follower of the Breton monk Cadfan, Sulien has dedications in Brittany and two churches in Cornwall at Tresilian and Luxulyan. Luxulyan means '*loc,* or chapel, of Sulien'. It is the only Cornish use of the prefix *loc*, a common feature in Breton place-names. The ancient church of Corwen in mid-Wales is dedicated to Mael and Sulien, and a well in Cwm parish on the slopes of the Clwyd range is also named after the two monks; its water cured eye diseases.[48]

TEILO

Teilo was a sixth-century monk and bishop, whose work and cult was centred on Llandeilo Fawr in south Wales. He may have been born in Penally, on the coast near Tenby. In about 1130 Geoffrey of Llandaff wrote a biographical sermon about Teilo, in which he relates that he was a pupil of Dubricius and Paul Aurelian. During the plague he went to Brittany for seven years, staying with Samson at Dol. He then returned to Wales and died in Llandeilo Fawr.

TRILLO

Another disciple of Cadfan, Trillo was said to have been a priest on Bardsey Island. The tiny medieval chapel of Llandrillo-yn-Rhos ('church of Trillo on the promontory') near Colwyn Bay is named after him. He is also honoured in the village of Llandrillo, 30 miles inland over the moors, on a tributary of the River Dee, where his medieval church stands beside an ancient yew tree. Across the river, at the foot of an oak, is Trillo's holy well, which cured rheumatism; it flowed until a hundred years ago.

TYSILIO

A younger son of Brochwel, King of Powys, Tysilio's name means 'dear Sunday's child', so he was probably born on a Sunday. He lived in the early seventh century and apparently studied under a hermit named Gwyddfarch at the monastery of Meifod in central Wales, five miles north-west of Welshpool. Tysilio later became abbot of Meifod. He is said to have spent time as a hermit on the island of Llandysilio in the Menai Strait. A number of churches dedicated to Tysilio are situated close to royal forts of Brochwel's household. Two more settlements are named after him in south Wales, with another to the south-east in the Wye Valley. Tysilio's Life was written by a Breton monk in the fifteenth century, but it is unreliable and may be a conflation of stories about two different men.

WINIFRED

The name Winifred means 'radiant Freda' (*gwen Frewi* in Welsh). In north Wales, Winifred's cult is ancient and widespread, but surprisingly little is known about her. When her relics were taken to Shrewsbury Abbey in 1138, its monks wrote the *Legend of St Winifred*. She is described as a princess who was beheaded by Caradoc, the son of a neighbouring prince, whom she had refused to marry. A spring flowed at Holywell where her head fell to the ground, but her uncle, Beuno, restored her to life. The legend is one of many in which a saint is decapitated and a healing spring flows where their blood touches the earth. Winifred is said to have established a convent at Holywell. According to her Life, Winifred later travelled inland and eventually settled at Gwytherin, where she died.

WINWALOE

Winwaloe was widely venerated in Brittany, where he has fifty dedications, and in Britain, where another six churches are named after him, including those of Gunwalloe and Landewednack on the Lizard in Cornwall. Abbot Wrdisten's late ninth-century *Life of Winwaloe* describes how he was born of noble British parents who had emigrated to Brittany. He was trained in Budoc's monastery, after which he founded a community on the Isle of Tibidy, and another at Landévennec, in Finistère, where he died.

Introduction

1. C. Thomas, *Celtic Britain*. London: Thames & Hudson, 1986, p.54.
2. Gildas, *The Ruin of Britain*, 10, in M. Winterbottom (trans.), *Gildas: The Ruin of Britain and Other Works*, London: Phillimore, 1978.
3. Thomas, *Celtic Britain*, p.54.
4. D. Keys, 'Archaeologists Unearth Capital's First Cathedral', *The Independent*, 3 April 1995.
5. D. Neal, *Lullingstone Roman Villa*. London: English Heritage, 1991, pp.8, 23.
6. R. Goodburn, *The Roman Villa, Chedworth*. London: The National Trust, 1994, p.24.
7. W.H. Davies, 'The Church in Wales', in M.W. Barley and R.P. Hanson (eds), *Christianity in Britain, 300-700*, Papers presented to the Conference on Christianity in Roman and Sub-Roman Britain, held at the University of Nottingham, 17-20 April 1967. Leicester University Press, p.140.
8. Ibid., pp.140-2.
9. M. Costen, *The Origins of Somerset*. Manchester: Manchester University Press, 1992, p.74.
10. Gildas, *Ruin of Britain*, 11.
11. Sulpicius Severus, *The Life of Martin of Tours*, in J. p.Migne, *Patrologia Latina*, Paris, 1844-64, vol. 20, cols 159-222.
12. N. Russell (trans.), *The Lives of the Desert Fathers*, Prologue, 10. London: Mowbray, 1981, p.50.
12. Ibid., pp.13, 18, 53.
14. P. Hill, *Whithorn and St Ninian: The Excavation of a Monastic Town, 1984-91*. Stroud: Sutton Publishing, 1997, pp.13-14.
15. Severus, *Martin of Tours*.
16. B. Ward, *The Lives of the Desert Fathers*. London: Mowbray, 1981, p.10.
17. Gildas, *De Poenitentia* 1.10, in Winterbottom (trans.), *Gildas*.

Notes

18. C. Thomas, *Britain and Ireland in Early Christian Times, AD 400-800*. London: Thames & Hudson, 1971, p.92.
19. Thomas, *Celtic Britain*, p.135.

Part One: Ireland

1. C. Thomas, *And Shall These Mute Stones Speak?* Cardiff: University of Wales Press, 1994, pp.33-4.
2. S. Lincoln, *Declan of Ardmore*. Cork: Aisling, 1995, p.43.
3. Ibid., p.32.
4. There is a summary of the *Navigatio* in Appendix I of Tim Severin's account of his re-creation of Brendan's epic journey: T. Severin, *The Brendan Voyage*. New York: McGraw-Hill, 1978, pp.265-73.
5. Luke 14.26.
6. T. O'Loughlin, *Journeys on the Edges: The Celtic Tradition*. London: Darton, Longman & Todd, 2000, pp.91-8.
7. Ibid.
8. B. Duffy, *Archaeology in County Sligo*. Sligo: Duchás – the Heritage Service, 1998, p.25.
9. H. G. Leask, *St Patrick's Rock, Cashel*. Dublin: Stationery Office, n.d., pp.8-9.
10. Ibid.
11. Ibid., pp.24-5.
12. C. Manning, *Clonmacnoise*. Dublin: Duchás, 1998, p.52.
13. J. Marsden, *The Illustrated Columcille*. London: Macmillan, 1991, p.60.
14. C. Manning, *Early Irish Monasteries*. Dublin: Town House & Country House, 1995, p.24.
15. E.G. Bowen, *Saints, Seaways and Settlements in the Celtic Lands*. Cardiff: University of Wales Press, 1969, pp.126-7.
16. Duffy, *Archaeology*, p.28.
17. M. Low, *Celtic Christianity and Nature*. Belfast: Black Star Press, 1996, pp.98-9.
18. L. Barrow, *Glendalough and St Kevin*. Dundalk: Dundalgan Press, 1992, pp.16-17
19. Manning, *Early Irish Monasteries*, pp.30, 36.
20. Duffy, *Archaeology*, p.24.
21. Ibid.
22. Manning, *Early Irish Monasteries*, pp.16, 29.
23. Ibid., pp.22-3.

24. J. P.Hynes, *Kilmacduagh: A Short Guide*. Mold: J. p.Hynes, 1986, p.8.
25. Ibid., p.9.
26. Duffy, *Archaeology*, p.26.
27. Low, *Celtic Christianity*, p.158.
28. 1 Kings 18.20-40.
29. O'Loughlin, *Journeys on the Edges*, pp.88-90.
30. Manning, *Early Irish Monasteries*, p.32.

Part Two: Scotland

1. N. Atkinson, *Aberlemno to Glamis*. Balgavies, Angus: Pinkfoot Press, 1997, pp.4-5.
2. B. Colgrave and R. A. Mynors (eds), *Bede's Ecclesiastical History of the English People*. Oxford: Oxford University Press, 1969, Bk. 5, ch. 9.
3. Atkinson, *Aberlemno to Glamis*, pp.8-9.
4. W.J. Watson, *The History of the Celtic Place-Names of Scotland*. Edinburgh: Birlinn, 1993, p.275.
5. Hebrews 11.38.
6. A. Macquarrie, *Cille Bharra*. Droitwich: Grant Books, 1989, pp.10-11.
7. Watson, *History of Celtic Place-Names*, p.278.
8. I. MacDonald (ed.), *Saint Mungo, Also Known as Kentigern, by Jocelinus, a Monk of Furness*. Edinburgh: Floris, 1993, pp.12-18.
9. J. Randall and C. Seymour, *Stobo Kirk*. Selkirk: Stobo Kirk, 1997, pp.8-9.
10. J. Marsden, *The Illustrated Columcille*. London: Macmillan, 1991, pp.32-3.
11. A. Chetan and D. Brueton, *The Sacred Yew*. London: Penguin Arkana, 1994, pp.47-9.
12. MacDonald, *Saint Mungo, Also Known as Kentigern*, pp.60-2.
13. P. Hill, *Whithorn and St Ninian: The Excavation of a Monastic Town*. Stroud: Sutton Publishing, 1997, pp.13, 28, 35.
14. J. Dunbar and I. Fisher, *Iona: A Guide to the Monuments*. Edinburgh: Her Majesty's Stationery Office, 1995, p.15.
15. Ibid., p.13.
16. Ibid., p.15.
17. Watson, *History of the Celtic Place-Names*, p.282.

Notes

18. Ibid., p.189.
19. I. Zaczek, *Ancient Scotland*. London: Collins & Brown, 1998, p.84.
20. J. Sinclair, *St Mackessog's Church, Luss, Loch Lomond*. Luss Church Promotions, n.d., p.1.
21. 'Early Christian church found on the Isle of May', *British Archaeology* 18 (October 1996), News, p.4.
22. A. Ritchie, *Meigle Museum: Pictish Carved Stones*. Edinburgh: Historic Scotland, 1997, p.6.
23. Ibid., p.16.
24. Ibid.
25. 'The Life and Miracles of St Cuthbert', in Colgrave and Mynors, *Bede's Ecclesiastical History*, ch. 6.
26. R. Fawcett, *St Andrews Cathedral*. Edinburgh: Historic Scotland, 1993, p.4.
27. Ibid., pp.4-5.
28. Ibid., p.6.
29. D. Smith, *Celtic Travellers: Scotland in the Age of the Saints*. Edinburgh: Stationery Office, 1997, pp.41-2.
30. Ibid., pp.44-5.
31. E.G. Bowen, *The Settlements of the Celtic Saints in Wales*. Cardiff: University of Wales Press, 1954, pp.74-8.
32. Smith, *Celtic Travellers*, p.30.
33. Colgrave and Mynors, *Bede's Ecclesiastical History*, Bk. 3, ch. 4.
34. Hill, *Whithorn and St Ninian*, pp.69, 300-1.
35. Ibid., pp.37-8, 52.
36. I. MacDonald (ed.), *Saint Ninian, by Ailred, Abbot of Rievaulx*. Edinburgh: Floris, 1993, p.39.

Part Three: Wales

1. F. Jones, *The Holy Wells of Wales*. Cardiff: University of Wales Press, 1992, p.152.
2. M. Chitty, *The Monks on Ynys Enlli*, Part 1, *c.* 500AD – 1252 AD. Aberdaron: Mary Chitty, 1992, pp.13-14.
3. Ibid, pp.14-15.
4. P.H. Jones, *Bardsey, its History and Wildlife*. Criccieth: Bardsey Island Trust, 1995, p.10.
5. Chitty, *Monks on Ynys Enlli*, pp.15, 21-2.
6. B. Colgrave and R. A. Mynors (eds), *Bede's Ecclesiastical*

History of the English People. Oxford: Oxford University Press, 1969, Bk. 1, ch. 7.

7. C. Knightly, *Mwynhewch Sir Ddinbych Ganoloesol*. Denbigh: Cyngor Sir Ddinbych, 1998, p.18.

8. E. G. Bowen, *Saints, Seaways and Settlements in the Celtic Lands*. Cardiff: University of Wales Press, 1969, pp.132-4.

9. F. Jones, *Holy Wells*, pp.108, 179.

10. A. Chetan and D. Brueton, *The Sacred Yew*. London: Penguin Arkana, 1994, pp.55, 153.

11. N. Edwards and A. Lane, 'Archaeology of the Early Church in Wales: An Introduction', in N. Edwards and A. Lane (eds), *The Early Church in Wales and the West*, Oxbow Monograph 16. Oxford: Oxbow Books, 1992, pp.9-10.

12. Jones, *Holy Wells*, p.70.

13. C. David, *St Winefride's Well: A History and Guide*. Naas, County Kildare: The Leinster Leader, 1993, p.20.

14. J. Griffiths, *A Short Guide to the Parish Church of St Asaph and St Cyndeyrn, Llanasa*. Llanasa: A5 Publications, 1986, pp.1-2, 5.

15. E.G. Bowen, *The Settlements of the Celtic Saints in Wales*. Cardiff: University of Wales Press, 1954, pp.53-5.

16. C. Guest (trans.), *The Mabinogion*. Dover/Constable: London, 1997, pp.52-8.

17. O. Davies, *Celtic Christianity in Early Medieval Wales: The Origins of the Welsh Spiritual Tradition*. Cardiff: University of Wales Press, 1996, p.23.

18. E.G. Bowen, *The St David of History. Dewi Sant: Our Founder Saint*. Aberystwyth: Friends of St David's Cathedral, 1982, pp.7-8.

19. D. Brown, *The Lichfield Gospels*. London: Pitkin Pictorials, 1982, p.6.

20. Jones, *Holy Wells*, pp.81, 198.

21. Bowen, *Settlements*, p.30.

22. M. Redknap, *The Christian Celts: Treasures of Late Celtic Wales*. Cardiff: University of Wales Press, 1991, pp.16-17, 20-5.

23. Bowen, *Settlements*, p.68.

24. Jones, *Holy Wells*, pp.74, 151.

25. V. Kelly, *Saint Illtud's Church, Llantwit Major*. Cowbridge, Glamorgan: D. Brown and Sons, 1993, pp.2, 8-9, 13.

26. Jones, *Holy Wells*, p.173.

27. W. p.Seymour Davies, *The History of the Church of St Tysilio*

and St Mary. Welshpool: Meifod Parish Council, 1984, p.4.

28. Bowen, *Saints, Seaways and Settlements*, p.203.
29. L. Macinnes, *Anglesey: A Guide to the Ancient and Historic Sites on the Isle of Anglesey.* Cardiff: Welsh Historic Monuments, 1994, p.22.
30. Ibid., pp.20-4.
31. I. MacDonald (ed.), *Saint Mungo, Also Known as Kentigern, by Jocelinus, a Monk of Furness.* Edinburgh: Floris, 1993, pp.31-4.
32. Davies, *Celtic Christianity*, pp.45-8.
33. R. Van der Weyer, *Celtic Fire: an Anthology of Christian Literature.* London: Darton, Longman & Todd, 1990, pp.71-2.
34. Bowen, *St David of History*, pp.9-10.
35. Jones, *Holy Wells*, p.69.
36. Ibid., p.191.
37. Redknap, *Christian Celts*, p.10.

Part Four: Cornwall

1. J. Meyrick, *A Pilgrim's Guide to the Holy Wells of Cornwall.* Falmouth: Meyrick, 1982, p.15.
2. N. Orme, *The Saints of Cornwall.* Oxford: Oxford University Press, 2000, p.131.
3. J. Chapman, *St Petroc.* Bodmin: Chapman, 1995, pp.4-5.
4. Orme, *Saints of Cornwall*, p.95.
5. Ibid., pp.100-1.
6. *The Life of Samson*, ch. 46 in D. Attwater (ed.), *The Saints of Cornwall by G. Doble.* Truro, 1960–70, vol.5, pp.87-9.
7. Meyrick, *Pilgrim's Guide*, p.52.
8. C. Thomas, *And Shall These Mute Stones Speak?* Cardiff: University of Wales Press, 1994, p.265.
9. F. Jones, *The Holy Wells of Wales.* Cardiff: University of Wales Press, 1992, p.94.
10. Orme, *Saints of Cornwall*, pp.169-71.
11. Thomas, *op. cit.*, p.291.
12. Ibid., pp.197, 285.
13. Meyrick, *Pilgrim's Guide*, p.129.
14. Ibid., p.23.
15. N. Johnson and p.Rose, *Cornwall's Archaeological Heritage.* Truro: Cornwall Archaeological Unit, 1990, p.19.

16. Orme, *Saints of Cornwall*, p.78.

17. Meyrick, *Pilgrim's Guide*, p.25.

18. R. Gradwell, *St Clether Holy Well*. Camelford, n.d., p.3.

19. C. Weatherhill, *Cornovia: Ancient Sites of Cornwall and Scilly*. Tiverton, Devon: Cornwall Books, 1985, p.119.

20. E. Rees, *Celtic Saints, Passionate Wanderers*. London: Thames & Hudson, 2000, p.152.

Part Five: Southern England

1. M. Carter, *The Fort of Othona and the Chapel of St Peter-on-the-Wall, Bradwell-on-Sea, Essex*. Essex: St Peter's Chapel Committee, 1966, pp.2-4, 7-9.

2. Ibid., pp.12-13, 16.

3. G. Webster, *The British Celts and their Gods under Rome*. London: Batsford, 1986, p.32.

4. P. Rahtz, 'Sub-Roman Cemeteries in Somerset', in M. W. Barley and R.P. Hanson (eds), *Christianity in Britain 300-700*, Papers presented to the Conference on Christianity in Roman and Sub-Roman Britain, held at the University of Nottingham, 17-20 April 1967. Leicester: Leicester University Press, 1968.

5. J. Jackman, *Brean, the Millenium Years*. Upton-on-Severn, Worcestershire: Square One Publications, 1999, p.2.

6. M. Costen, *The Origins of Somerset*. Manchester: Manchester University Press, 1992, p.76.

7. R. Brunning and R. Croft, 'Somerset Archaeology 1998', *Council for British Archaeology South West, 2* (Winter/Spring 1999), p.42.

8. P. Hill, *Whithorn and St Ninian: the Excavation of a Monastic Town*. Stroud: Sutton Publishing, 1997, p.297.

9. P. Rahtz, 'The Dark Ages, 400-700 AD', in M. Aston and I. Burrow (eds), *The Archaeology of Somerset*. Taunton, 1982, p.103.

10. P. Rahtz, *The English Heritage Book of Glastonbury*. London: Batsford/English Heritage, 1992, pp.54-7.

11. D. Keys, 'Archaeologists Find Iron Age Gateway to the Cotswolds', *The Independent*, 5 June 2000.

12. M. Costen, 'Some Evidence for New Settlements and Field Systems in Late Anglo-Saxon Somerset', in *The Archaeology and History of Glastonbury Abbey*. Woodbridge: Boydell Press, 1991, pp.50, 55.

13. D. Millward, 'Finders Keep Roman Coins', *The Daily Telegraph*, 10 November 1999.

Part Six: Northern England

1. B. Colgrave and R.A. Mynors (eds), *Bede's Ecclesiastical History of the English People*. Oxford: Oxford University Press, 1969, Bk. 3, ch. 14.
2. Cumberland and Westmoreland Antiquarian Society, 'St Martin's Church, Brampton', *Transactions of the Cumberland and Westmoreland Antiquarian Society*, vol. 82 (1982).
3. I. MacDonald (ed.), *Saint Mungo, Also Known as Kentigern, by Jocelinus, a Monk of Furness*. Edinburgh: Floris, 1993, pp.11-12.
4. E. Cambridge, *Lindisfarne Priory and Holy Island*. London: English Heritage, 1995, pp.14-15.
5. E. Eckwall, *The Concise Oxford Dictionary of English Place-names*, 3rd edn. Oxford: Oxford University Press, 1951, p.318.
6. D. S. Dugdale, *Manx Church Origins*. Lampeter: Llanerch, 1998, pp.20-3.
7. Ibid., pp.24-5.
8. A.M. Cubbon, *The Arts of Manx Crosses*. Douglas: Manx Museum and National Trust, pp.38-9.
9. Ibid., pp.18-20.
10. W.C. Corlett, W. K. Kermode, p.Cadman, *et al.*, *Annual Report of the Manx Archaeological Society* (1909), pp.19-26.

Part Seven: the Saints

1. B. Colgrave and R.A. Mynors (eds), *Bede's Ecclesiastical History of the English People*. Oxford: Oxford University Press, 1969, Bk. 5, ch. 15.
2. D. Smith, *Celtic Travellers: Scotland in the Age of the Saints*. Edinburgh: The Stationery Office, 1997, p.30.
3. W.J. Watson, *The History of the Celtic Place-Names of Scotland*. Edinburgh: Birlinn, 1993, p.271.
4. Colgrave and Mynors, *Bede's Ecclesiastical History*, Bk. 3, ch. 5.
5. Ibid., ch. 3.

6. Ibid., ch. 5.

7. A copy of the hymn, trans. W. F. Ewbank (1980), can be seen at St Bega's church, Bassenthwaite.

8. M. Bragg, *Credo*. London: Sceptre, 1996.

9 E. Rees, *Celtic Saints in their Landscape*. Stroud: Sutton Publishing, 2001, pp.77-8.

10. E. Rees, *Celtic Saints, Passionate Wanderers*. London: Thames & Hudson, 2000, pp.79, 83-7.

11. Watson, *History of Celtic Place-Names*, p.274.

12. See Part One, BRANDON CREEK.

13. D. p.Mould, *Ireland of the Saints*. London: Batsford, 1953, pp.63-4.

14. M. Costen, *The Origins of Somerset*. Manchester: Manchester University Press, 1992, p.46.

15. C. Thomas, *And Shall These Mute Stones Speak?* Cardiff: University of Wales Press, 1994, pp.145-51.

16. N. Orme, *The Saints of Cornwall*. Oxford: Oxford University Press, 2000, p.198.

17. Rees, *Celtic Saints, Passionate Wanderers*, pp.68-71

18. Colgrave and Mynors, *Bede's Ecclesiastical History*, Bk. 3, ch. 23.

19. Ibid., ch. 22.

20. Ibid., ch. 23.

21. Ibid., ch. 25.

22. Ibid., ch. 23.

23. C. Manning, *Clonmacnoise*. Dublin: Dúchas, 1998, pp.10, 52.

24. Orme, *Saints of Cornwall*, p.89.

25. Watson, *History of Celtic Place-Names*, p.278.

26. J. Marsden, *The Illustrated Columcille*. London: Macmillan, 1991, p.33.

27. Ibid., pp.46, 96.

28. Orme, *Saints of Cornwall*, p.95.

29. S. Lincoln, *Declan of Ardmore*. Cork: Aisling, 1995, p.32.

30. F. Jones, *The Holy Wells of Wales*. Cardiff: University of Wales Press, 1992, pp.102, 118.

31. Orme, *Saints of Cornwall*, p.120.

32. T. O'Loughlin, *Journeys on the Edges: The Celtic Tradition*. London: Darton, Longman & Todd, 2000, pp.101-10.

33. Orme, *Saints of Cornwall*, pp.100-1.

34. J. Meyrick, *A Pilgrim's Guide to the Holy Wells of Cornwall*. Falmouth: Meyrick, 1982, p.60.

35. C. Guest, *The Mabinogion*. New York: Dover Publications, 1997, p.56.
36. I. MacDonald (ed.), *St Mungo, Also Known as Kentigern, by Jocelinus, a Monk of Furness*. Edinburgh: Floris, 1993, pp.11-12.
37. Ibid., pp.29-30, 31-7, 42-3.
38. D. S. Dugdale, *Manx Church Origins*. Lampeter: Llanerch, 1998, pp.113-15.
39. Watson, *History of Celtic Place-Names*, p.305.
40. Orme, *Saints of Cornwall*, pp.185-6.
41. Ibid., pp.200-1.
42. Colgrave and Mynors, *Bede's Eccesiastical History*, Bk. 3, ch. 4.
43. A full account of the excavations at Whithorn is found in p.Hill, *Whithorn and St Ninian: The Excavation of a Monastic Town*. Stroud: Sutton Publishing, 1997.
44. T. O'Loughlin, *St Patrick: The Man and His Works*. London: SPCK, 1999, section 16, p.61.
45. Orme, *Saints of Cornwall*, p.212.
46. 'The Life of Samson', ch. 46 in D. Attwater (ed.), *The Saints of Cornwall by G. Doble (1860-70)*, vol. 5, Truro, n.d.
47. Jones, *Holy Wells*, p.142.
48. Ibid., p.178.

INDEX

243

Index

Index

Index

Index

Index

Index

Index

Index

Index

Index